GROWING UP FAST

FOR MY MOTHER

Who Gave me Life and Showed me Strength

CONTENTS

	AUTHOR'S NOTE	IX
1	PITTSFIELD	1
2	AMY & BERNARD	53
3	LIZ & PETER	105
4	COLLEEN	135
5	SHAYLA & C.J.	167
6	SHERI	217
7	JESSICA	267
8	COMMUNITY	317
	NOTE ON METHOD	367
	NOTES	371
	BIBLIOGRAPHY	405
	ACKNOWLEDGMENTS	417

Picador® is a U.S. registered trademark and is used by St. Martin's Press under license from Pan Books Limited.

www.picadorusa.com

Design by Nick Wunder

Library of Congress Cataloging-in-Publication Data

Lipper, Joanna.
    Growing up fast / Joanna Lipper.—1st ed.
        p.   cm.
    Includes bibliographical references (p. 405).
    ISBN 0-312-42222-9
        1. Teenage mothers—Massachusetts—Pittsfield—Social conditions.
    2. Teenage mothers—Massachusetts—Pittsfield—Psychology.
    3. Pittsfield (Mass.)—Social conditions. 4. Pittsfield (Mass.)—
    Economic conditions.   I. Title.

HQ759.4.L57 2003
306.874'3—dc21

2003049862

First Edition: November 2003

10 9 8 7 6 5 4 3 2 1

GROWING UP FAST

Text and Photographs

by

Joanna Lipper

PICADOR   NEW YORK

AUTHOR'S NOTE

This is a work of nonfiction. All its characters are real, as are the places where they live and the details of their personal lives. Quotes from the subjects and dialogue I have used were taken directly from edited scenes I videotaped, as well as from edited transcripts of interviews I conducted and either videotaped or audiotaped.

All the teen parents seen in the photographs I took for this book are referred to by their real names. They embarked on this project knowing that their true stories would become public and that their identities and the identities of their children would not be hidden.

Their courage, their honesty, and their long-term commitment to sharing their stories over the course of four years made this book possible, and for that I shall always be extremely grateful.

Most of the other people who appear are referred to by their real names. Some names have been changed. Every instance in which a pseudonym is used is accounted for in the endnotes.

I was interested in presenting the subjective stories of these individuals, who spoke from the heart of their personal experiences and shared their unique perspectives on their lives and the world around them. I accepted what they said without judgment, not necessarily as the only truth, but as their genuine perception of the truth.

For the first and last chapters, I did substantial research and am greatly indebted to the work of experts, scholars, and writers in many fields. Details about the sources of the information and statistics in those chapters can also be found in the endnotes.

chapter one

PITTSFIELD

BILL AND DORIS WERE ADDICTED TO SKYDIVING. FALLING through space and time, their survival instincts kicked in. The adrenaline rush was pure and unparalleled. Parachutes snapping open, they surrendered to a blissful sensation of weightlessness, drinking in a bird's-eye view of the world, far above the burdens, frustrations, and disappointments that awaited them down on the ground back home, in Pittsfield, Massachusetts.

During the week, Doris drove a long yellow school bus. She had started this job when her two daughters were little, intending to move on to something else once they were older. Fifteen years later she was still driving the same bus, thankful for the benefits and paid vacations.

As Doris watched her daughters grow up, she felt her own youth slipping away. When she looked in the mirror, she saw barely any trace of the young woman who at nineteen had given birth to Jessica. Doris had subsequently divorced Jessica's father and married Bill, with whom she had her second daughter, Catherine, all before the age of twenty-three. All that seemed so long ago. As Doris studied the thin lines trailing out from the corners of her eyes, she worried that her life had been defined solely by the roles she played in relation to others. She was afraid that she hadn't done nearly enough for herself.

Skydiving was the only activity Doris indulged in solely for the purpose of her own enjoyment, but there was one hitch—each jump was wickedly expensive. Doris maneuvered her way around this obstacle by getting a weekend job at the drop zone, packing parachutes and videotaping other sky divers from a small camera strapped onto her head. In exchange for performing these duties, Doris was given a special pass that allowed her unlimited jumps at a huge discount.

Bill, a machinist, put extra money aside to support his skydiving habit, but as the years went by and jobs became more and more scarce, decent work was harder to come by. Starting out as an apprentice, Bill had worked his way up the ranks, taking time off to fight in Vietnam. His steadiest employment had been at a steel company that relied on subcontracts from General Electric. In the late 1980s, as GE pulled out of Pittsfield, that company went bankrupt and Bill found himself unemployed. He subsequently worked various jobs spinning steel, but none lasted very long or provided the steady income and security he longed for.

Bitter and disillusioned, Bill languished at the bar, passing long, uneventful hours reminiscing and joking around with his buddies while Doris, at home waiting up, covered his plate in Saran Wrap and stared out the window, watching as the trees in the backyard turned ashen and then disappeared, engulfed in darkness. The hours blurred into one another. Her eyes grew heavy. Sometimes she dozed off.

When the doorknob finally turned and Bill stumbled through the front door, Doris jolted herself awake and summoned up the last of her remaining strength. She fought and pleaded with her husband about his alcoholism. The sound of their arguing voices—his slurred, hers tired and high-pitched—wafted through the thin walls to where Jessica lay in her bed with a pillow over her head, doing her best to sleep through it all.

Bill acknowledged that his drinking and reckless spending put a tremendous strain on his marriage. "But guess what?" he remarked. "When you're screaming through the air at one hundred and twenty miles per hour, a bad day at home doesn't really come up!"

In the summertime, Bill and Doris crammed as many jumps as they could into a day, stopping reluctantly only when thunder crackled or the sun sank. Meanwhile, down below, fourteen-year-old Jessica and her younger sister spent lazy, humid afternoons in an overgrown field adjacent to the runway, listening to music, cooking hot dogs on the grill, bouncing on the trampoline, and stretching out on the hoods of cars in their bikinis, competing to see who could get the best suntan. When Jessica heard the plane's engine idling overhead, all she could do was hope for the best as she craned her neck upward and squinted into the glare of the sun, holding her breath, always terrified that her parents' next jump might be their last.

For the first few minutes Jessica often couldn't see her mother and stepfather at all. At such high altitudes, clusters of thick, fluffy white clouds usually obscured the rough contours of their bodies. With her heart pounding against her ribs, Jessica learned to force herself to imagine what she couldn't see—their canopies gracefully unfurling, creating the gentle tug of resistance that would cut the velocity of their steep, rapid descent.

Finally, after what seemed an eternity to Jessica, her parents would float into view, two small black specks on the distant horizon with nothing but thousands of feet of air between them and the hard, unforgiving earth. "No way would you ever catch me jumping out of a plane with a parachute," said Jessica. "A piece of cloth? No, no, no. I like my feet right on the ground, thank you very much!"

Blond, blue-eyed, willowy, and a stellar student to boot, Jessica entered high school with substantial potential. She rotated from one after-school job to another, unable to last long at places like Burger King, Pretzel Time, and Bonanza. Convinced that a good education would be her ticket out of Pittsfield, Jessica much preferred to spend her spare time working hard to get good grades.

Among her peers, Jessica hid her intelligence and ambition under a flippant, giggling, exaggeratedly feminine persona, often inviting comparisons with the character Phoebe on the hit television show *Friends*. Despite her widespread popularity and her movie-star looks, Jessica suffered from low self-esteem. She was unable to feel special unless she was the special girl in some guy's life. She explained, "I was one of those girls who just always had to have a boyfriend."

While Jessica steered clear of risks as extreme as skydiving, she was less careful when it came to sex. At the age of sixteen, she got pregnant. Too frightened to confide in anyone, Jessica hid her pregnancy for six months, hoping that the problem would just disappear so that her life could go on uninterrupted.

"I was in denial," she recalled. "I didn't want to be pregnant. All my friends would say, 'You're getting bigger. . . . Your stomach's getting bigger. . . .' I'd shrug and say, 'Oh, I'm just eating a lot.'"

Every day at school, Jessica felt sick and anxious. It was hard for her to concentrate on anything. Most nights she spent awake, tossing and turning in her bed, inhabiting the lonely, dark space carved out by insomnia as the clock beside her bed ticked and ticked. As she entered her third trimester, Jessica took a long, hard look in the mirror and saw a dramatically different body reflected back. She was enormous. None of her clothes fit. After one too many sleepless nights, she decided to break her silence. Too terrified to face her mother in person, Jessica chose to put her thoughts down on paper.

"I wrote a letter to my mom. It said, 'Please don't abandon me, I love you and I'm so sorry.' My mom was going skydiving, so I asked my sister to put it in her parachute bag, so she'd find it before she jumped!"

After reading Jessica's note on the plane, Doris floated down toward the ground. Airborne beneath her unfurled canopy, she had time to reflect on the sixteen years she had spent building up her hopes, dreams, and plans for her studious, spunky, beautiful daughter. Now all that would have to change, or at least be deferred indefinitely. In tears, she drove back to Pittsfield to confront Jessica.

"When my mom got home, she sat me down and said, 'Are you going to have this baby?' I said, 'Yeah.' I was already six months pregnant. There was nothing I could do. I wasn't gonna have an abortion. My parents—they weren't angry, but they were very disappointed. I had so much going for me, and it was all thrown in the garbage."

Jessica promptly transferred out of Taconic High School into the Teen Parent Program, affectionately dubbed "TPP" by its students. This alternative, nonresidential day school was located five minutes from the center of Pittsfield, in a small building attached to St. Teresa's Church. Upon enrolling, Jessica gained access to an array of special services, including one-on-one tutoring, child-development and parenting classes, medical care, counseling, and day care. Under the auspices of this support system, Jessica carried her fetus to term, gave birth, and nurtured her son through his first year of life while simultaneously completing the requirements she needed to graduate on time with her high school class.

Jessica was surrounded by many other pregnant and parenting teens. Between 1995 and 2000, an average of fifty-nine teenagers from Pittsfield gave birth each year. Approximately 81 percent of these teen mothers were white, reflecting the demographics of city's overall population, which the U.S. Census 2000 officially calculated as 92.6 percent white.

Prior to transferring into the Teen Parent Program, most teen mothers were registered at one of Pittsfield's two public high schools, which enrolled a combined total of approximately 1,570 students: 730 boys and 840 girls. Within these locker-lined corridors, every student had some exposure to teen pregnancy and parenthood, if not through their own direct experience, then through classmates or, in many cases, through elder siblings, cousins, and other family members. When Jessica was asked why she thought there were so many teen mothers in Pittsfield, she didn't mention the words "abortion," "adoption" or "choice."

"Pittsfield is very boring," she said. "There's nothing for us to do. I used to just drive around in my car with all my friends and hang out at the parks or hang out at some friend's house. We don't have anywhere to go. Nowhere . . . That's probably why there are so many pregnant people around here, because there's nothing else to do but have sex. I mean, there is nothing else to do!"

Jessica's negative impressions of her hometown were echoed by many of her contemporaries. When talking about Pittsfield, these teenagers often resorted to using words like "dead," "boring," "frustrating," and "hate." Many of their parents shared this extreme pessimism. Pittsfield's history illuminated the backdrop against which the dramas of these individual lives unfolded.

Located in western Massachusetts, approximately 150 miles from New York City and Boston, Pittsfield evolved throughout the nineteenth and twentieth centuries as one of several major pockets of industry. Imposing and strikingly urban, Pittsfield—with its towering smokestacks and gigantic, fortresslike factories—was always a bit of an anomaly, surrounded by the predominately mountainous and pastoral, picturesque terrain of Berkshire County, a region renowned for its sweeping open landscapes and the meticulously preserved elegance of its small Old New England towns with their Gilded Age mansions, world-class resorts, pristine spas, and thriving summer communities.

With its clear blue lakes, peaceful hiking trails, burnished autumn leaves, and necklace of cultural gems, Berkshire County never fails to attract throngs of tourists. Year after year visitors from all over the world are irrepressibly drawn to Tanglewood, the Williamstown Theater Festival, Shakespeare & Company, the Berkshire Theater Festival, Jacob's Pillow, and MASS MoCA. Adding to its allure is the fact that the region has been home to several major artists and intellectuals, including painter Norman Rockwell, psychoanalyst Erik Erikson, and legendary American authors Edith Wharton and Herman Melville.

Less often highlighted in Berkshire County's tourist brochures, but impossible to ignore in the context of teen parenthood, is Pittsfield's long, bittersweet industrial heritage, inextricably intertwined with the General Electric Company.

In its glory days, Pittsfield was endearingly referred to as "the Plastics Technology Center of the Nation." In addition, numerous industrial buildings housed GE's Power Transformer Division and its Ordnance Division, a major producer of armaments during World Wars I and II and the Cold War. GE's defense activities included contracts for the Polaris missile, naval ballistics missiles, and the Bradley Fighting Vehicle.

During the early postwar period, approximately three-fifths of Pittsfield's workforce was employed by General Electric. Then in 1960, Jack Welch joined GE's Plastics Division as a chemical engineer. For the next seventeen years Welch lived and worked in Pittsfield as he evolved into the legendary CEO whose leadership, vision, and strategy helped the corporation arrive at and maintain its enviable position as one of America's most profitable and valuable companies.

Throughout most of the twentieth century, GE maintained a vested interest in preventing other businesses from coming to Pittsfield, determined to control the workforce and the wages. The company's management exerted influence over the city council to ensure that protective measures were taken so that Pittsfield remained securely under GE's jurisdiction, conveniently isolated from competition. As anthropologist Max H. Kirsch explained: "The community was dependent on the corporation for the tax dollars that maintained the city's infrastructure developed to house its workers; workers were dependent on the corporation for jobs; families on wage earners; and secondary industries on the wages the workers generated."

Then, quite abruptly, GE's happy marriage to Pittsfield came to an end when Jack Welch led the corporation into a period of major downsizing and globalization, shifting the focus of U.S. operations from production to high technology and financial services, dramatically scaling back the blue-collar labor force; replacing thousands of U.S. workers with robots and cheaper nonunionized foreign labor; increasing efficiency, productivity, and profits while cutting costs. It was inevitable that high-tech solutions would eventually replace old-fashioned assembly lines, and as operations became more streamlined, jobs were tailored to those with higher education and expertise. Many blue-collar workers were laid off as GE edged its way toward the twenty-first century, wholeheartedly embracing the spirit of capitalism.

On Wall Street, shareholders' pockets jingled with profits. Jack Welch was hailed as a hero, and competitors around the world sought to emulate his strategies once they saw just how seductively lucrative they were. As globalization became more and more widespread, the purchasing power of the average American increased, thanks to the availability of goods that, because they cost less to manufacture, subsequently cost less to buy. Nevertheless, there are two sides to every coin, and as Janet Lowe, author of *Welch: An American Icon,* concedes: "As visionary as his leadership has been, Welch has also ushered in many ugly problems. Companies the size and scope of GE invariably raise questions about the way they affect lives everywhere, and though Welch has defended himself and the company, troubling conflicts still exist. . . . Nobody has figured out a way to build a world in which all people live in a just, humane society that rewards them adequately for the work they perform."

In 1986 GE announced the closing of the Power Transformer Division and began its withdrawal from Pittsfield. The city's unionized blue-collar jobs were sucked up into a vacuum. In 1988 defense production was sharply curtailed, and by the early nineties GE had sold many of its weapons businesses, cutting more jobs. GE Plastics' Global Headquarters housed the corporation's advanced Plastics Technology Center, which was the only division that remained in operation in Pittsfield, staffed primarily by a small number of highly educated, skilled employees who focused on research and development.

As GE stock shot way up, in Pittsfield the quality of life plummeted. The bottom fell out of the middle class. After being laid off, many former GE employees who had served the company loyally for decades were forced to take on lower-paying service and retail jobs that, in addition to being mostly unregulated by the unions, offered relatively meager compensation and few, if any, benefits. As a result of these dramatic economic shifts, society became increasingly polarized. The Pittsfield Economic Revitalization Corporation published a comprehensive report, warning that as the availability of "upwardly mobile types of jobs" quickly diminished, left behind were "a large group of single mothers, young people, and displaced blue collar workers for whom there is little hope for achieving a middle-class lifestyle."

———

At the time these unsettling economic changes took place, Jessica and her classmates at the Teen Parent Program were, for the most part, between the ages of five and eight. Their parents were in the prime of their working years. Quite suddenly, the manufacturing base of their region had virtually disappeared, with no prospect of recovery on the immediate horizon.

Bill described the traumatic time of transition that followed. "Pittsfield, once upon a time, was General Electric," he explained. "Thousands upon thousands of jobs were supplied by GE. Anybody that was anybody worked at GE. Everything else in town catered to the people who got their money from GE. Then, GE slowly but surely left town. When GE left, it wasn't that you were laid off; you weren't fired . . . your jobs just didn't exist anymore.

" 'Generous Electric' was the only union shop in town, and the company I worked at got a lot of the subcontracts from GE, so when GE went down the toilet, we were definitely affected. One Saturday morning I went in to do overtime, and there were padlocks on all the doors and NO TRESPASSING signs because the bank had just confiscated the building. The boss didn't see fit to tell anybody. We had no warning. Nothing. So everybody shows up at work to get the overtime, and you find out you don't even have a job!

"It leaves you in a strange predicament. Unemployment lasts only so long. And you're out of money. Basically, you have no skills because you've been a monkey and a button. You wind up working at McDonald's, a gas station, or whatever. After a while, even those jobs start petering out, because everybody and their brother is competing for those jobs."

In the wake of GE's departure, Pittsfield's shops, restaurants, and small businesses began shutting down as those families who once had money to spend left town in search of decent-paying jobs and healthier communities. "There is cause for alarm," warned the Berkshire County Development Commission in response to a study on Pittsfield's population, which rapidly dwindled from 57,020 in 1970 to 45,296 in 1999. The U.S. Census 2000 identified Pittsfield as one of the five metropolitan areas in America that on a percentage basis had experienced the steepest population drop during the 1990s. According to the census, only 12.4 percent of Pittsfield's remaining residents over twenty-five years of age held bachelor's degrees. Only 8.1 percent held graduate or professional degrees, and 79.5 percent had no college degrees at all.

Many of those who remained in Pittsfield could not afford to leave. North Street, once a bustling center of activity, quickly assumed the aura of a ghost town as this working-class community was thrown into an era of social and economic catastrophe. These sudden, pronounced demographic and economic shifts paved the way for the increasingly severe presence of a host of social ills, including drugs, crime, and teen parenthood.

Panic about a toxic-waste crisis compounded the economic disaster Pittsfield faced. In 1976 the federal government had banned PCBs (polychlorinated biphenyls) in light of substantial evidence that these synthetic chemicals posed an increased risk for cancer in humans, in addition to an array of other serious health problems. Manufacturing power transformers had traditionally been one of GE's core businesses in Pittsfield, and PCBs were part of a compound that comprised Pyranol, a fire-resistant insulating lubricant used in production and sealed inside of power transformers. These hazardous chemicals regularly spilled all over areas inside the factory buildings where the transformers were tested. "The Pittsfield Operations processed 140,000 pounds of PCB each week," reported Thomas F. O'Boyle, "several thousand pounds of which spilled on the floor, down the drain and into the Housatonic River."

Mickey Friedman, a local documentary filmmaker, interviewed many GE workers who were employed in the Power Transformer Division. "These guys spent their days slogging through this constant layer of liquid on the floor," he said. "The chemical was so potent that the boots GE would give them would be worn down if they stood in the liquid for too long—it would just eat the rubber right off the soles of their shoes.

"So because the floor was wet all the time, just drenched in chemicals, GE would use this absorbent dirt," explained Mickey. "It was a kitty-litter-like substance called Fuller's Earth, and they would throw it on the floor so that it would soak up the liquid. They were generating hundreds of barrels of this stuff. The first place they would take it was the old Pittsfield landfill. Two or three tractorloads would go out every single day into the city dump for years and years and years, to the point where they filled up the dump.

"Then in the 1940s," continued Mickey, "somebody at GE got the idea to create a fill giveaway program. They would encourage GE workers and local building contractors to come in and take away these barrels of contaminated Fuller's Earth to use on construction sites. GE also contracted with several local trucking companies to actually take the contaminated Fuller's Earth and deliver it to people's homes and, in fact, asked people to sign a waiver of liability when they received the fill, saying that they were, in fact, receiving 'clean-fill.' "

The contaminated fill looked just like regular dirt, so some people who had low spots in their backyards due to the river occasionally flooding used the fill to even out their land. Some workers used the fill to kill the unruly weeds that kept persistently nudging their way through cracks in the sidewalk. The fill was spread across dirt roads to keep the dust down and was suspected of being used to straighten out the oxbows in the Housatonic River, apparently in an effort to make the river more efficient, as it meandered through the center of the city. Over the years, truckloads of the fill were dumped at various sites in Pittsfield. By the time PCBs were declared to be a serious health hazard, there were pockets of contaminated soil all over the city, and the Housatonic River was horribly polluted.

In 1992 Mickey cofounded the Housatonic River Initiative, a coalition made up of activists from various walks of life, including GE workers, environmentalists, fishermen, scientists, sportsmen, and small-business owners whose commercial properties had been polluted by PCBs. All these people were united by their interest in protecting the environment and human health and by their desire to expose the truth about PCBs in Pittsfield. As this group became more vocal, public consciousness about the pollution grew. In 1997 members of the Housatonic River Initiative pressured the Massachusetts

Department of Environmental Protection to set up an anonymous tip line so that people could phone in and report whatever knowledge they had regarding where toxic waste had been dumped without fearing that GE would retaliate.

"Once we did that," said Mickey, "several people who had trucked toxic material called up and said, 'Listen, fifteen years ago, I took old transformers and barrels to what is now . . . this park . . . this children's park.' Slowly people started turning in sites, and that was the major breakthrough. It was a continuing battle because the state would say to us, 'You're just exaggerating. We don't necessarily be-lieve this.' For years the environmental agencies were saying, 'Listen, this stuff did not really leave the factory.' We would have to convince them case by case that in fact—the unthinkable was true."

Pittsfield residents were alarmed when land was finally tested and PCBs were identified as the responsible agents in contamination of local sewer lines, residential basements, private gardens, an elemen-tary school, the Housatonic River, and acres and acres of GE's former plant sites.

"First you have people coping with the fact that the jobs are leaving and then you have this added trauma," said Mickey. "These same people who worked very hard in the factory for years with enormous loyalty no longer have jobs and are now worried about their exposure. They are coming home to the house that they are so proud of and discovering that their backyard is contaminated. You have people discovering that the elementary school that their children go to was built on contaminated land. You have people on the west side of town whose kids have been playing basketball in Dorothy

Amos Park discovering that their kids have been exposed to unacceptable levels of PCBs. You have people who have beautiful homes along the Housatonic River who are now worried about the fact that their little children used to go down to the riverbank to play. So you add all that onto the first trauma of the economic engine of the community leaving and the burden of walking down the main street and seeing store after store that's been closed and seeing no vibrant downtown, and you're talking about an enormous psychological blow. It's hard enough when the economy crumbles around you, but then to fear for your public health? To worry about the air you're breathing? Psychologically, many people felt like they were living in a dying town."

Among certain circles of friends and neighbors, the incidence of cancer appeared to be rising at an alarming rate, and former GE employees who had worked in the Power Transformer Division found themselves frequently reaching into their closets to pull out the black suits they wore to funerals. Needless to say, the presence of PCBs made the already gloomy city an even less desirable destination for residents, tourists, and prospective new businesses.

The damage caused by this toxic-waste disaster was so extensive that it merited evaluation and federal intervention by the Environmental Protection Agency (EPA). Acres of GE's polluted plant sites and the Housatonic River with its PCB-laden sediment were the subjects of a legally binding consent decree involving the EPA, the Department of Justice, state officials, the city of Pittsfield, and General Electric. GE agreed to a $150–$200 million settlement of claims. They were required to pay for portions of the cleanup of the river and for the eventual redevelopment of the contaminated plant site.

Although they fought hard against it, GE was ultimately forced to dredge a polluted section of the Housatonic River. Beginning efforts have been made, but there is still a long way to go before the cleanup will be finished. The EPA estimated that the total price tag of resolving the toxic-waste crisis in Pittsfield would end up somewhere in the range of $300–$700 million, figures hotly contested by GE.

An EPA report warned that "teenagers growing up near portions of the river face a 1 in 1,000 cancer risk due to exposure to contaminated river soils. . . . Young children and teenagers playing in and near portions of the river face non-cancer risks that are 200 times greater than EPA considers safe. Non-cancer effects from PCBs may include liver and nervous system damage and developmental abnormalities including lower IQ's."

When asked for her theory about why teen parenthood had become such an epidemic in Pittsfield, Shayla, a teen mother who got pregnant in 1998, replied half jokingly, "It must be something in the water." Born to a fifteen-year-old mother and a seventeen-year-old father, Shayla was exposed to teen parenthood the moment she took her first breath. Sixteen years later, Shayla and her boyfriend, C.J., intentionally conceived a child together. "I really wanted to have a baby because all my friends had babies," explained Shayla. "I thought it would bring my popularity up because people would be like, 'Hey she's got a baby and that's cool.' I thought that C.J. and me and the baby would be a family."

A study conducted by the Alan Guttmacher Institute looked at a sample of teen mothers in California who, like Shayla, had *intended* to get pregnant:

> In the analyses including the father's intentions, young women who reported that their partner had wanted them to get pregnant were nearly fifteen times as likely as others to have intended the pregnancy (as opposed to having not intended it). In these young women's circles, early childbearing was not uncommon. Nearly seven in ten had close friends or teenage siblings who were pregnant or already had children. In addition, many respondents reported unhealthy past or present dating relationships. 47% had been in a controlling or abusive relationship, either prior to or with their baby's father.

"I definitely think my environment influenced me to get pregnant," said Shayla. "When you're around people that are constantly doing something, eventually, consciously or unconsciously, you're gonna pick that up. If I had hung out with people that were more school-oriented or more focused on the bigger picture, then I don't think I would have gotten pregnant. I really don't."

Framed by the majestic Berkshire Mountains, poverty in Pittsfield wore a prettier face than inner-city poverty but nevertheless was immediately visible. On residential streets, contemporary apartment complexes and public housing projects were interspersed with older single-family homes, many of which had been converted to house several families. Peeling paint, sliding shingles, cluttered porches, fractured windowpanes, and boarded-up storefronts silently reflected the reality that this city, home to one of the oldest minor-league ballparks in the United States, had definitely seen better days.

On North Street the once-spectacular Colonial Theatre remained the focus of a slow but steady restoration effort. After its construction in 1903, the theater was renowned throughout the country for its ornate interior and exceptional acoustics. Back in the theater's heyday, legendary performers including John Barrymore, Sarah Bernhardt, and Eubie Blake graced its stage. Sold-out shows included *The Ziegfeld Follies* and other hits of the era. The curtain closed for the last time in 1952, and when the property changed hands, the new owner converted it into an art-supply shop without making any major structural changes. Forty-six years later, in 1998, the city's determined efforts to salvage this run-down architectural jewel received a huge boost from the visit of then–First Lady Hillary Rodham Clinton. In association with the National Trust for Historical Preservation, she honored the theater by making it the first stop on the prestigious "Save America's Treasures" tour.

Sadly, other areas of Pittsfield were not the recipients of such special attention.

On the outskirts of town, giant abandoned manufacturing plants loomed ominously, weathering rain, sleet, snow, and the beating sun. Season after season, GE's former factory sites remained completely deserted, surrounded by tall chain-link fences emblazoned with imposing KEEP OUT and NO TRESPASSING signs. There was no need to enter. From the outside, the view through the cold, metal diamond-shaped slats was achingly clear: Pittsfield's most vital organs had died.

"When GE split, the heart and soul of Pittsfield pretty much went to shit," said Bill. "And when the money left town, all the supporting businesses went with it. So, you've got people losing their homes. You know, you worked for GE for twenty-six years, then you're out of work, you've still got five years left on your mortgage . . . bad news. You've got despair, depression—the whole nine yards. And, of course, the drug dealers come in. They start with the kids. And I hate to say it, but the parents follow suit. The kids see what's going on with their parents, and life can look pretty stinking grim. Kids get discouraged when they see their parents going down the toilet. They think, 'Is this what I have to look forward to?' "

In this morbid atmosphere, a thriving underground drug economy exploded, primed to exploit the unskilled labor force and the city's vulnerable youth.

"As General Electric left town and the population decreased, crime started to rise largely because of crack cocaine and the influx of drug dealers into this community," explained Captain Patrick Barry, a native of Pittsfield and the proud descendant of several generations of resilient police detectives. After joining the police force on Christmas Day in 1988, Barry became a narcotics investigator. By 1997 the raven-haired officer had impressed his superiors with his insight, diligence, and dedication. They promoted him to sergeant. Before long he was promoted to captain and given command of the Drug Unit and the Detective Bureau. He was subsequently named special operations commander, and his responsibilities expanded to encompass the Crime Scene Services Unit and the Anti-Terrorism Unit.

Divorced from his wife, who lived with their young daughter out of state, Captain Barry devoted himself to fighting Pittsfield's war on drugs. During his tiny slivers of leisure time he played golf, skied, and hiked up the Berkshire Mountains accompanied by his beloved beagles, Snoopy and Snoopy Two. However, as crime in Pittsfield escalated, those carefree moments of peace became increasingly rare and what little free time he had was spent visiting his daughter or catching up on sleep.

Usually Captain Barry was up all night on the midnight shift, patrolling the streets, often undercover. Most mornings he saw the sunrise with bleary eyes while breakfasting on an Egg McMuffin. On cold winter afternoons, when he had a moment to spare, he liked to warm up at the Elm Street Luncheonette, sipping hot coffee while thumbing through the newspaper, which often included articles about his department's latest arrests.

Throughout the 1990s, the drug scene in Pittsfield centered on crack cocaine. Starting in 1992, the Pittsfield Police Department's Drug Unit implemented an aggressive policy to win back the streets. Using undercover officers to purchase crack cocaine from street-level dealers, the unit made more than seven hundred arrests with a high rate of subsequent convictions.

"We would send a patrolman down and kick the dealers off the street corner, and then we would take over the street corner for that evening," said Captain Barry. "I had a beard and we'd wear different types of clothes to help disguise ourselves. We knew what the street-level dealers were like—what kind of clothing they wore and where they stood to deal. So we would try to be like them. People are desperate for the drug, and sometimes, even if they suspect you're a cop, if you're willing to sell it to them, they're willing to take it and they hope they'll get away.

"The population of users includes a vast range of people. They come from right here in the community in Pittsfield. We've had doctors out of Williamstown down here buying crack cocaine and well-to-do people out of South County as well.

"We've also encountered prostitution. That came along with the drug dealing. I worked as an undercover john to get hookers. I got several of them working the streets of the city of Pittsfield. Usually they're looking to buy crack cocaine and they don't have the money, so they want to turn a trick."

Captain Barry and his colleagues regularly apprehended drug dealers who conducted business in public places, including parking lots at McDonald's, Burger King, Big Y Supermarket, Harry's Supermarket, and the Pittsfield Plaza—all locations where many teenagers worked for minimum wage after school, during the summer, and on weekends. In these and other local settings, the culture of adolescence blended with the narcotic subculture. Thus, the social lives of some teenagers and some drug dealers began to merge. This was beneficial for the drug dealers because every new teenager they befriended or supplied could introduce them to more teenagers who were viewed as potential customers, potential runners, and potential girlfriends, who were valued because many helped dealers establish fronts in their apartments in exchange for money and the illusion of love.

Raised in Pittsfield, Nicole was always considered pretty. Her almond-shaped eyes defined her pale face and her long honey-blond hair cascaded down her back.

"My parents—they were into drug use," explained Nicole, "so I was around it pretty much all the time. As a young girl, I hung out with the older crowd. I was drinking at nine years old and smoking cigarettes. In sixth grade I started smoking pot, and basically it took off from there. I did cocaine, and then the higher high was crack. When I started getting into crack, everything went downhill.

"I was eighteen my senior year in high school and I went to my first rehab. I tried to stay clean and then I got back into it because I never changed the people I hung out with or the places I went. Every time I got back into it, I got in deeper and deeper. I couldn't function without crack. I had a couple of car crashes, and still nothing. I did some time in jail for my behavior. I knew nothing of life and how to live it without drugs."

Between 2000 and 2002, the drug trade in Pittsfield careened toward heroin with a velocity, intensity, and violence that stunned law enforcement and garnered headlines all across Berkshire County. Because of the widespread availability of extremely pure, potent heroin, users could now sniff or smoke the drug and still get a terrific high. The removal of the needle barrier made heroin more socially acceptable and increased its popularity among teenagers. The influx of drug dealers into the community was accompanied by an alarming surge in the numbers of vicious dogs that populated the city streets.

"Pit bulls are a status symbol for drug dealers and other young males," said Captain Barry. "So people want to have them just for that, but they're also used to intimidate people and to protect the drug houses."

Inside their mouths, often under their tongues, open street-level drug dealers hid small plastic bags containing a tenth of a gram of crack cocaine. These bags were sold on street corners for twenty dollars and could be swallowed easily if a guard dog's growl alerted the dealer to the approach of a cop. The dogs were equally vigilant indoors, where most heroin deals took place in the privacy of dank, musty apartments with the shades drawn.

"The drug dealers I knew would let their dogs fight for fun," said Nicole. "These dogs were very mean and very abused. By beating a dog, you're provoking them and they start going at it—and when pit bulls start going at it, they're really aggressive, especially when they're being beaten. They have no tolerance for anything, so it doesn't take much to get them to start fighting. If the dog got badly hurt, it became meaningless. They'd just let them go and not care for them. I seen two dogs left to die. It was horrible."

Just attending a dogfight is a felony in most states. The blood sport is widely condemned as a dehumanizing, criminal activity that frays the very threads of civilization. Such savagery demonstrates the power of two-legged monsters to create four-legged monsters by molding their minds and behavior through abusive, traumatic conditioning.

As dusk fell over Pittsfield's deserted alleys, slowly enshrouding abandoned industrial lots, it was not unusual to see a small group of youths goading and cheering on a pit bull as he leapt up to a low branch of a forlorn tree in an attempt to grab a sweatshirt that his owner had wrapped in fresh meat and hung as bait. Sometimes entire branches bent and snapped as they bore the brunt of one these "training sessions," during which, on command, the dog would do his best to jump as high as he could, pawing and clawing, sweating, drooling, and panting, until the sweatshirt, shredded like torn paper, dangled limp in the vise of his sharp teeth.

Terrified of incurring the wrath of their masters, these dogs stood alert, ready to pounce on command, discouraging nosy neighbors, inquisitive social services representatives, and law enforcement, making it safer for their owners to conduct business with maximum protection and minimal interference. Meanwhile, innocent members of the Pittsfield community lived in daily fear of being attacked. Numerous formal complaints were filed, including one from the U.S. Postal Service, whose representatives threatened to install cluster boxes so their employees wouldn't have to keep making door-to-door deliveries and risk being bitten. Policemen, firemen, paramedics, and postal workers took the extra precaution of arming themselves with Mace or pepper spray before leaving home to go to work.

The Berkshire Eagle featured headlines about the vicious dog problem. The city council responded to the community's widespread concern by approving an ordinance to identify and track vicious dogs and their owners. Owners of dogs designated as terrorizing dangers to others were forced to "pay for tattooing and/or implanting a microchip" and "to obtain liability insurance in the amount of at least $100,000, naming the city as an 'additional insured.' " They were also required to place large signs on their property, warning pedestrians to BEWARE.

Nicole doubted that the signs would do much good. She believed that the dogs and other persistent dangers would exist as long as Pittsfield remained infested with drugs. "Drug dealers just have no respect for themselves, so I think that they have no respect for humans or animals," she said. "Everybody out in the drug world—everything's abusive, no matter what it is."

"We have a lot of domestic-violence crime in Pittsfield," confirmed Captain Barry. "In fact, probably most arrests that we make are definitely for domestic violence. It's a problem here, and it's aggravated by drug and alcohol abuse. The chief and the district attorney's office take domestic violence very seriously. They have several victim advocates in the D.A.'s office for that, and the police department recently applied for a grant, which I believe we've been awarded, so that we could have a special domestic-violence officer just to work on reducing domestic-violence crime."

Colleen, a teen mother who attended the Teen Parent Program with Jessica and Shayla, described life with the abusive young heroin addict who was the father of her baby. "My boyfriend on heroin was like . . . he'd be quiet at times—or he'd be so nice to me. He could be this wonderful person, but yet it was the drug that was making him that happy. When he was down from the drugs, it was just awful. He was mean, terrible. He would say, 'Get me money, do *whatever* you have to!' He'd get so mad at me if I didn't give him any money for the drugs. He'd say I didn't love him and call me names. . . . Horrible verbal abuse. When I would get mad and want to leave, it would turn into physical abuse. The physical abuse at our apartment was really bad."

Sheri and Amy attended the Teen Parent Program the same year as Jessica, Shayla, and Colleen. At one point, several of these young women lived near one another with their children at the Dalton Apartments, a subsidized housing complex located on April Lane, near the border between Pittsfield and Dalton, ten minutes by car from a huge strip mall. For drug dealers, the fact that this housing project was slightly off the beaten path made it very seductive, as they were always on the lookout for places to temporarily shack up without attracting too much attention.

Amy got pregnant for the first time when she was fourteen. Unmoved by her mother's repeated attempts to convince her to put the baby up for adoption, Amy gave birth and kept her daughter. At seventeen, Amy gave birth to a son and moved to April Lane with the two kids and her son's father, Bernard. She hoped that this environment would be better than Riverview, the more urban project where they had previously lived, right beside the polluted Housatonic River. With its grassy communal lawns, rusty swing sets, and sparsely wooded play areas, April Lane did indeed initially seem quieter and more peaceful. But soon after moving there, Bernard, Amy, and her two young children discovered that life on April Lane wasn't always as peaceful as it appeared to be upon first glance.

One afternoon, in broad daylight, a gunman pulled into the parking lot behind Amy and Bernard's apartment and sprayed six bullets into the communal yard before backing out and zooming away. Luckily, no one was hurt, but a bullet was found in Amy and Bernard's apartment. The police dug it out of a wall not far from their son's bed. Thankfully, Amy, Bernard, and the kids had not been home at the time of the shooting. The perpetrator was never found, but a rumor circulated that the shooting was drug-related. When questioned by police, Amy and Bernard said that the bullets were not intended for their apartment. They insisted that the gunman's choice of where to shoot had been completely arbitrary.

"I was in charge of the Detective Bureau at the time," said Captain

Barry. "I remember interviewing people at the scene and seeing the bullet holes—you know, bullet holes, right in the house. We had nine shootings in 2002, and it's absolutely amazing that we haven't had a homicide as a result. My biggest fear is that an innocent by-stander—someone just walking down the street—will be shot and killed."

After the shooting at April Lane, residents started a neighborhood watch in an effort to deter the drug dealers and related violence. Amy's father, James, doubted that such minor measures could even make a dent in Pittsfield's massive drug problem. A Pittsfield native and a second-generation GE employee, James realized that the city of his boyhood was long gone. He worried constantly about his grand-children growing up in what had evolved into a considerably more dangerous environment.

"At one time April Lane was a project built for middle- to low-income working families," explained James. "I guess that's still what it's supposed to be, but people have to live in fear because there's guns. That comes along with the drug trade. Mayor Giuliani takes credit for cleaning up New York City, but my guess is that he drove the drug dealers into the small towns throughout New England and upstate New York. Instead of them dealing their drugs in the city, they're dealing them here now. We're easy pickings, which is not a very good thing."

The rapidly increasing migration of drug dealers from New York City to Pittsfield dates back to the early 1980s, coinciding with a short transitional period predating managed health care, when instead of being controlled by tightly regulated management on the insurance side, companies, organizations, and states were allowed to establish private contracts with various units of hospitals. In the arena of addiction services, this period of premanaged care was regarded as open season, in part because when it came to making money, detox units were relatively cheap to run and brought in a steady clientele—for some hospitals, these addiction units were cash cows.

Facing shrinking dollars and business in the local community, the McGee addiction unit at Hillcrest Hospital in Pittsfield reportedly took advantage of this friendly bureaucratic climate and allegedly set up lucrative contracts with New York Medicaid and a few other New York–based companies. The result was that hundreds of drug addicts from all boroughs of New York City were shipped straight to Pittsfield. Residents recall seeing busloads of addicts disembarking and entering the hospital, where they spent four weeks in detox. Many locals suspected that after being released, not all of the addicts hopped on the bus and went straight back to New York City. Many of those who did eventually returned to Pittsfield.

"I believe that the McGee unit worked hard to get contracts and established a contract with New York Medicaid," one doctor explained. "I still hear rumors that McGee was bringing bad characters into this community, and some were staying here and setting up shop. I am sure it happened. Drug dealers especially were causing disruptions. They found ways to get integrated into the system here, especially through the twelve-step programs. When they were in treatment, they met people and made connections."

"We had heard that the McGee unit was rehabilitating crack cocaine addicts that were being sent here from New York under their state Medicaid program," confirmed Captain Barry. "We heard that from a couple of different sources. Some of the people that were released into the community chose to stay here, and that began the demand for crack cocaine. There were a lot of other communities affected with crack cocaine in the 1990s, but because we're centrally located between New York City, Boston, and Springfield, we became a magnet."

"Here in Pittsfield, there's a much bigger profit, and dealers caught on to that," explained Nicole. "If you were to get a rock of crack around here, it's twenty dollars for a piece. That same piece would be five dollars in New York because of the fact that it's so much more readily available in New York than it is here. So they jack up the prices here."

As soon as Nicole was old enough to get her driver's license, she began transporting drug dealers back and forth to New York City. In exchange for acting as chauffeur and using her own car, Nicole was paid in cash or, more often, in grams of crack.

"A lot of the dealers that I know are actually users," she said. "A lot of their profit is their head money. They're supporting their own habit with the drugs that they're selling—that's like ninety percent of the drug dealers I hung out with."

Parked on street corners in Brooklyn and the Bronx, Nicole waited in her car while the drug dealers she was working for entered buildings and replenished their supplies. When they exited she had the motor running, ready to whisk them back to Pittsfield.

"When they go get drugs in New York City, lots of them don't want the same car traveling back and forth and they don't want to be the one driving back and forth. So they get someone like me to drive them," said Nicole. "A lot of them don't have a license when they come to Pittsfield and they don't pursue it," she explained. "They don't want to show their faces in the public eye, as far as like the Registry and police stations and that sort of thing."

Another major point of entry for out-of-town drug dealers was the local bus station. The Pittsfield Police Department's Drug Unit placed this location under tight surveillance. They regularly made arrests and seized large quantities of drugs from dealers arriving by bus from Springfield, Albany, and New York City.

"The drug dealers obviously have the money to have a vehicle, but they won't drive their own vehicles and flash them, because that would draw more attention to them," explained Nicole. "So once they got to Pittsfield, taxis were their means of transportation locally. Taxi drivers would support them with a ride, and the drug dealers would support the taxi driver with their drug habit, so it was an even trade-off."

Over the years, Nicole witnessed drug dealers flowing in from New York City, sometimes with relatives in tow. "The drug dealers let their brothers and their sisters know that in this area they made three times the profit, and the word kept being known through the families. The mothers of the families liked it in the Berkshires because they weren't in the high-rises and the whole city mode. They thought Pittsfield was like a vacation, so the whole family would move here. That's when it started getting really bad.

"In my experience," said Nicole, "about eighty percent of the drug dealers in Pittsfield are ethnic. I knew a lot of families that moved here from the Bronx because of the simple fact that their children were making more in Pittsfield. Dealing drugs is a way of life out there, and they were fine with that. That's their way of bringing in money for the mothers, for the babies. So they come here and make a life, and along with making a life, they make three times more money here and they start overpopulating different areas."

Pittsfield's crack cocaine and heroin epidemic had what law enforcement referred to as "an umbrella effect," spawning an array of spin-off crimes. "People need money for drugs," explained Captain Barry, "so there's theft and prostitution. Every hooker I bagged wanted the money for crack. People steal to get drugs. They'll ask a drug dealer, 'What do you want?' The drug dealer will pick out clothes. He might say, 'I want a size thirty-four-inch-waist pair of Tommy Hilfiger carpenter jeans and I want a green sweatshirt to go with it and a pair of Timberland work boots. The drug dealer will give an addict a shopping list, and they'll steal and trade the stolen goods for drugs. A guy was arrested a couple of weeks ago coming out of Price Chopper. He had stolen six hundred dollars' worth of steaks and lobsters. He tried to hide them with a couple of rolls of paper towels shoved over the top, and he got busted on his way to trade that food for drugs. People on public assistance abuse that and use that money for drugs. For example, they'll take food stamps and trade them for drugs."

Often drug dealers carried weapons, including guns, knives, box cutters, razor blades, and brass knuckles, ostensibly for protection in case someone tried to rip them off. Thus, innocent people lived in fear of being robbed and wounded, and children were surrounded by a culture of violence at an early age. Vulnerable, naive young girls in these environments were exposed to older males who were often sexual predators. Within the narcotics subculture, it was not uncommon for a drug dealer to father multiple children with several local teen mothers.

Once these young mothers got on welfare and got subsidized housing, their apartments were frequently used as fronts by the fathers of their babies. In exchange for cooperating, the girls often got money, gifts, and drugs. Many of these relationships were emotionally sadistic and addictive, and lots of girls found it hard to break free of them, especially after they had the dealer's baby. As Marjorie Cohan, the executive director of the Mental Health and Substance Abuse Services of the Berkshires, explained, "I think that these guys come to town and they can easily find somebody who will take them in because they have a lot of money and they can be very generous with their money and buy things—a nice new couch, a new this and a new that—and then the next thing we know, that apartment becomes a center for drug activity and as soon as the police hear about the drug traffic, the dealers move on. In the meantime, some nice young kid is pregnant and kind of left there. And that pattern repeats itself."

The idea behind a drug dealer's using a young woman's subsidized housing as a front is that in the event of a raid, if drugs are found on the premises tucked away in a drawer, buried beneath a pile of baby clothes, it is harder to tie the crime to the dealer whose name is not on the lease, and thus ultimately more difficult to prosecute the case and get a conviction. Pittsfield police have caught on to this strategy and cracked down. Before they make a raid, they gather information from informants who buy drugs from that particular apartment, so they know ahead of time exactly who the dealer is. If a drug raid takes place and drugs are found and the dealer is nowhere in sight, the young mother on the premises is often faced with a frightening choice: rat on your baby's daddy, or take the rap yourself.

"We tell the girl she could be charged with possession and with attempt to distribute," said Captain Barry. "We ask her to get on board and cooperate against the actual dealer so that in turn she won't face as much jail time and possibly won't even be charged in court. The girls usually cooperate," he said, nodding, as the corners of his mouth turned up in the slightest hint of a grin.

"The first offense for any drug possession is a misdemeanor, and you're probably not gonna go to jail," said Captain Barry. "They're probably gonna get you rehabilitation. But if you're caught selling, that's distribution—it's drug dealing, and the penalty for selling crack cocaine is a one-year mandatory minimum state prison term. The maximum is ten years. The penalties increase for multiple offenses and for larger quantities of the drug."

The state of Massachusetts is also tough when it comes to prosecuting assault and battery. Because of an avalanche of assault and drug-related charges, several of the teen mothers saw the fathers of their babies repeatedly going in and out of jail as if there were a revolving door. A few of their babies saw their fathers for the first time through the barrier of the glass partition that separates visitors from prisoners.

Incarceration is a legacy often passed down from one generation to the next, and compared with children born to older mothers, sons of teen mothers are at a higher risk of ending up in prison, and daughters are at a higher risk of becoming teen mothers themselves. Just as teen motherhood is a rite of passage for some girls in the absence of other valid landmarks and marked transitions, jail is a rite of passage for some boys. Jail culture offers inmates the structure, routine, rehabilitation, and predictability many never got from their broken homes, as well as a hiatus from a world driven by inequality and brutally divided between those who have money and power and those who have neither.

"Some people are incompetent to deal with society," said Nicole, speaking from own her experience as a young woman behind bars. "Some people get used to the jail world. It's almost like a form of retardation. Being in jail, you're a lot more accepted. You can deal with the mentality of the jail level, and you have a roof over your head, you have a meal, you have a bed, and some people are fine with that; but you put them out into society, and they're lost. They feel really out of control. To break a law is of no consequence to them. They don't mind going back in. So I think they don't think twice about it."

In jail, some young fathers feel liberated from the daunting adult responsibility of providing for themselves and their families. By the time they get out, many feel like survivors. Getting through their sentence is a tangible accomplishment and many view their time behind bars as a period of maturation and spiritual growth. In the real world with its laws, standards, and challenges, some of these young men experience little if any sense of achievement. More often there is just the daily grind, the escape route offered by drugs, the rage and shame associated with failure, and the constant need to prove one's manhood through repeated attempts to rebel against the perceived injustice of being stuck on the bottom rung of the ladder.

At the Teen Parent Program in Pittsfield, many infants born to teen mothers were of mixed race, which is interesting in light of the fact that according to the U.S. Census 2000, the city's officially registered total population was 3.5 percent black or African American, 2 percent Hispanic or Latino, and 91.6 percent white. Given that 81 percent of Pittsfield's teen mothers were white, the prevalence, significance, and implications of interracial relationships within this specific segment of the city's population cannot be underestimated.

Captain Barry said, "We've noticed a lot of interracial births among young white females from a lower socioeconomic background and young black males, many of whom are drug dealers from out of the area, many of whom have been convicted of using drugs."

"Interracial relationships are really well known in Pittsfield," confirmed Nicole. "The teen music is R&B and hip-hop, and that's the 'in' thing, and obviously most of the groups are ethnic groups, so for a white woman to be with a black guy . . . that's the fad, it's the thing to do, along with wearing the pants low and the whole thing. If you see something going on in the music world, it's usually going on in the teen world."

Sitting beside her daughter and son, whose brown skin contrasted with her own white skin, Amy said, "I know a lot of black people who don't like white and black couples, and I know a lot of white people that don't like black and white couples. They think biracial kids are wrong, but I don't see the difference. People who are racist learn from when they're young because their parents teach them that there is a difference between black and white, and then they just make stereotypes. My daughter doesn't have no problem with that 'cause she's not raised that way. She's four and she already asked me if she was brown or white. She came to me herself because she was wondering. I told her she was both. When she gets older, she'll understand."

Jessica talked openly about the strange experience of sometimes not being recognized as her son's mother, because she is fair and blond and he is brown with jet-black hair.

"My friend Tamika, she's black, and sometimes we'll go out and she'll be holding my son and people will go up to her and say, 'Oh, your son is so cute,' and I'll be like 'No, he's *mine!*' I don't really mind, because people don't really talk about mixed races anymore. It's not a big deal, because you see it everywhere. It's, like, not a new thing."

Shayla defied her father, who prior to his separation from her mother had ordered her never to date white guys. "I wasn't surprised that my baby came out very light because of his father's color," she said. "Sometimes when I walk around, people ask me whose baby he is because he doesn't look anything like me and because he's so light."

Liz grew up in a series of foster homes, and after several years of gang involvement, she ended up in Pittsfield at a juvenile lockup facility. Shortly after being released, she got pregnant at the age of sixteen and joined the other girls at the Teen Parent Program.

"My mother's ethnicity is Italian, and my dad's background is Hispanic," Liz explained. "My son is Puerto Rican and Chinese. We have a little nickname for him, 'Puerto-chink.' It's either 'Puerto-chink' or 'Chink-o-rican.' It's kinda cute, but I really don't want to say it that loud, because you say 'chink' and that's insulting Chinese people."

Liz's boyfriend, Peter, discussed the marriage of his Anglo-Saxon mother to his Chinese father, who, after being abandoned by his biological parents, grew up in a series of foster homes in Massachusetts.

Peter said, "I'm a mixed breed from my ethnic background. My son's background doesn't really make a difference. He's still human and he's mine. That's all that matters."

Bernard, the father of Amy's son, was raised in Africa. He immigrated to the U.S. as a young adult. "I think that issue of black and white should be over by now," he said. "We're living in the twenty-first century and this thing should stop. We had enough. People who have ideas of racism should learn more and teach their kids. I always think that people that hate black people end up being family with black people. I have seen a lot of white folks that hate blacks, and either their son or daughter becomes friends or family with black people. We are all equal. That's the way it's gonna be, and we should all move on."

The views and experiences of these young parents of multiracial children reflect some of the major developments and trends that are changing the face of America. The number of children who are multiracial is roughly double the percentage of adults and is likely to keep growing at an exponential rate. An article in *USA Today* cited the following projection made by demographers: "By the year 2050, 21% of Americans will be claiming mixed ancestry." In response to the release of the census data, national newspapers were flooded with scholars speculating that "as race fades as a basis for social distinctions and government policies, new lines may be based on socioeconomic class, geography, education and other factors."

As the significance of race diminishes as a basis of social distinction, many social disadvantages that go hand in hand with teen parenthood are coming into even sharper focus: most prominent is the sharp disparity between socioeconomic classes. Not since the Great Depression has America been so polarized between those who have access to money and resources and those who don't. The United States has the largest gap between rich and poor among industrialized nations—and also the highest teen pregnancy rate.

Sociologist Kristin Luker has done extensive research on the links between financial hardship and teen pregnancy. In stark contrast to teenagers from mid- and high-income backgrounds, who are much more likely to have abortions, *poor and low-income teenagers account for approximately 83 percent of adolescents who have a baby and become a parent and 85 percent of those who become an unwed parent.* Luker sees teen parenthood as "the province of those youngsters who are already disadvantaged by their position in our society. The major institutions of American life—families, schools, job markets, the medical system—are not working for them."

Luker identifies "early childbearing as a symptom—not a cause, but a marker of events, an indicator of the extent to which many young people have been excluded from the American dream." Reflecting on the statistic that almost three-quarters of all teen pregnancies are described as unintentional, Luker explains that "youngsters often drift into pregnancy and then into parenthood, not because they affirmatively choose pregnancy as a first choice among many options, but rather because they see so few satisfying alternatives. As Laurie Zabin, a Johns Hopkins researcher on teen pregnancy, put it, 'As long as people don't have a vision of the future which having a baby at a very early age will jeopardize, they won't go to all the lengths necessary to prevent pregnancy.' "

In light of the hard evidence that disadvantaged teenagers are much less inclined toward the options of abortion and adoption than girls from mid- and high-income families, Luker concludes that "the decision whether to terminate a pregnancy is powerfully affected by class, race and socioeconomic status. The more successful a young woman is—and more importantly, expects to be—the more likely she is to obtain an abortion."

Hope is the ingredient that is missing from the lives of so many young women who become teen mothers. In depressed communities such as Pittsfield, where positive role models, supportive mentors, fulfilling job prospects, decent incomes, happy marriages, and tangible achievements are hard to come by, the fantasy of motherhood promises unconditional love, an identity, and a sense of self-worth that comes from being vital to the survival of a tiny human being. Motherhood draws upon one of the few precious resources that a discouraged teenager may believe she has inside her: the capacity to nurture and give love to another human being. In some particularly dark environments, a girl's fantasy of finding comfort and intense intimacy through sex that results in a baby may be the only sparkle in her otherwise bleak vision of her own future.

Researchers have discovered strong links between childhood abuse and the sexual risk behaviors in young women that often culminate in teen parenthood. As head of the Department of Preventive Medicine at Kaiser Permanente, one of the largest HMOs in America, Dr. Vincent J. Felitti has been working in collaboration with epidemiologist Dr. Robert F. Anda from the Centers for Disease Control (CDC) on the ACE Study, a landmark, decade-long inquiry into the far-reaching, long-term medical and social consequences of Adverse Childhood Experiences and their link to self-destructive high-risk behaviors such as unprotected sex and addictions to food, cigarettes, drugs, and alcohol. These patterns of behavior frequently originate as coping devices used to deal with psychological stress stemming from severe family pathology. Dr. Felitti, Dr. Anda, and their colleagues have determined that over time and in excess, these self-destructive behaviors often trigger serious chronic health problems, many of which ultimately lead to the diseases that are the leading causes of death in adults.

For the purposes of their research, Dr. Felitti, Dr. Anda, and their colleagues created a seven-point checklist defining categories of Adverse Childhood Experiences. Three categories related to childhood abuse, including psychological abuse, physical abuse, and contact sexual abuse. Four categories related to childhood exposure to household dysfunction, including witnessing the violent treatment of a mother or stepmother, substance abuse, mental illness or suicide, and criminal behavior within the household.

One section of their study focused specifically on sexual risk behaviors in women. Based on information gathered from more than five thousand female participants, Dr. Felitti, Dr. Anda, and their researchers concluded that "each category of Adverse Childhood Experience was associated with an increased risk of sexual intercourse by age fifteen, and that the chances that a woman first had sex by age fifteen rose progressively with increasing numbers of such experiences from odds of 1.8 among those with one type of adverse childhood experience to 7.0 among those who had been exposed to six or seven categories."

Liz, Amy, Shayla, Jessica, Colleen, and Sheri were all sexually active by the age of fifteen. They conceived and gave birth with the determination that through their children, they would revise and rework the traumatic aspects of their childhood. Some of them viewed their babies as vessels for their own thwarted hopes, dreams, and ambitions. This attitude was reflected in the time and energy these girls spent altering conventional spellings of names, in an effort to ensure that their babies' would be special.

In a crib placed in one corner of the stuffed-animal-and-makeup-cluttered, half-adolescent, half-infant bedroom that Sheri shared with her daughter and her younger sister was a handmade pillow that had her baby's name and date of birth embroidered onto it. Instead of *Leah* being spelled with only one *e*, there were two *es* stitched on, to spell *Leeah*. When asked about the unconventional spelling, Sheri explained that she wanted her daughter to have a name that no one else had. She had seen the name "Leah" in a "what to name the baby" book, and although it was not a common name in Pittsfield, she had wanted to add the extra *e* to make the name unique.

Jessica named her son Ezakeil, a name that appears in the Bible with the spelling Ezekiel. Jessica purposely changed the *e* to an *a* and reversed the *ie* to *ei* in order to create a more original spelling. Jessica's friend Mary Ann had named her daughter Karesse after meeting her friend's daughter whose name was Caressa. Mary Ann explained that she thought the name she chose for her daughter was unusual and liked the way it sounded but had changed the spelling because she, like Sheri and Jessica, wanted her baby to be one of a kind. For the exact same reason, Amy named her daughter Kaliegh, after seeing the name spelled as Kaylie and as Caleigh in a name book. For these young mothers, the act of naming was weighted with power. They shared a strong, conscious desire for their babies' names to be unusual and somewhat exotic, which could be interpreted as an expression of their collective wish that the lives of their children would transcend the ordinary, surpassing the boundaries and limitations they perceived within themselves and their environment.

Robert Coles has written poignantly about encountering a similar mind-set while interviewing a pregnant fourteen-year-old girl in a Boston ghetto. Coles found "a conviction on her part that the word 'success' belonged to others. Yet she considered her baby, still inside her, as quite possibly one of those 'others.' He or she would grow up to be 'different.' He or she would 'escape.' "

At age sixteen, Shayla, like many of her peers in Pittsfield, didn't clearly see other possible ways of doing something that even came close to the magnitude of bringing another life into the world. For Shayla, having a baby was the only dream that at that particular moment seemed to be remotely within reach. Conceiving a child was a way of bringing drama and significance and purpose into her life; it was one definite way of taking control of her destiny.

"I felt that if I had a baby, it would change things," Shayla sighed. "I thought it would make my life a lot better."

David Simon and Edward Burns encountered a similar mind-set when writing their book, *The Corner,* which chronicles the lives of people living in a drug-infested neighborhood in West Baltimore, a city that has one of the highest teen pregnancy rates in the country. On the subject of teen parenthood in that particular community, they wrote: "These children have concluded that bringing about life—any life whatsoever—is a legitimate, plausible ambition in a world where plausible ambitions are hard to come by. This they can do."

Robert Coles encountered a similar point of view when he interviewed a teen mother who recounted the following mother-daughter dialogue: "My mother said, 'Don't you have a child until you're good and ready.' When I got pregnant I told her, I said, 'It may be early for me, but to tell you the truth, I'm good and ready.' Then I told her why: because I wasn't getting any place any other way, and so this was the way for me."

Education might appear at first glance to be one of the few accessible routes out of a place like Pittsfield. For some students it was, but for many others it most certainly was not. After expensive structural renovations and modernization of Pittsfield's school buildings, the two public high schools were so stretched for costs that in 2002 there was talk of merging them under one roof to save money. Students were acutely aware of the lack of resources. They organized bake sales in order to help fund sports and extracurricular activities and did what they could to stave off the threat that at any moment, these too could be slashed.

Their teachers lived with the same uneasiness and precarious instability. In May of 2002, *The Berkshire Eagle* reported that "the School Department issued layoff notices to fifty-eight teachers, and put them on a recall list. Those teachers could be recalled based on their seniority in the areas in which they are certified to teach if funding for those positions becomes available. The remaining thirty-eight teachers were given termination notices, based on classroom performance and certification issues." These ups and downs ensured a reasonably high turnover of faculty and made many teachers feel that they and their services were undervalued.

Mary arrived fresh from out of town to teach in Pittsfield's public school system. Youthful, energetic, and idealistic, she entered the classroom on the first day fully prepared to give the sixth grade her very best effort. She had many ideas about what she wanted to teach, but as her enthusiasm was dealt one heavy blow after another, she was forced to rein in her objectives.

"I've never done anything as challenging as teaching at Reid Middle School in Pittsfield," she said. "I was asked to get the kids to write creatively and also to teach them punctuation and grammar and spelling. I would be given a certain amount of pencils and paper, and sometimes if we ran out I'd be told, 'There's no more.' We would have to wait or the kids would have to provide their own; and some of them couldn't really provide their own materials, because they didn't have the resources to do it. So if a school can't provide a pencil and paper for a kid, then that kid doesn't have the basic tools to even begin to write.

"For my class, there were no materials for them to read in school or to take home, and I think you can't really learn to write unless you read other writers. Grammar lessons are really boring for kids—practicing where to put commas and that kind of thing—it's just not interesting unless you can put it in context and show the kids why it's useful. So here's what I tried to do. I went and photocopied excerpts from Anne Frank's diary and from Frederick Douglass's autobiography. I wanted to give the kids the idea that like Anne Frank, kids their age write and express themselves, so that it wasn't such a foreign idea.

"I handed those excerpts out at the beginning of the semester and then I was told, 'You have to stop doing that, because you're going to exceed your photocopying limit.' This happened during the first six weeks of the semester. So I then realized, okay, I can't provide them the materials that I need to help inspire them to start journals. So what am I supposed to do?

"I decided I'd try to make up really simple exercises that only required pencils and paper and their imagination. Some days it would just be my saying, 'I want you to go look out the window for two minutes and I want you to remember whatever you see and write about it. . . .' I thought to myself, *I'm failing these kids, every day.*

"I observed a group of very dedicated teachers. Many of them had been there for twenty-five years and they wanted to help. But they had reached a point, they sort of . . . their behavior was . . . Well, the message I got was 'Don't rock the boat. You're breaking the code by questioning the fact that we can't have glitter for Christmas decorations. We can't afford that stuff!' To question that and complain about it? I really felt like I had stepped out of line when I did that.

"The thing that has to be said over and over again until anybody who cares about education feels like a broken record is that the public school system has got to be supported. It has to have resources, and it has to be reorganized so that it functions. Right now, at least judging from my own experience, that system is completely dysfunctional. It just doesn't work. It doesn't serve the educators or the children. People should be able to have an education so that they can achieve their full potential. That should be a right, but that's completely gone. I don't think that right exists."

A year after Mary taught at Reid Middle School, President Bush signed the historic No Child Left Behind Act of 2001. Among its many provisions, this bold new federal law promises to hold public schools more accountable for the performance of students; promises to give parents of children from disadvantaged backgrounds the option to transfer a child out of a failing school into a better public or charter school; and, where failure persists, allows federal funds to provide supplemental education services, including tutoring, after-school services, and summer school programs.

This sweeping educational reform occurred a year or two after Jessica, Colleen, Amy, Shayla, Liz, and Sheri had gotten their high school diplomas or their GEDs, so they did not have a chance to reap any of its benefits. Instead, they were stuck scrambling to comply with the stringent demands of the 1996 welfare reform bill, which had replaced Aid to Families with Dependent Children (AFDC) with Temporary Assistance to Needy Families (TANF), ending sixty years of welfare entitlement, limiting each person's eligibility for federal assistance to a maximum of five years per lifetime and requiring with very few exceptions that teen parents who were minors live with a parent or responsible adult in a supervised setting. It became mandatory for teen mothers with children over a year old to attend school or college or professional training full-time and/or work—in some cases, up to forty hours a week. Failure to abide by these and a host of other strict rules raised the possibility of sanctions that potentially included the abrupt suspension of benefits.

This shift in policy rendered the myth of the welfare-incentive argument obsolete. It no longer made sense for disgruntled taxpayers to accuse adolescent girls and young women of having children on purpose out of sheer laziness in order to milk the government for free money and housing rather than going to school or getting a job. After welfare reform, the system was anything but user-friendly, especially when it came to teen mothers.

Although Jessica, Colleen, Amy, Shayla, Liz, and Sheri worked and went to high school and longed to be independent and self-sufficient, they confessed that they had never taken the SAT, nor did they remember ever being told that this test was required for application to most four-year colleges. They had never been told about the different ways of financing a college education and were not aware of the existence of need-blind admissions. Most just assumed that if they continued their education, they would choose between two local institutions: Berkshire Community College or the Mildred Elly Business School, which was located a few minutes away from North Street, in a strip mall next to the Misty Moonlight Diner. To these teenagers, life began to look more and more like a one-way dead-end street that ended not far from where it began . . . in Pittsfield.

chapter two

AMY & BERNARD

"When I met my first boyfriend, it wasn't really about the sex part. It was the fact that I had a boyfriend that was so great. My friends kind of looked up to me because my boyfriend was in high school. I was hanging out with the popular clique. I wanted to be friends with everybody who was cool. I ended up getting pregnant around the end of my eighth-grade year."

CONTINUITY AND TRADITION WERE THE CORNERSTONES of Amy's family history. She grew up on a quiet street in a neighborhood populated almost exclusively by white married couples with children. Her parents owned a three-bedroom ranch house just two doors down from her mother's nearly identical childhood home.

Born in Italy, Amy's maternal grandfather came to Pittsfield at the age of ten. In his early twenties, he married an Irish woman with whom he had five children, including Amy's mother, Donna. While making a living painting houses and factories, Amy's grandfather was exposed to high levels of asbestos. During a routine health examination administered by his labor union, he tested positive for high levels of chemical poisoning. He was subsequently diagnosed with a rare, fatal form of lung cancer. He received several small settlements from some of the companies responsible for manufacturing the products that had made him so gravely ill. When he died at the age of sixty-one, he bequeathed his business to his son.

Amy's paternal grandfather was of Irish Catholic descent. He devoted the prime years of his life to General Electric. He and his wife had thirteen children, including Amy's father, James. In 1973, at the age of nineteen, James followed in his father's footsteps and reported for his first day of work at GE. He was assigned to the Power Transformer Division. Several years later, he was transferred to the Ordnance Division, where he served as a cog in the giant machine that orchestrated the complex multistep process of manufacturing guidance systems for missiles launched from submarines.

During his years at GE, James was called upon to fulfill a variety of functions: welder, fabricator, burner, and assembler. Proficient at wiring, he often built circuit boards. After putting in a grueling forty-hour week at the plant, James liked to spend his leisure time hunting and fishing with his buddies. He also enjoyed relaxing with his family and tending to the pale pink roses that bloomed in his spacious backyard.

Calm and reserved, with gray hair and a thin mustache, James was a man who appreciated what he had. He took pride in his home and was content with his solid marriage to his wife. Donna stayed home during the week with their three kids, until they were all old enough to go to school; then she worked part-time, driving for a local transportation company and waiting tables at a local restaurant on weekends. Secure in their daily routine, James and Donna divided their time between their respective jobs and raising their three beautiful children—Shalene, Michael, and Amy, who was the youngest.

Amy and her siblings attended catechism at St. Mark's and maintained strong ties to the local Catholic Youth Center. Under the umbrella of this organization, they participated in a variety of sports and extracurricular activities. Michael was a star basketball player, and his parents proudly videotaped his games. Amy and Shalene were cheerleaders. On Saturday afternoons, as Donna and James relaxed on the deck above the backyard, they could see their daughters enthusiastically practicing their routines. On Sundays, the family went to church. Every Christmas Eve, Donna and James stuffed stockings full of small gifts for the children and placed larger gifts under a glittering tree. There were Little League games, barbecues, birthday parties, and hearty Thanksgiving dinners. Overall, life was good.

James had expected to work at GE until he was old enough to retire and get his pension, just as his father had done. He was alarmed in 1988 when GE shut down the Power Transformer Division. Many of his friends were among the thousands of workers who lost their jobs.

James continued working at the Ordnance Division, anxious about his fate. He felt as if he were sitting on a time bomb. The amount of his retirement package would be contingent upon his years of service and his salary at the time he stopped working for GE. He was only thirty-seven, and he worried that if he was laid off, he might have to wait until he was sixty in order to receive his pension. He wondered how he would support his wife and his three school-aged children if he lost his job. As GE scaled back its Pittsfield operations, James feared that Jack Welch's strategy of downsizing and globalization might end up costing him and his family their security and the way of life they had until then taken for granted.

"GE is a union shop, so the pay is pretty high," James explained. "It's probably double of what most workers make around here. Fifty, sixty, even seventy thousand dollars a year: for a factory worker, that's pretty good. You can make a decent living. It's enough to support a family and send your kids to college. That's what you want to do now, because they're not gonna have the factories anymore. You always want better for your kids. You want to be able to send them to college."

In the early 1990s, when GE sold most of its weapons businesses, James's worst fears were realized. Nearing forty, with almost two decades of service under his belt, he was laid off, and the lifestyle he and his family had became accustomed to was thrown into jeopardy. Uncertainty crept into their lives, spreading its tendrils in every direction.

Amy was ten when her father lost his job at GE. Stress in the family escalated. Her mother began working longer hours for the transportation company, sometimes chauffeuring clients as far as New York City, Boston, and Albany.

Included in the severance package GE had given James were funds earmarked for education and job training. James left his family in Pittsfield and temporarily moved to Vermont to attend a trade school. He took courses on how to be a professional wallpaper applier. James hoped that GE would recall him to another plant, but as a backup plan, he made tentative arrangements to join forces with his brother-in-law who had inherited his father's painting business. Since wall-papering often went hand in hand with painting, the idea was that when James got back to Pittsfield armed with a new set of skills, he and his brother-in-law would share clients.

In the wake of GE's departure, the city James had grown up in was evolving in ways he had never dreamed of. During his childhood, there had seemed to be a public school on every other block. Back then each school reflected the character of its distinct neighborhood and offered both parents and children a sense of cohesion and community spirit. Now many local neighborhood schools had shut down, and instead of walking a few blocks to school, students were packed onto buses and transported to a handful of public schools near the center of town. As James observed the modern world of fractured single-parent families encroaching on his old-world values, he worried about his kids.

After completing his course at the trade school in Vermont, James returned to Pittsfield, where he was forced to come to terms with the fact that locally there was no work that would offer him wages and benefits that were comparable to what he had gotten from GE. After a year, his hope of being recalled by GE gave out. One afternoon James found himself behind the wheel, driving to the local stationery store to place an order for business cards for the wallpapering company he intended to run out of his home. His backup plan was now his game plan.

James remembered that among his coworkers at GE there had been a saying: "Last one in, first one out!" This adage and the seventeen years of service James had racked up proved to be his salvation. After wallpapering houses for six months, he was one of the chosen few who were recalled to the GE plant in Schenectady, New York. Ecstatic after hearing the good news, James tossed his wallpapering business cards into the garbage, grateful to his union for coming through for him.

At the Schenectady plant, James was assigned to a team that manufactured generators. His relative seniority in Pittsfield meant very little at this new job, where he was regarded as both a newcomer and an outsider. There had been massive layoffs in Schenectady, and many native workers deeply resented that a handful of Pittsfield workers had been imported to take over a few of the remaining scarce, coveted positions. Hostile coworkers dubbed James and his Pittsfield colleagues "the Massholes."

James was given the undesirable night shift, where he subsequently spent the next six years. Back when he was a young man just starting out, he had worked nights in Pittsfield until he had enough seniority to be transferred to days and could have a life again. With his new schedule in Schenectady, James was on his way out or already gone by the time his kids came home from school, and he was either fast asleep or just waking up when they left for school in the morning. Donna worked during the day, so the couple's time together was sharply reduced. After sundown James was on the road, alone amid the glare of headlights, coasting along the interstate beneath the sleek, black, often starless sky.

The new job in Schenectady made James feel that he was being forced to start all over again at the bottom, largely surrounded by younger guys who were less experienced. Very few of his old pals had been rehired. The camaraderie that had brought humor, friendship, and team spirit to the job was gone. Despite his many reservations, James resigned himself to the monotonous labor, the nocturnal hours, and the sixty-mile commute, determined to work the fifteen years he had left until he would be eligible for his pension. After all, GE had given him a "good-paying job," and good-paying jobs were few and far between.

Burdened by her husband's frequent absence, Donna struggled to shepherd her three children through adolescence. Amy's friends made jokes about her father never being home. They teased her, saying that her father probably had a secret life that she knew nothing about—maybe he even had another family. Amy insisted that that wasn't the case and explained that her father had to work all the time. But when asked, she had to admit that she wasn't quite sure about what he did, for although Amy had attended several family nights at GE, she had never been allowed to actually watch her father work. Her imagination ran wild as she wondered what his all-consuming, important job really was and concocted outlandish stories to appease the curiosity of her friends.

"My dad is very busy and very important and he's not allowed to talk about his work," Amy explained to a circle of rapt eleven-year-old girls. "I think he's an FBI agent," she would whisper. "He works part-time as a private eye. That's why he drives that long detective's car and gets home so late."

Later that same year, when Amy had her first period, she locked herself in the bathroom and cried. Donna knocked on the door and then handed her a worn-out old book her own mother had given her at the same point in her life. The book contained diagrams about menstruation and reproduction. Donna assumed the book contained all the information Amy needed to know at that early juncture. Amy barely even glanced at it.

Eager for more adult company and additional income, Donna started working at a shop that sold arts and crafts. She did her best to help the kids through the painful transition to puberty. The two elder children were self-motivated and functioned well independently, excelling at school and remaining focused on grades, sports, and college, but Amy had a hard time academically and failed to find her niche. In the congested hallways of her school, she often felt that aside from her beauty and popularity, she was interchangeable, just one of the crowd. It seemed as if the teachers gave most of their attention to the tiny group of "star" students who got their pictures printed in the newspaper when they won awards.

Amy had a hard time just passing her tests, let alone acing them. She longed for some defining talent or special attribute that would distinguish her, something that would shift the spotlight away from her siblings onto her, something that would make the teachers and her parents reach out and pay more attention to her. Feeling outshone by her siblings and overlooked by her teachers, Amy became disenchanted with school. She gave up on her classes and diverted her energy to her social life. Failing to find support or direction or goals to anchor her, in seventh grade Amy began smoking and drinking at parties with her friends.

"When Amy went to middle school, she got tied in with some other girls," said James. "I think every single one of them was from single-parent families with, like, no control whatsoever. Those girls got ahold of Amy and kinda took control of her life. That's the way I see it."

Strongly susceptible to peer pressure, Amy was prepared to do whatever it took to be part of the popular clique, no matter how risky. She enjoyed the thrill of walking the tightrope of adolescence without a safety net, boldly putting one foot in front of the other, showing off, and never thinking for a moment that with one false move she might come tumbling down.

Amy didn't know how to say no to her friends. Despite her

mother's protests, the family home became a late-night hangout for a horde of wild teenagers. At thirteen, Amy was dying to be older than she was. She viewed her mother as an adversary, envied her elder siblings, and yearned for the extra privileges that were bestowed upon them as a result of their perceived maturity. She became enraged when her mother denied her these same privileges, insisting that she was still too young.

Amy's rebellious behavior far exceeded what James and Donna had gone through with their other children. They adopted a strict, no-nonsense attitude, set more rules, and tried to monitor their teenage daughter's every move. Whenever Amy went out at night, they called other parents to verify her whereabouts and grounded her when she broke her curfew and lied about whom she was with or where she went. Amy was infuriated by her parents' surveillance. Determined to break loose from their jurisdiction, she became sly, sneaky, and secretive about her social activities.

Behind her parents' back, she began dating Trevor, a senior at the local high school. Amy's romantic link to a black guy who was seventeen raised her status immeasurably within the competitive social hierarchy of the eighth-grade girls who occupied coveted positions in the "popular" clique. This social circle included girls from various ethnic backgrounds who wholeheartedly embraced hip-hop fashion and music and interracial relationships, which were considered to be extremely cool and in vogue.

Having Trevor as her boyfriend gave Amy a false sense of superiority over other girls her own age. Her advancement in the arena of dating compensated for her lack of distinction in academics, art, music, and sports. Amy wanted to be among the first of her friends to go all the way with a guy. When she achieved this goal, her friends showered her with questions, congratulations, and admiration.

"The fact that I had a boyfriend was so great," explained Amy. "All my friends looked up to me."

While on a superficial level being part of a couple validated Amy's insecurities about being attractive and desirable, on a deeper level her relationship with Trevor was immature and emotionally unrewarding. Their interactions revolved around public displays of affection intended to maintain an appearance of being sexy, cool, popular, and in love. This role-playing mimicked behavior they saw in movies and on television shows, but behind all their posturing, Amy and Trevor's relationship was characterized by a total lack of communication. They rarely discussed their thoughts or emotions, and during their many sexual encounters, the question of contraception was never raised.

Amy described Trevor as "extremely quiet," terms similar to those she used to describe her father. According to Amy, she and her father rarely had conversations or connected in a significant way that made her feel whole and recognized. She interpreted her father's frequent absences and silence as a lack of interest in her. At night, while her father was away at work, Amy made life miserable for her mother. She was rude, disrespectful, and provocative. When no one was looking, she would sneak out of the house and meet her older friends around the corner. They would whisk Amy away in their cars, leaving her mother to discover an empty bed when she opened the door to Amy's room.

Amy quit catechism and refused to abide by any of her mother's rules. Donna resented the fact that her husband wasn't there to help discipline their teenage daughter. After working the night shift, he'd come home to find the entire household fighting. James got caught between Amy and Donna. Amy complained to her father that her mother was exaggerating and being unreasonable. Donna was put in the awkward position of having to defend herself. She insisted to her husband that Amy's behavior was indeed inappropriate and out of control, and demanded that he intervene. When he tried, Amy argued and did her best to drive a wedge between her parents. She often succeeded in turning her father against her mother. Donna deeply resented that her husband allowed their adolescent daughter to poison the tiny slivers of time they shared together as a couple. It wasn't long before Amy's rebellious, manipulative, attention-seeking behavior began to shake the very foundation of her parents' marriage.

Finally, after the police came to the house and found Amy a her underage friends with booze, Donna told James she had enough.

"My wife—she actually moved out of the house," he rec "She couldn't handle Amy. They couldn't be in the same roc gether. Donna came to me and said, 'That's it, you deal w can't take it anymore,' and she left. I was shocked. I kept as to come back, but she was firm on it. She said, 'No. I'm n back until Amy straightens out.' "

Donna moved in with one of her friends. James requ transferred off the night shift, citing family problems. His denied. He was reminded that shifts were allocated or seniority and was told to wait his turn.

James resorted to putting his son, Michael, who was in the tenth grade, in charge of keeping Amy out of trouble. Amy continually disobeyed her elder brother. Fed up with screaming matches that sometimes escalated into knock-down-drag-out fistfights, Michael threw up his hands and told his father that, short of calling the police, he knew no way of preventing his crazy little sister from having friends over on weeknights when she was supposed to be doing her homework and going to bed early.

"Amy would have people over," James recalled, "and I'd get home at midnight and tell them all to get out, but they never wanted to leave."

One night, after arguing with a group of Amy's friends who refused to depart, James exploded.

"You know what you're doing," he shouted at Amy, hoping to elicit a confession.

Amy played dumb.

"I'm working second shift, I come home at midnight, and you got all these guys in here, sitting on the couch with you and your girlfriends and . . ."

James paused awkwardly, wishing his wife were there to help him through this delicate moment. He took a deep breath.

"If you keep this up, you're gonna get pregnant," he told Amy. "It's gonna happen."

Silent and mortified, Amy remained seated, hugging her knees s she rolled her eyes. James stared at his daughter, waiting for her) respond. Averting her gaze, Amy got up, stomped into her bed-m, and slammed the door.

James took a few steps toward Amy's closed door. When he

opened it and peered in, he saw her curled up on her bed, facing the wall. Strains of blaring rap music spilled out of her headphones as she deliberately ignored her father's presence.

Feeling very tired, James left the room and shut the door behind him. What James did not know was that he had initiated the right conversation at the wrong time. As another month went by, Amy continued to hide her pregnancy.

Eventually, Amy decided to confide in her best friend. Unbeknownst to Amy, her best friend's mother had picked up the extension to make a call and had heard the girls chattering away about Amy's pregnancy. After eavesdropping on the rest of the call, her best friend's mother then telephoned her good friend, Amy's aunt.

Donna was ringing up a sale at the crafts store when the call came.

"It's your sister," shouted her coworker.

Donna picked up the receiver.

"Hello?"

"Donna, I think you'd better come home," her sister said.

"Why?" Donna asked. "Is something wrong?"

"I don't know how else to put this to you, but Amy is five and a half months pregnant."

"She's *what?*"

Despite their problems, Donna hadn't expected this. Images of Amy as a little girl scrolled through her mind. She remembered how all her friends used to compliment Amy and say that she was such an angel.

"It was a big shock," said Amy. She giggled. "Everyone thought I was still a virgin."

Since Donna had left home she had not noticed that Amy had been gaining weight. For the first three months Amy had been tiny and had even dared to wear a bikini on several occasions without anyone's noticing her condition. The biggest hint had been Amy's irritability, which both parents had interpreted as her standard belligerence.

"My mother was really upset," Amy recalled. "She was over having babies. She didn't want any more babies in the house. It was too late to have an abortion, but she didn't want me to keep the baby. She thought it was going to ruin my life."

"I was the last to know," said James, "and I was *pissed*—*real* pissed. My question to Amy was, *Why?* Why would you do something like this?"

"I think my pregnancy happened because I was so young," said Amy. "I didn't think something like that could happen to me. I didn't think I could get pregnant. It was just something that never crossed my mind. I never really talked to my parents about sex. I had it in health class, but it really didn't faze me."

Amy paused, allowing herself a rare moment of introspection.

"I also think the fact that me and my parents weren't that close contributed to the fact that I got pregnant," she said. "I didn't think they had any expectations of me. They didn't really tell me how to do things. They never gave me a path to go toward."

The moment Amy's pregnancy was out in the open, the question of what path she would take became the central topic of every family discussion. All other issues in her parents' lives paled compared with Amy's present condition and her questionable future.

At Donna's insistence, Amy made her first visit to the doctor, who confirmed that she was almost six months pregnant. Abortion was no longer an option. At that juncture, James and Donna made their expectations clear: They wanted Amy to continue with school, go on to college, and make something of herself. They did not feel it was feasible for her to raise a child at fourteen. They wanted her to put the baby up for adoption.

Donna viewed Amy as a wild child who could barely take care of herself. She knew that a baby wouldn't change Amy's nature and could see that on top of battling over curfew, unwanted visitors, homework, and her own job at the crafts store, she would become a full-time baby-sitter. Whatever little free time she and James might have together would be devoured. Raising another infant was not something Donna was willing to take on after having raised three children. She wanted to be the kind of grandmother that grandchildren visited once or twice a week, and had no intention of becoming a primary caregiver.

Donna contacted adoption agencies. Feeling guilty for all the stress she was causing her family, Amy went through the motions with the adoption agency that her mother selected. Several weeks later, Amy received a photograph of the couple who wanted to adopt her baby as soon as it was born. As her pregnancy continued into its final weeks, Amy agonized over her decision to give up the baby. Finally she decided that there was no way she could go through with the adoption. She mustered up the courage to stand up to her mother.

"Mom, I'm keeping the baby," she announced.

"What do you mean? You can't back out now," Donna said. "What about that lovely couple who have their heart set on adopting the baby?"

Amy could see her mother's lower lip trembling. She took a deep breath and stuck to her guns.

"Mom, I can't carry a baby in me for nine months and then give it away to somebody. That just isn't me."

Though Amy had the authority and right to defy her mother with her decision to keep her baby and could refuse to sign the adoption papers, she lacked the power to make Trevor take full responsibility for the pregnancy.

"My daughter's father was seventeen," Amy recalled. "When I brought up the situation, he didn't really say anything. He didn't know what to make of it. I didn't really know what to make of it. I went through a phase where I was screaming and yelling at him. Telling him that he needs to do something with his life, telling him to get off his butt and take care of me. It was just too much pressure for him.

"I thought that maybe we could be together and everything, but as the pregnancy went along, we were in school and he was, like, hiding under the stairwells from me because I was walking around pregnant and I was humongous. He and his friends were into cheerleaders and stuff like that, so he didn't want anything to do with me. Behind closed doors, it was fine and he was supportive and everything. But when it came to his friends . . . he just didn't want to be around it near his friends. I didn't think it was going to be like that. I didn't picture going to my first year of high school pregnant and having my boyfriend *ignore* me . . . but that's what happened."

Amy gave birth to a beautiful baby girl. With her pale brown skin, almond-shaped eyes, and jet-black wavy hair, Kaliegh was a perfect combination of both her parents.

"Donna came back when Kaliegh was born," recalled James. "Things were okay for a while. Amy and Donna were getting along better. Then all of a sudden, it got worse. Amy saw us as instant baby-sitters, so she'd say, 'Oh, I'm going out.' And we were left watching the kid."

Amy thought that because she was now a mother herself, she was automatically an adult and her mother no longer had any right to tell her what to do. Donna disagreed. As long as Amy was fifteen and living under her roof, she had to abide by whatever rules were set, regardless of whether or not she had a child.

One chilly winter night, Amy wanted to go to a party. Her mother forbade her from leaving the house, saying that she didn't want to baby-sit. Amy picked up her daughter, who was several months old, and said, "Fine. Then I'll take Kaliegh with me," and headed out the door.

Donna grabbed Amy and dragged her back inside. Amy started yelling and screaming at her mother. Donna picked up the phone and called the police.

"I've got a fifteen-year-old thinking she's an adult," she said, then begged the officer to stop Amy from leaving the house with the baby. "It's way too cold and she's in no condition to go anywhere alone with the baby," Donna explained.

The policeman went to the house. Donna was shocked when he greeted Amy by name. He had encountered Amy on other occasions during parties that had been busted. In an effort to break the tension in the household, the policeman took Amy to a friend's house, leaving Kaliegh in the warmth with her grandmother. The next morning, Donna decided to file a CHINS petition against Amy. She called the

Department of Social Services (DSS) and announced that she had a Child in Need of Services.

"Me and my mother had a lot of arguments about how to raise my daughter," recalled Amy. "I was still young. I still wanted to go out with my friends. I wanted to party like regular teenagers do once in a while. My mother really didn't know how to control me. She wanted somebody to be able to come in and have more authority over what I was doing, so she called DSS and got them involved. I needed guidance, and they were more stern—you know, straight down to the point with me. I had to listen to them. There were consequences if I didn't."

"It was no joke," was James's view. "DSS—they take control of your life. They tell you what you're gonna do and how you're gonna raise your kids. If you don't like it and you don't do it, they'll take your kids away from you."

Faced with the threat of having her daughter removed from her custody and placed in foster care, Amy got her act together. She enrolled in the Teen Parent Program and moved forward with her studies. She began working part-time as a waitress at Friendly's.

"Having a baby turns your life around," Amy said. "You have to grow up so fast."

Trevor went off to the army, leaving Amy to raise their child on her own. Right after Trevor signed up, Amy's father went to talk to the recruiters. He wanted to make sure they knew that Trevor had a daughter and was obliged to pay child support. As James had suspected, Trevor hadn't written anything on the forms about being a father, nor had he mentioned it in his interview.

James presented Kaliegh's birth certificate to the recruiting officer

on duty. The officer suggested that James contact his local congressman, John Olver, who was widely respected in the county for being
a strong advocate for working families, youth, child care, and afford-
able health care. James called the congressman's office and spoke to
a page who helped him file the necessary paperwork so that child-
support payments would be automatically deducted from Trevor's
monthly salary. They also made sure that Kaliegh was placed on the
army's health insurance plan. Soon after being recruited, Trevor was
stationed in Colorado. He called Amy and told her that he'd be
spending only a few weeks a year in Massachusetts. He said he hoped
to see his daughter for a few days at Christmas.

While attending the Teen Parent Program, Amy was separated from
most of her friends at Pittsfield High School. Her life was boring
compared with what it used to be. She did her best to prove herself
a fit mother, and after a year of relatively good behavior, she succeeded in convincing DSS that she could handle the responsibility of
raising a child.

"They dismissed my case because they thought I was doing good,"
she said.

Amy left the Teen Parent Program and went back to Pittsfield
High School. With DSS out of her life, Amy, now sixteen, felt it was
time to find a way to escape from her parents' house. She felt trapped
living at home and longed to be free of her mother and father's
watchful, critical eyes. She had rapidly lost the weight she had gained
during her pregnancy, and with her long, luxurious brown hair, her
perfectly applied makeup, her stylish clothes, and her long painted

fingernails, she was a magnet for the opposite sex. When Kaliegh was one and a half, Amy's friend introduced her to Bernard, a young African who was working in Pittsfield and taking classes at Berkshire Community College.

"The first time I met Amy, she had a little girl with her," Bernard recalled, "and I was like, 'Who is she?' She said, 'My daughter.' Well, I didn't believe it. I was, like, 'Oh no, I don't think so.' I said to myself, 'It's probably her sister or something, her little sister.' "

Amy was immediately captivated by Bernard's exotic, thick French accent. She was intrigued to learn that he had recently

come to America from Ivory Coast to live with relatives and pursue his studies, in fulfillment of his parents' dream. Bernard's mother and father wanted their son to become rich and successful in America.

Amy had not traveled far from Pittsfield and had never been outside the United States. She loved the idea of spending time with a man who had grown up in Africa, in the midst of a different culture and with a set of values and experiences that were so completely fresh and unlike anything she was familiar with. Compared with other guys Amy knew, Bernard seemed more serious about his education, more ambitious, more idealistic, and more conscious and appreciative of the opportunities America offered. He adored his part-time job at the Center for Disabled Children and spoke enthusiastically about the children he worked with.

"Bernard's an intelligent guy," said James, "but he was older, so I wasn't too hip on the situation. Bernard was, like, at least twenty-two years old. I don't know. I think he was attracted to Amy 'cause she's good-looking."

Amy was extremely impressed by the fact that Bernard had his own car, his own apartment, and a steady flow of income. She told Bernard that because of a medical condition, she couldn't get pregnant again. They had sex and never used any contraception. After they had been dating for three months, Amy missed her period.

"I ended up getting pregnant again," she said. "It was just another mistake. People make mistakes."

"Amy told me that she couldn't get pregnant," said Bernard. "I was so stupid. I didn't even think about it."

"I was on the Pill and then I was off," Amy explained, "but I didn't think I could get pregnant. I thought that . . . I don't know what I thought . . . I just wasn't thinking!"

Amy's father had a different theory about what motivated his daughter's second pregnancy.

"Amy was living here at home, and she was still battling all the time and fighting with everybody. So I think she got pregnant on purpose, just to get out of the situation she was in here."

Amy didn't hide her second pregnancy. She told Bernard right away.

Bernard recalled, "When Amy told me she was pregnant, I said, 'Amy, the baby is not a baby yet. It's just a development. It's just a little egg that is growing inside you. If you do an abortion, it would be so fast. If you let the baby grow inside you, the process will be so much harder.' I said, 'Please, Amy, let's do an abortion.' "

Bernard shook his head. "She said, 'No!' "

"When I was pregnant with my daughter, I didn't want to get an abortion," explained Amy. "Being pregnant the second time around, I looked at my daughter and I figured that I couldn't kill a baby. That's all."

The decision about what to do with the fetus was ultimately up to Amy. The appropriate time for Bernard to make a clear, definitive statement about not being ready to become a father had long passed. Now that the situation had progressed to this stage, Bernard was forced to live with Amy's decision, whether he agreed with it or not.

Amy went to the doctor. After checking the results of the tests, the doctor put her hands on her hips and asked Amy, "So, what are you going to do?"

The condescending tone of the doctor's voice caused Amy to

shrink away from the cold metal of the stirrups around her feet. The rough white paper crackled beneath her back as she sat up and stared into the cold, hard eyes of the forty-something, instrument-wielding female gynecologist. In a clear voice, Amy stated her wish to have the baby and raise it herself. There was a palpable current of silent condemnation in the stark, white institutional room. Amy felt it settle on her like a cloud of dust. She felt dirty, ashamed, and defiant. She hated the doctor for making her feel that it was expected she would want an abortion, given her age and circumstances.

Rather than having a conversation about her options and emotions and her relationship with Bernard, Amy remained silent and furious throughout the rest of the examination. This encounter sealed Amy's dislike and mistrust of doctors. They didn't respect her, so she didn't respect them. She would show them she was capable of raising two children. They'd see. She would prove to everyone that she could be a good mother.

"No, not again!" James and Donna screamed when they heard that Amy was planning on keeping the second baby. They reminded their daughter of the enormous additional responsibility of clothing, feeding, and educating another child, not to mention the extra time, love, emotional energy, and attention a second child required. Amy told them that she had made up her mind and that nothing anyone said would change it. She packed up her and her daughter's belongings and moved in with Bernard. James and Donna disapproved.

"Bernard had an apartment at this place called Riverview," James recalled. Located at the bottom of a ravine behind shrubs and foliage, the river was barely visible from the high-rise building; it was the contaminated Housatonic River, where PCBs from GE had been dumped. "It was kinda a low-middle-income project," said James. "There were drug dealers in there. It's not a place I would want to live."

Amy didn't like the project, either, but she did her best to make it as nice as she possibly could, decorating it with pretty curtains and other knickknacks. She was relieved to have escaped her parents' house. She desperately wanted Kaliegh to have a father figure in her life, and Bernard seemed willing to take on that role, at least initially. Since her life already revolved around motherhood, Amy thought a second baby would solidify her life with Bernard. It wasn't quite that simple.

Bernard was in turmoil about the impending arrival of the baby. For months, he couldn't bring himself to tell his parents that he was going to be a father. They had worked hard to be able to send their son to America and harbored high hopes for what he would be able to accomplish, armed with a degree from an American college. The last thing Bernard wanted to do was dash their expectations and wound their pride. Yet in order to help support Amy, the baby, and Kaliegh, Bernard would have to work full-time, which would entail postponing his studies indefinitely.

Not wanting to break his parents' hearts, Bernard kept finding excuses to avoid telling them. Finally, toward the end of Amy's pregnancy, he picked up the phone and made the international call to Ivory Coast. As expected, his parents were devastated. When Bernard recalled the telephone conversation that transpired, he bowed his head and fixed his eyes on the ground. His voice sank into his throat, weighed down by a sense of shame and failure.

"My father, he sent me to America to go to school," he explained.

"For my father—seeing his son having a baby and dropping out of school . . . It was a big disappointment for him."

While Bernard and Amy were adjusting their lives to accommodate parenthood, Amy's brother and sister were on a completely different track. They left Pittsfield and enrolled in college. Amy's sister majored in environmental science. Her brother studied communications in the hopes of someday fulfilling his dream of becoming a sportscaster.

College was not in the cards for Amy. After giving birth to her healthy son, Marcus, she struggled to balance the demands of being a teen mother of two children with the challenge of completing her high school education. She transferred back into the Teen Parent Program and continued working part-time as a waitress at Friendly's.

Marcus was admitted to the Teen Parent Program's nursery, but Kaliegh, now three, had to attend different day care. The rule at the Teen Parent Program was that once kids were old enough to walk, their mothers had to find alternative day-care facilities for them. Amy found private home day care that would accept her vouchers. On weekdays, when school let out at three o'clock, Amy strapped Marcus into his car seat and drove to the place where Kaliegh spent most afternoons.

It took Amy ten minutes to get to the street that led to the gravel driveway of the run-down private home that doubled as a day-care center. As Amy turned the knob, the screen door swung open into a dusty room that was dingy and poorly lit. Children lay strewn around on the floor, looking bored and lethargic.

Kaliegh ambled over in a daze and threw her arms around her mother in a prolonged embrace, glad to be picked up. The gaunt middle-aged woman who looked after the children didn't say much more than hello and good-bye. Her mind was elsewhere. She moved as if caught in slow motion. Kaliegh ran outside, eager to breathe some fresh air. She hopped into the car beside her little brother, who gurgled a warm greeting. Amy drove through Pittsfield, past the Friendly's where she worked. She turned the corner and pulled into the parking lot of the tall subsidized apartment building that she, Bernard, and the kids called home.

For Amy, getting her daughter and infant son out of the car and up three flights of stairs to their apartment was a major daily ordeal. That afternoon Kaliegh bounded up the stairs, way ahead of her mother, who yelled out to her to be careful and slow down. Nervous about Kaliegh's being way ahead of her and out of sight in the unsafe drug-infested apartment building, Amy fought to balance her son in one arm and his carriage in the other, along with her school bag, which was casually slung over her shoulder. It was a heavy load to carry up three long flights of stairs, and when she got to her front door, she was panting and out of breath. As Kaliegh wailed impatiently, Amy set everything down and fumbled for her keys. She heaved a deep sigh of relief as the door swung open. Once the kids were safely inside, Amy finally had a chance to catch her breath.

Without any help, Amy faced these and other practical challenges every single day. Even the simplest, most mundane tasks that most people take for granted were rendered exponentially more difficult by the presence of two young children. Complicating matters, Amy and Bernard's relationship remained strained. The birth of their son had increased the tension between them rather than alleviating it, as Amy had hoped.

Although Amy deeply appreciated Bernard's presence and the fact that he fulfilled his duties as a father to both her daughter and their son, they were constantly fighting. Bernard resented not being able to go to college because of his obligation to work to support his family. He came from a home where the male was the sole bread-winner, and he was uncomfortable with Amy's working and making as much money as he did. Amy didn't like being told what to do by her boyfriend. She became extremely frustrated and upset when Bernard criticized her friends and tried to exert control over how she spent her free time.

Amy and Bernard's shared sense of responsibility for the two kids was the glue that held their fragile relationship together. Although all relationships require compromise, the longer two people know each other, the more aware they become of exactly what those compromises are going to be. Then when they make a decision to commit to a relationship for the long term, the choice is ideally an informed decision. Amy and Bernard went about it the opposite way, committing to a person each barely knew and then slowly learning about the other as they went along, balancing their personal conflicts with the added pressure of raising two children and the challenge of living together in a small apartment while struggling to make ends meet.

When Marcus was a few months old, Amy heard some ugly rumors. She had good reason to believe that Bernard was being unfaithful to her. Her fears came to the surface at the Teen Parent Program in May, when for an hour each week she attended a series of writing workshops conducted by visiting psychologist Carol Gilligan and her colleague Normi Noel.

Carol and Normi used Edith Wharton's novel *Summer* as a starting point for discussions and writing exercises. Set in the early 1900s in North Dormer, a bleak fictional town believed to be a composite of Pittsfield and surrounding areas of Berkshire County, Wharton's novel describes the plight of a teenager named Charity Royall. Following a passionate love affair with Lucius Harney, a rich architect from out of town, Charity finds herself pregnant. Just as she is wondering how and when she should break the news to her lover, she hears some upsetting gossip: Harney is, in fact, already engaged to a rich socialite from one of the city's finest families.

Amy sat very still as she listened to Carol Gilligan read the following passage aloud:

> Sometimes as Charity lay sleepless . . . she planned many things. . . . It was then she wrote to Harney. But the letters were never put on paper, for she did not know how to express what she wanted to tell him. So she waited. . . . Since her talk with Ally she had felt sure that Harney was engaged to Annabel Balch. . . . She was still sure that Harney would come back, and she was equally sure that, for the moment at least, it was she whom he loved and not Miss Balch. Yet the girl, no less, remained a rival since she represented all the things that Charity felt herself most incapable of understanding or achieving. . . . The more she thought of these things, the more a sense of fatality weighed on her:

She felt the uselessness of struggling against the circumstances.

After reading the passage, Carol described how Charity subsequently feels unworthy of getting what she wants, so she writes a short, self-effacing letter to Harney that completely misrepresents her true feelings, hides the reality of her pregnancy, and masks her desire. She pointed out how Charity's options shrink and her future darkens as a result of her silence and fear of speaking the truth.

Carol then set the novel down and asked Amy and the other teen mothers in the workshop to write two letters to the fathers of their babies: one that they would be willing to send, and another that they wouldn't dare send, for fear of the implications of expressing their real thoughts and feelings. When it came time for the teen mothers to read their letters out loud, Amy adjusted her glasses and began:

> Dear Bernard,
>
> I wanted to let you know I am very happy. But I am also very unhappy. I wish we could take this relationship to another level. I am tired of the rumors. I am tired of the lies. I want a picture-perfect relationship. I want so much more than I have at this point.

Smiling nervously, Amy paused and picked up the letter that she *wouldn't* send.

"Okay," she warned her attentive peers. "This is the bad one. This is the one I wanted to write to him."

Dear Bernard,

    *I hope you did not sleep with my friend. I don't understand why
my friend would say such things to me. I'm not sure what to believe.
But I hope to God that you care too much for me to be so stupid.*

Amy took off her glasses, wiped the tears from her eyes, and
fought to compose herself.

"This just makes me really mad," she said. "Because I want to kill
somebody right now."

Later, when asked to respond to Amy's worries about his infi-
delity, Bernard was evasive. He addressed the issue in an indirect,
inconclusive way that neither affirmed nor denied Amy's fears about
his cheating on her. He shrugged his shoulders, squirmed on the
couch, took a deep breath, and tried to justify himself.

"I would consider myself like Bill Clinton," said Bernard. "He's
got a family. He got a job, I have a family, I have a job, and I would
do the same thing, too. He's raising his family, and I have to do the
same. Everybody should do the same."

"That letter that I wrote to Bernard was kind of nasty," Amy
acknowledged a few weeks later. "But I guess things are working out
right now; they're going really good. Bernard supports me really
well. He helps me. He pays bills. He takes my daughter to the doctor.
He watches my daughter. He's really supportive."

"I have to support my family," said Bernard. "That's the way my
father raised me. My mom was a teenager, too, when she met my
father. My father never ran away. He stayed there for my mother.
They were both young. He stayed there, stayed there, worked,
worked, worked. . . . Now things are getting better."

Refusing to be held back, Amy graduated from Pittsfield High School with the rest of her class. The ceremony was held in the neighboring town of Lenox. Cloaked in purple caps and gowns, the class of 1999 filed into the spectacular Seiji Ozawa Hall at Tanglewood, home of the world-renowned music festival.

When Amy's name was called, she ascended the podium. Onstage, the mayor of Pittsfield handed her a white rose and her diploma. Later that afternoon, James and Donna hosted a big party at their home. While Amy and her friends celebrated, a group of small children congregated on the lawn and had a party of their own. The young sons and daughters of the class of '99 drove their plastic cars in circles, admired one another's balloons, and devoured hot dogs drenched in ketchup.

After graduation, Amy enrolled in a cosmetology course offered at the vocational school attached to Pittsfield High School. For two years, she trained to get her license, focusing on hairdressing. She was required to put in one thousand hours of training before she could take her state boards and be certified. Amy started out cutting hair on mannequins and then moved on to real people. She was taught how to do manicures, facials, and waxing. On days when she didn't have class, she continued waiting tables at Friendly's.

"My hours are from as early as six-thirty in the morning until six o'clock in the afternoon," she said. "I don't work nights anymore because nights are too much."

"Welfare's a little different now," James explained, " 'cause the federal government clamped down on that. Before, it was like you could be on welfare all your life and they'd just send you a check every month plus food stamps, free medical, and all that. They're a little tougher on that now. Amy works full-time so her income is up to a point where she doesn't get any money.

"When I say Amy doesn't get any money—her rent is subsidized, so welfare's probably paying five hundred dollars a month toward her rent. Her health insurance is MassHealth, so if she goes to the hospital, she don't pay anything for that. The state pays that. I guess if you're working, you can get health insurance, rent subsidies, and food stamps, but lots of times nowadays, they don't give out money."

Bernard continued to work at the Center for Disabled Children. He structured his schedule to complement Amy's. In order to make it possible for him to spend time with the kids during the week while Amy was working, Bernard worked thirteen- or sixteen-hour shifts on Fridays, Saturdays, and Sundays. He regretted that he had to work on weekends because that's when most of his friends were going out and having fun.

Although the pay was minimal, Bernard got tremendous satisfaction out of working with handicapped children and seeing them learn and progress. His work experience gave him insight into children's thoughts and behavior. Bernard felt strongly that this insight made him a better parent. He used many of the concepts and techniques he learned on the job at home to guide him in his attempts at understanding and teaching his son. While Bernard enjoyed his work, he remained troubled by a sense that he was failing to achieve his full potential.

"I love the job that I do, but it's not something I want to do for the rest of my life. It's a beginning," he stated emphatically. "I do what I have to do to have my family live under a roof and eat something."

Amy and Bernard were alarmed when the rent for their apartment skyrocketed. James explained what had caused the sudden increase.

"These subsidized housing projects were built by the state, but these large corporations own them, and they're always buying and selling them. This one company bought the project where Amy and Bernard lived and then went in there and renovated it and then jacked the rents up, double or triple. The low-income people who were living in there were asked to pay eight or nine hundred dollars a month. That's outrageous for this area, so Amy and Bernard moved out to another housing complex on April Lane.

"In subsidized housing," said James, "the state has a formula based on what you can afford to pay for rent, and they figure out what you can afford. So Amy—she hardly makes anything. At April Lane it's probably six hundred a month, but because it's subsidized, Amy probably pays eighty dollars a month. Taxpayers pay the rest."

Amy and Bernard and the two kids settled in to a duplex apartment on April Lane. Although drugs were still a concern, as was the rare drive-by shooting, these apartments were on the whole more child-friendly, surrounded by grass and trees and swing sets. The doorways were all at ground level, so Amy was spared the hassle of hiking up three flights of stairs.

Wanting to increase her income beyond what she was making at Friendly's, Amy began looking for a second job. When a position opened up at the Teen Parent Program, she called and submitted her name for consideration. She was hired to take care of babies while their mothers were being tutored. Amy returned to the grueling night shift at Friendly's so that she could be free to work at TPP during the day.

On a typical day, Amy woke up at seven and dropped the two kids off at day care on her way to work.

"My job was really tiring," she said. " 'Cause I just watched babies all day and then I'd come home to my own babies. And it was just— ugh . . . sometimes I just . . . I would just go home and fall asleep."

Amy had a few hours off in the late afternoon, and when she could keep her eyes open, she used this time to run errands, shower, change into her uniform, and make dinner for the kids. She would then drive to Friendly's, where she worked until midnight.

Bernard had mornings to himself. Usually he relaxed, did errands, watched TV, and caught up with his pals during his daily workout at the gym. After lunch he would head out to pick up the kids from day care. He spent most weekday afternoons playing with the children in the park or at home.

Bernard felt that his role as a father combined teaching with discipline. He did his best to teach the children to respect adults and avoid violence. He believed that children should have "less toys and more books."

"I want my kids to be wise," he said. "One day, I want to be proud of them. To teach kids to love books, you have to start from a young age. The more reading they do, the more they learn—the smarter they get."

Overloaded with the dual responsibility of being a mother of two and providing for her family, Amy had absolutely no time to herself. Going to and from work, she and Bernard passed each other like ships in the night. Most days she felt physically, emotionally, and spiritually drained.

"I'm nineteen going on twenty, and I feel like I'm fifty," she said. "I'm just so tired. I do what people are supposed to do when they're thirty, or in their late twenties. I'm running around all the time, getting up early, working, and chasing kids. A lot of people my age don't get up early and get two kids ready. I have to get them dressed and feed them breakfast and take them to school. It's frustrating that I can't work every day because I have to work around the kids' schedules, so I'm not free to make as much money as I want to. It's hard. I feel like I'm old."

Amy shook her head in wonder, remembering how naive she was back at the beginning of eighth grade, before she got pregnant for the first time.

"I never thought I'd be in the situation I'm in now," she said. "I was just a normal teenage girl who thought that nothing could faze me, that nothing bad would ever happen to me—that nothing bad *could* ever happen to me."

Kaliegh, nearly five years old, entered the room, dressed up as a bride. The little girl had used bobby pins to attach a piece of white lace to her hair. The lace draped across Kaliegh's face like a veil, as she put one foot in front of the other, pointing her toes, making every effort to walk gracefully in a perfectly straight line. Holding her son, Marcus, Amy turned to look at her daughter.

"What are you doing, Kaliegh? Getting married?"

Kaliegh broke into a huge smile, nodded, and continued her walk down an imaginary aisle.

Amy laughed at her daughter's pretend game, and shook her head. For Amy, marriage seemed far off in the distant horizon. "I want to get married someday," she said, "but Bernard and I are both still young, and we have a lot ahead of us. When I get married, I want to be settled down, having a house, doing the right thing, making lots of money. . . . I don't see that happening in the next two years, but eventually . . ."

Bernard agreed that marriage was not something he was ready to dive into.

"You don't say, 'I want to get married,' because it's fun," he said. "I've seen people that got married and got divorced in less than two weeks. I want to get married eventually, but right now I'm just waiting. Right now there is commitment between Amy and I. We act like we're married. Because of the kids we have, we each fulfill a parent's life. Once in a while I tease Amy and say, 'Oh, I wanna marry you,' you know, stuff like that. She knows I do that just to tease her, and we laugh about it."

"I know he's kidding me," Amy snapped, "because he knows not to come to me without a ring."

"How much does a ring cost? Thirty dollars?" Amy frowned as Bernard shrugged his shoulders, a wide grin on his face. To him, it was all a big joke.

"Thirty dollars?" Amy glared at him. "An engagement ring better be way more than thirty dollars, or I'll return it."

"I can go to New York and buy you a fake one. You know, those crystals."

"Yeah, right," said Amy. "If you ever buy me a ring to get married, I'll bring it to the jeweler and make sure it costs way more than thirty dollars."

Eighteen months after graduating from high school, Amy looked pale and haggard. She had chopped off almost all her hair and covered what remained with a bandanna. Working two jobs was getting to her. At home she could be found curled up on a chair, lost in a deep sleep, oblivious to the sounds of the kids playing, undisturbed by the drone of a game show on TV.

In spite of their initial resistance to Amy's having children at such a young age, James and Donna had fallen deeply in love with their grandchildren. They often stepped in to help Amy, appreciating that she was doing her very best to stay afloat under extremely difficult circumstances.

"I see Kaliegh and Marcus three or four times a week," said James. "Kaliegh learned how to use the phone and she's constantly calling here saying, 'Grandpa, I wanna sleep over your house tonight.' I always say, 'Okay, come on over.' They're here all the time."

"My parents have taken my kids to Disney World, the Jersey Shore, and the Bahamas. At age six, my daughter has gone more places than I have in twenty years," said Amy, her voice tinged with envy, her eyes brimming with gratitude.

On Halloween, rather than trick-or-treating around April Lane, Amy and Bernard decided to take the kids to James and Donna's neighborhood, which they felt was much safer. While Amy and her mother stayed at home and offered hungry ghosts and goblins handfuls of candy, Kaliegh dressed up as an angel and set out on her own candy-hunting mission, accompanied by her little brother, who was trick-or-treating for the first time. James and Bernard led the kids from house to house, laughing as Marcus unabashedly ran straight inside every door with his arms outstretched and palms open, eager to grasp the next Tootsie Roll, Starburst, or lollipop.

Having lived in the neighborhood for more than twenty years, James was on familiar terms with his neighbors. Their houses and yards were decorated with all sorts of ghoulish displays, including plastic skeletons and gigantic spiderwebs dangling from trees, as well as glowing, grinning pumpkins of all shapes and sizes. They appeared to enjoy the annual ritual almost as much as the kids did.

As each door opened, James introduced Bernard and his grand-children to the mostly white neighbors who lived on his street. Some of them were meeting Bernard and the children for the first time. Their eyes traveled from James to Bernard to the children, mentally inserting Amy, the missing piece of the family portrait.

As November swept through the Berkshires, the trees lost the last of their leaves and the temperature plummeted. Amy bundled up to face the bitterly cold New England mornings. Back on the breakfast shift at Friendly's, she poured coffee and took orders for eggs over easy, occasionally glancing out the steamed-up windows into the parking lot, where snowflakes fell onto windshields as customers hurried inside, shivering as they removed their hats, gloves, and parkas. Amy was always ready with her pad and pencil. She took pride in her work and always tried to be at her best for the people she served.

Amy's fluctuating hairstyles provided the best indication as to what was really going on behind her pretty smile. The novelty of having two kids had worn off, and Amy was looking for new ways to captivate and startle people. In efforts reminiscent of her old need to get attention from her preoccupied family, Amy changed her hair length, color, and style several times a month. It went from brown to red to blond to a different shade of brown. On one occasion, she braided straw-blond extensions into her short brown hair to make two-tone cornrows. Though it was easy for Amy to change her hairstyle or her nail polish, it was much harder to change other aspects of her life.

Amy finished her one thousand hours of training and passed her state boards for her cosmetology license. During the exam, she used her mother as a model and gave her a haircut. Now certified, Amy longed to get a job as a hairdresser so that she could give up her job at Friendly's. She enjoyed hairdressing because it allowed her some creativity, unlike waitressing.

"I've gone out looking for jobs for hairdressing, but a lot of the hours that people want me to work are hours that are impossible for me because I have kids. I can basically work thirty hours a week during day-care times. I can't work weekends, 'cause Bernard works weekends."

The division of labor between Bernard and Amy meant that there wasn't a single day of the week that the entire family could spend together. The time each spent with the kids became increasingly stressful.

"Money is a big problem," Amy said. "We fight over bills, and bills, and more bills. Neither one of us has jobs that we make tons of money at. We both have a limit. Bernard's okay because he pays for a lot. It's hard for me to pay for a lot because my job isn't that good."

Bernard's eyes narrowed as he chastised Amy.

"Don't sit down and talk about how we fight for money, we fight for this, we fight for that! We have arguments. We don't fight! We talk. When we don't compromise, I go my way, she goes her way."

Amy sat absolutely still, saying nothing, looking weary and slightly embarrassed by Bernard's harsh rebuke. Exasperated, Bernard sighed and shook his head.

"My stress—my stress is not money. My stress is that I'm not accomplishing the things that I wished for. I will accomplish something. It has to be with school. I hope I go back. I want to finish what I started. Right now we're at a young age and we're raising two kids. It's not easy."

Like many immigrants, Bernard came to America with high expectations based on fairy-tale impressions of a culture he knew only from TV shows such as *Beverly Hills 90210* or *Friends*. Bernard dreamt that the education he would receive in America would open door after door, eventually empowering him to ascend the ranks and make lots of money. He envisioned himself living a lifestyle not unlike those he had seen night after night on television in his parents' modest home in Ivory Coast.

After several years of living in Pittsfield, Bernard had become much more jaded. He recognized his lost innocence in the hopeful faces of his friends who remained in Africa, clinging to their dreams of someday going to America and transforming their lives.

"A lot of my friends in Africa think that America is the country of opportunity," Bernard explained. "Why? Because they know that by coming here, they can do better than back home. It's not easy back home, and by seeing stuff on TV all the time, they wish to be here; they think America is paradise. I went home this summer and I told them, 'You think America is a paradise, but it's not easy to live there. It's a lot of struggle, and you gotta work through your whole entire life. You get a job, and your whole paycheck could be gone in less than a minute. You work to pay bills. You work, and they take your money. You work and you pay insurance for your car. You pay rent. Even food is expensive. It's not easy.' I tell them that. I tell them, 'The people you see on American TV shows, they're doing well. But many of us are suffering. It's not only me.'

"It's not easy, but my dream will come," promised Bernard. "My dream is to be somebody one of these days, to be able to have a house. . . . I don't want to be a millionaire, but I need something for my family to be happy. I don't want my kids to struggle."

Bernard paused, deep in thought. Suddenly his face lit up and his mood shifted. He sat up straight, his shoulders back, his head held high.

"I brought my son to work today, and everybody was saying, 'Oh my God, I can't believe it. Look how fast Marcus can talk. He's only two. He's so active. He's learning so quick.' It makes me feel good when my coworkers talk about how good my son is. It makes me feel like I'm raising him the right way. I'm gonna see it go further," said Bernard. "I'm gonna do a lot with my son."

The tension between Amy and Bernard escalated as Bernard tried to assert more control over Amy's life. He complained about her choice of friends and made it clear that he didn't approve of her going out and partying. Amy was furious. She had moved in with Bernard to get away from her parents, and now she felt that Bernard was acting as if he were her father. She told him that she wouldn't tolerate his behavior and that she would do what she wanted, when she wanted, with her own money.

Bernard and Amy usually made about the same amount of money per week but occasionally Amy made more, because of tips. Bernard was uncomfortable with Amy's role as a breadwinner who made all her own decisions, spent her money as she pleased, and had no qualms about running out to bars and nightclubs with her friends whenever she felt the urge to party.

"You can't do that," protested Bernard as Amy ran out of the apartment, jumped into the car, and drove off, dressed for a night out on the town. "You have children!" he yelled. "It's your job to stay home and take care of the children!"

Bernard's words fell on deaf ears. Amy wanted her freedom and balked at Bernard's efforts to rein her in. Since Bernard was so far away from his own family, he sometimes turned to Amy's father for advice on how to deal with Amy.

"Bernard, this is America," James told him. "Women aren't slaves in this country. If they want to go out, they get a night out."

"But she goes out with those bad kids," Bernard complained.

"That's a different story," said James, knowing from his own experience exactly what Bernard was up against. "I hate to tell you, Bernard, but Amy chooses the people she hangs around and there's nothing you're gonna be able to do about that. If you think you're gonna keep her tied down in the kitchen, barefoot and pregnant— that's not gonna happen." James chuckled. "Bernard, if you think you're gonna control Amy's life, you might as well forget it."

Seeking peace and a bit of a break from the tumultuous situation with Amy, Bernard made plans to go back to Ivory Coast to visit his family. He stayed in Africa for a month, during which time Amy and the kids stayed behind in Pittsfield. Unbeknownst to Bernard, Amy viewed that time as a trial separation. She was surprised at how well she managed taking care of the two kids on her own.

"Amy and Bernard's relationship is pretty stormy," said James, his face graying in the rapidly fading winter light. He paused for a moment, looking out the window, gathering his thoughts. "I think a lot of it could be their age difference. Bernard seems like a calm, mature guy, but Amy—she's kinda immature and stubborn. I know Bernard wants to continue his education. I told him, 'Well, if that's what you want to do, go ahead and do it.' If he thinks that having a child and Amy are holding him down, I don't know, maybe he's gotta choose. . . .

"Bernard comes from a different culture," explained James. "He says to me, 'In Africa a woman doesn't do this or that.' I tell him, 'You're not in Africa. This is America and I don't know if you guys are ever gonna make it.' "

"We broke up," reported Amy shortly after Bernard's return from Ivory Coast. "Bernard's a jerk and I don't want to be with him anymore. We fight all the time. I'm sick of him, and he's sick of me. We shouldn't be together. We have absolutely nothing in common at all. All Bernard does is bitch at me for everything I do. He doesn't like me to go out, and I like to go out a lot. He don't let me do nothing. He acts like he's my father. He's not my father, and I will not be pushed around like that. I don't like to be stepped all over, so I'm moving out. My kids are gonna live with me. I'm gonna be raising them.

"I applied for Section Eight housing. For some people, it takes up to a year to two years to get it, but there was an opening on the list and they ended up sending me a letter that I got it. I don't have any furniture yet. I got money back after I paid my taxes from working all year. I'm gonna use that to get some furniture."

"If you make under a certain amount of money," explained James, "then, I believe it's the federal government, they give you fifteen hundred dollars per child. You don't claim it against your income. So Amy, she gets a big tax return, twice as big as I get. She's got two children, so that's three thousand dollars. They just give it to her."

James and Donna helped Amy get the bare essentials for her new apartment, a duplex in the April Lane housing project, less than a minute's walk across the parking lot from Bernard's front door. As Amy settled in with the two kids, Bernard sharply reduced the amount of time he spent with them. He told Amy that he didn't feel he had any responsibility to Kaliegh, since she wasn't his daughter.

He saw his son much less than Amy had expected, given that he lived practically next door.

One night a week, Marcus slept over across the yard at his father's apartment. The rest of the week the family rarely saw Bernard, not even in passing. Often when Amy was overwhelmed with work and exhausted after looking after the two kids, she would call Bernard and ask him if they could work out a schedule where they shared custody of Marcus; she would take care of the little boy four nights a week, and Bernard would take him the other three nights. Bernard refused, claiming he was too busy to make that commitment.

Bernard continued working at the Center for Disabled Children and enrolled in a course at the Mildred Elly Business School. After completing the course, he got a job designing websites for a local company. He loved this job. Trained by his coworkers, Bernard was constantly expanding his capabilities and learning new skills. His bosses were very pleased with his progress. When the company traveled to New York City for trade shows and conferences, Bernard was one of the employees chosen to attend.

Amy started working at a hair salon at the mall in Great Barrington. It was the job she had been hoping for. Her boss adored her, and she had many regular customers. She worked forty hours a week but remained financially strained because despite the success Bernard was enjoying at his new job, he didn't regularly pay child support and, aside from a few small gifts here and there, he left Amy with the responsibility of providing for their son.

"Bernard throws a few bucks here and there," said James, "but as far as a monthly payment? No, he don't pay. I'm trying to encourage Amy to take him to court."

Amy was amazed at how fast the kids were growing up. Kaliegh attended summer camp at the Girls Club. Marcus celebrated his fourth birthday at a pizza parlor. Bernard attended the party with some of his friends. He, Amy, Kaliegh, and Marcus posed for a rare family snapshot.

Amy turned twenty-one and began to outgrow her hard-partying ways as she saw more and more of her friends from high school succumbing to serious drug addictions. She began saying no when her friends asked her to do things that she thought might be unsafe. Gradually Amy began figuring out which of her friends were worth keeping.

"Amy had a couple of girls come over, and I think they were drinking," said James. "They wanted Amy to give them a ride home, and Amy couldn't because of the kids. So she let the girls take her car. One girl got dropped off, and the other girl went to another party, got loaded, and ended up upside down in a river with a fractured skull. Somehow she survived it. Amy was out of a car, but dear old dad took care of it."

James bought Amy a new car. He sensed that although Amy still had a long way to go, she was starting to make some real progress. He knew life wasn't easy for her, and he did whatever he could to help out with the kids.

When Amy wanted to go on a vacation, Donna and James assured her that they would look after the kids while she went away. Amy

collected travel brochures about Florida. For months, she saved up tips from work, stuffing her cash into an empty champagne bottle that she kept hidden in her closet.

One night, Amy's childhood friend Bridget stopped by for a drink. Once a member of the popular clique in high school, Bridget had become a teen mother and, like Amy, had given birth to two children at a very young age. Whereas Amy had buckled down and was devoted to her career as a hairdresser, Bridget had become addicted to crack. When she visited Amy, she talked about how the Department of Social Services had removed both her children from her custody. They were now in foster homes.

After spending roughly an hour at Amy's apartment, Bridget gave Amy a hug and departed. The next morning as Amy was getting dressed, she looked into her closet and realized that her champagne bottle stuffed with cash was gone. Convinced that Bridget had stolen it, she drove over to the apartment where Bridget was staying and confronted her boyfriend. He said that Bridget was gone and claimed to know nothing about a champagne bottle.

That same day, Bridget skipped out of town. There were rumors that she had gone down South. Most people suspected that she was holed up somewhere on a binge. Amy never heard from her again.

Months later Bridget's former boyfriend confessed to Amy that he had indeed seen broken glass all over the floor of their bedroom. Amy had no doubt that the shards were from her shattered champagne bottle. She knew that her former best friend had stolen her hard-earned savings, probably to buy more crack.

Amy started saving up her tips again. When James and Donna celebrated their twenty-fifth anniversary, Amy, her sister, and her brother all chipped in to buy them tickets to Ireland. James was thrilled. He had always dreamed of traveling to the country where his ancestors had lived. A rare smile illuminated his face, and Amy was delighted to see her father looking so happy.

chapter three

LIZ & PETER

"When I was seven I got molested by my mom's boyfriend. Charges were pressed. He was put in jail for two years. After that, he came out on parole and it was sort of weird because I knew he was out there somewhere still and I just didn't feel too comfortable. After that, life was just sort of about trying to get my life back together."

LIZ WAS BORN IN SPRINGFIELD, AN HOUR AWAY FROM Pittsfield, where she ended up at the age of fourteen when the Department of Social Services placed her in a juvenile correctional facility. Between stints in lockup, Liz lived in a series of foster homes. She became pregnant at the age of seventeen and enrolled in the Teen Parent Program. Her luminous brown eyes traversed the cracks in the ceiling as she searched for the right words to describe the jagged shards of the years that had constituted her childhood.

"My childhood? I got deprived. That's how I'd put it. I grew up in a violent home, so it wasn't easy. There were a lot of beatings in my house, other than me. My dad would always beat up my mom and yell at her and throw stuff. My mom would do the same. Since I was born this was happening.

"In my neighborhood there were shootings, stabbings, rapes, murders, hit-and-runs. . . . I had to deal with it," said Liz, "because I lived there no matter what. Everyone there was—you can't say poor—but you could say that it was hard to get money. People would do dumb things to get cash. You'd see hookers, drug dealers, people robbing other people, that kind of stuff. There were lots of gangs, too."

Liz could not remember a time when her mother, Paula, wasn't dependent on welfare. Paula worked sporadically at an array of fast-food restaurants and went through long periods of unemployment. Liz shrugged her shoulders as she rattled off a few adjectives that described her mom:

"White, Italian, about three hundred pounds, long hair, wears glasses . . ." Liz sighed and collected her thoughts. "I don't know how to explain my mom any more than that," she concluded. "She's got five different people all inside one person, so it's hard to describe her personality. It's easier to describe what she looks like."

When she was an infant and toddler, Liz stayed home with her biological father, who had come to the United States from Puerto Rico. He spoke Spanish to his daughter and could not read to her because he was illiterate.

"When I was five years old, my dad left me to be on his own," Liz explained. "He got tired of my mom and tired of me, I guess, from what my mom tells me. I really haven't seen him that much since then.

"As a kid, I saw him once in a blue moon, whenever he felt like stepping in. It kinda bothered me that my dad would come in and out of my life whenever he wanted, but my mom let it happen. It was like everything was okay, but it really wasn't. I couldn't say 'I love you, Dad,' and really mean it, 'cause I didn't know the guy."

Enraged after Liz's father walked out, Paula redirected her anger toward the one thing he had left behind: their daughter. In what became a pattern throughout Liz's childhood and adolescence, her mother frequently beat her. Paula once explained this violence by saying that she couldn't look at Liz without being reminded of her father. As the blows were falling, Liz recalled crying out, "How can you see my father in me? I am so different from him!"

Liz looked Hispanic like her dad, not white like her mom. Her identity as a child of mixed race was a huge issue in her life.

"The kids, they'd point at me and say, 'Oh, look at that, eeww. . . .' They'd call me a 'Gringo,' which in Hispanic slang means 'white girl.' People would also call me a half-breed because I'm Spanish and Italian. I didn't like being called those things. It was rude. I liked the fact that I wasn't all one person; I was white, I was Hispanic and a couple of other things, a whole bunch of breeds."

In conversations with Liz, it was impossible not to notice her high level of self-awareness and her excellent ability to express herself verbally. It was hard to believe that this spirited, alert, observant, articulate teenager had been held back in first grade and had subsequently failed many of her classes from that point on. The reason for her bad grades was not her aptitude or her lack of intelligence: it was her chronic absenteeism, a warning flag of child abuse.

The obstacles between Liz and an education did not originate within her. They were rooted in her unstable home environment. Teachers failed to effectively intervene, despite strong clues that this young child was living in a destructive, malignant home environment. Liz associated her early years with a sense of resignation, powerlessness, and loss. She described being held as a virtual prisoner in her own home, isolated from other children, forced to cater to her demanding mother's every need.

"I almost never went to school, because my mom preferred me to stay home and take care of her. She wanted me to be her 'duty girl,' fixing her things to eat, bringing her coffee. . . . It was just

'Liz, can you do this for me? Liz, can you get that for me? Can you light my cigarette for me?' I was like her slave girl. When kids in my class made fun of me, sometimes they would actually call me a slave because they knew why I was home. I don't know how they knew, but they knew.

"I had no friends. I was basically on my own. It was me, Liz, and Liz. That was all I could focus on because none of the kids at school ever wanted to get along with me. They used to laugh at me because of the way I looked. I had bowl haircuts and I looked like a boy. I dressed funny, in corduroys and butterfly collars, always in very funky colors—you know, pink with green. Very stupid-looking colors that I would never choose. My mom put that stuff on me 'cause that was all she could afford. So I can't get mad at that. All the other kids at school had the name-brand clothes on. I used to go to school and they'd say, 'What did you get at the Salvation Army yesterday?' I don't know how they knew, but they knew I went to the Salvation Army.

"My mother wasn't an alcoholic or a drug user, but she was a very lazy person. Not to be rude, but she really was the lazy kind. People say I should've focused on myself more, but it was kinda hard when you have one person like your teacher telling you that you should be in school and your mom saying, 'You should be home, listening to me and doing what I'm telling you.' As a child, I was really confused."

Liz was very self-conscious about the fact that her mother was obese. Paula's imposing three-hundred-pound frame often prompted nasty jeers and jibes from kids as well as from random people on the street, rude phrases along the lines of "Hey, fat lady walking down the street, how you doin'?" Liz felt guilty for not being able to defend her mother against these verbal assaults, but as a small child, she was too scared and too shy to open her mouth about anything to anyone.

Soon after Liz turned six, her mother gave birth again. According to Liz, her half sister's paternity remains a mystery. Now struggling to support two children on welfare, Paula pulled herself out of unemployment and started a new part-time job several nights a week.

Liz was too young to look after her baby sister, so her mother would often leave her daughters in the care of her boyfriend at the time, a man by the name of Ted. During Paula's extended absences, Ted began physically abusing Liz and her infant sister. This violence was conducted under the guise of discipline. It increased in severity as time went on.

One night Ted kicked open the door to Liz's bedroom and molested her, brutally forcing his hands inside her vagina as she sobbed. After sexually assaulting Liz, he went on to the infant. When Liz tried to intervene, Ted pushed her away. Liz was forced to watch helplessly as this man inappropriately fondled her little sister. Ted threatened Liz, telling her in no uncertain terms that he would kill her and her mother if she ever told anyone what had happened.

Midway through the evening, Vivian, a friend of Paula's, came in to check on the kids. She was greeted by the sight of Liz crouched in a corner, holding her body, clutching her nightgown, tears streaming down her face. When she asked Liz what on earth had happened, Liz tried to explain but was interrupted by Ted, who stormed in and began arguing with Vivian, denying everything and saying that Liz was lying. Unsure of whom to believe and not wanting to get involved, Vivian took the children to the home of Liz's biological father and left them in his custody. Ted insisted on accompanying them. He would not let Liz out of his sight. In addition to being her mother's boyfriend, Ted was a close friend of Liz's biological father, and to Liz's utter horror, her father welcomed this man into his home.

Later that night when Paula came to pick up the kids, Ted told her that Liz had misbehaved terribly. Liz's mother spanked her as punishment for her supposed misconduct. Then her father took her into the bathroom and spanked her again, even harder.

In the days that followed, Ted kept threatening Liz, assuring her that if she told anyone about the molestation, he would kill her mother. He further terrorized the little girl with threats of vague, dark, unspeakable things he would do to her, things that would be more terrible than anything she could possibly imagine, more terrible even than death. Liz could barely imagine what could be worse than what he had already done to her and certainly didn't want to find out.

In the wake of being molested, Liz shut down emotionally and spiritually. She continued to be absent from school and was forced to repeat first grade. By law, teachers must report sexual abuse if a child discloses it. However, some teachers neglect to pursue clues less overt than disclosure, such as extensive and unexplained absence, impaired social skills, and poor academic performance. Liz was exhibiting all these indicators of sexual abuse, but the teachers, possibly overwhelmed trying to control the rambunctious students in their classrooms, failed to question the child and did not launch a detailed investigation into her home environment before or after the molestation took place. At the young age of seven, Liz felt invisible, isolated, and fearful, trapped in her mother's tight grasp, victimized in her own home, and forgotten by those who might have helped her.

Liz's grandmother and friends of the family began to comment on the little girl's strange, withdrawn behavior. After observing her over the course of the year, her mother's friend Vivian became convinced that Liz had been telling the truth. After struggling internally about what to do, she confronted Paula with her suspicion that Ted had molested Liz. Paula went ballistic, chased Vivian out of her apartment, followed her home, and proceeded to smash through the terrified woman's front door with a baseball bat, leaving a gaping hole.

Next, Paula confronted her eight-year-old daughter. When Liz confirmed what Vivian had said, her mother demanded to know why she had never been told about the molestation a year ago, when it happened. Crying, Liz told her mother that she had tried to tell her many, many times. She vividly described moments when she had been trying to get her mother's attention and recalled fragments of the numerous conversations she had tried to interrupt as she searched for a way to confide in her mother, who had always been dismissive— too busy, too frazzled, or too distracted to listen.

After hearing Liz's detailed account, her mother finally began to piece together the truncated sentences her daughter had uttered over the past year, along with the very strange, worrisome behavior that many people had noticed and commented on when in the presence of the little girl. The truth was staring Paula in the face. Her child's agonized eyes were unwavering and unforgiving.

Paula contacted Vivian, who agreed to help her press charges. Liz was taken to a doctor, who examined her and confirmed that the molestation had taken place. The doctor completed the necessary paperwork for the courts. Liz courageously made a statement to the authorities describing the sexual abuse that had occurred. Ted pleaded guilty. The result? He was sent to jail for two years and was served with a restraining order prohibiting him from going near Liz for the rest of his life.

Although Paula was initially furious with Ted, her anger soon subsided. She confessed to Liz that she was still head over heels in love with him, in spite of the molestation. Paula made it clear to Liz that she resented her for coming forward. She held her eight-year-old daughter responsible for the fact that she was now separated from her lover, and blamed her for ruining her romantic relationship. Her mother's bitter accusations only added to the guilt and self-loathing Liz already felt. Bombarded with memories of the sound of her mother's harsh, reproachful voice, Liz cringed and shrugged her shoulders, justifiably incredulous after all these years.

"I don't know how a mother could love a guy that molested her daughter. I don't understand my mom's thinking," sighed Liz. "She just—it's like her mind slipped somewhere. . . . I don't know where. She always told me that she loved him. I got confused. I'd be, like, 'Why would you want him still here, knowing what he did to me? Would he do that again?' "

To Liz, Ted's jail sentence seemed much too short. Before she knew it, he was out on parole, back on the streets of Springfield, haunting her neighborhood. The ten-year-old lived in constant fear of running into the man who had molested her.

Liz rarely visited her biological father, except when she got into huge fights with her mother or when her mother was with a guy and didn't want her around, but one afternoon when she was at his apartment, she heard a knock at the door. When her father asked who was there in Spanish, Liz froze at the sound of an eerie, familiar voice. It was Ted.

Her father walked to the door and, without a second thought, turned the knob and let Ted in. Liz was in shock. Her own father was allowing this sexual predator to be under the same roof as her, in blatant defiance of the court's restraining order. Liz panicked and looked for a place to hide. Queasy with fear and repulsion, she cowered in the bedroom, pressing her full weight against the closed door in a forlorn protective gesture. But even as she covered her ears with both hands, she could not block out the sound of the men's voices.

She overheard Ted confronting her dad, telling him that she was a liar. Ted told her father that the only reason he had pleaded guilty to Liz's charge of sexual abuse was to spare her mother the agony of a long, drawn-out trial. Liz's father chose to believe Ted instead of his daughter. To Liz's disgust, the two men remained friends.

Overcome by feelings of seething rage, guilt, and resentment, Liz felt utterly betrayed by both her parents. Her self-esteem was already low, but her spirit sank even further, weighed down by her disappointment in their failure to protect her in the most basic, vital way. All through her tainted childhood, Liz internalized her mother's lack of concern for her daughter's physical and emotional safety and incorporated this maternal recklessness and negligence into her own view of herself. As a result of being convinced that no one gave a damn about how she was treated or cared whether she lived or died, Liz failed to develop either a strong sense of ownership or boundaries in relation to her own body. As she entered an extremely turbulent adolescence, she carried her precariously damaged body image with her.

By the age of ten, Liz was already making out with boys. At age eleven, she hit puberty and became confused, embarrassed, self-conscious, and alarmed over the changes she observed in her body. To Liz, it seemed as if her mother was in denial about the implications of her maturing body and emerging sexuality.

"I was developing different and that was hard because my mom never wanted to talk me about it. She never wanted to help explain what was going on. So, I had to figure it out for myself," Liz recalled. "I had to go to school and ask teachers what this meant, why this had to happen, why my breasts were growing, that kind of stuff."

By the time she entered the sixth grade, Liz was dating lots of different guys, most of whom were fifteen or sixteen years old. By engaging in this precocious, sexualized behavior, Liz cut short what ideally should have been a period of latency, a developmental phase that takes place roughly between the ages of eight and twelve, during which girls generally tend to turn away from boys and have mostly female peers. Ideally, it should be a time when girls develop skills and assert themselves in sports, academics, and the arts— learning about the world and building up confidence in their own abilities, laying the foundation for a strong sense of self defined independently of the opposite sex.

Having leapfrogged over this essential developmental phase, Liz struggled to fill her inner void by acting out "adult" roles, dressing provocatively and precociously, mimicking the sexualized behaviors that she saw in music videos, movies, and magazines—and at home. Her mother never drew any clear lines regarding what kinds of boys were appropriate or inappropriate for Liz to date, nor did she set a good example for her daughters when it came to relationships and the kind of men she associated with.

"My mom was dating all sorts of men," said Liz. "Every week there was a new guy I was introduced to. I thought that was her focus, to have these guys in her life to take care of her, which was wrong. One week this guy would try to be my father, and the next week some other guy would try to be my father. It was awful. I had all these guys trying to be my dad and I knew they weren't, so I defied them. That caused more problems between me and my mom. The fact of all these guys trying to be something they weren't for me, or to me . . . I didn't want to be around that situation and I didn't want my little sister to be around it, either. But I couldn't take my little sister, 'cause back then I didn't even know how to take care of myself."

Instead of reaching within and building up reservoirs of strength, conviction, and self-confidence, Liz searched outside herself for affirmation of her identity. She desperately craved acceptance, love, and validation. Her self-esteem was a completely unstable entity—dependent upon male attention of a sexual nature.

Liz's early re-initiation to sex occurred with a series of predatory adult male partners. Beginning at age thirteen, the sexual situations she found herself in were unquestionably defined by the same features as her molestation at age seven: a tremendous inequality in power, strength, and age, and her own objectification and exploitation.

"After I got molested at the age of seven, the next time I had sex was at the age of thirteen, which is quite young, now that I think about it. It was hard because I kinda went crazy. I liked the feeling of being near people. Being near a man, to me, was great. I thought I was being loved. I ran away after I first had intercourse. I stayed with the guy I slept with because I was scared to go home. I didn't want my mom to hit me or anything, because she was quite violent.

"The guy I was with when I was thirteen, he was twenty years old, he was Hispanic. He was a gang member, one of the Latin Kings. To me, he was good-looking at the time. Probably right now I wouldn't say that anymore. I felt like I was loved, so that's why I did it.

"I stayed at his house. I didn't go to school. I had to worry about cops. I had to worry about seeing my mom because I was only three buildings down from my own home. After that I ran away like thirty more times within two years. I never wanted to be home.

"It wasn't fun being on the run. You had to hide all the time. You were always scared. Like, if you saw a police officer, you ran the other direction because you didn't want him to take you back home. When I ran away, I felt more grown-up. I didn't feel like this little thirteen-year-old girl."

Liz was quickly exposed to the seedy underworld of hookers and drug dealers. Although Liz deluded herself into thinking that the older men who offered her shelter loved her and cared for her, the reality was that they were exploiting her. During many of these early sexual encounters, Liz didn't use any contraception.

"I was always trying to get pregnant," she recalled. "I always wanted to have a baby." Liz cited two primary motives for this unrelenting desire for a child: a deep sense of loneliness and the desire to have something that no one could ever take away from her.

Following the advice of some of her friends on the street, Liz started using condoms at least some of the time. It was only because of sheer luck that her high-risk unprotected sex with older men did not result in an earlier pregnancy, infertility due to a chronic STD, or AIDS. One night, exhausted, frightened, and tired of prostituting herself, Liz reached out for help. She called the hotline of a local organization for children in need. When they bluntly and unsympathetically advised her to turn herself in to the police, she hung up on them.

Unlike some less fortunate runaways who link up with pimps who drug them, kidnap them, and transport them across state lines, where they often meet with ugly fates, Liz never left the immediate vicinity of her hometown. She would run away for a while and then return to her mother's apartment, where she faced physical and verbal abuse. It was a vicious cycle. When Liz finally left home for good, it wasn't to go to a shelter where there was support and guidance. Instead, at age fourteen, she was sent to court in shackles and handcuffs.

"The violence between me and my mother got to the point where my mom would slap me a lot. She'd just start hitting me," said Liz. "One day I came home . . . I was like fourteen years old, and I was staying at my mom's house again. She told me I could go with my friends to the mall. So I did. She said to be back by eight o'clock. I was back two minutes after eight. I was slammed in the corner when I walked in the door. I was getting slapped in my face. Getting yelled at . . . 'Where were you for the two minutes?' She really flipped out on me. I had no other defense other than pushing my mom off me. So I slapped my mom, and that's when everything really changed.

"The cops got called. I got arrested for the first time. Charges were pressed on me from my mother. She accused me of assault and battery, which I don't think was right, because she was really hitting me hard. She was abusing me, literally abusing me. Physically, mentally, verbally, it was just all there.

"I went to court after my mom pressed charges. The first time was to be before the judge, and the second time was—they call it a sentencing. In the courtroom, I had handcuffs and shackles on. If I tried running, I'd fall on my face. You only have enough space with the chains so that you could walk. Then you had a chain coming up from your feet to your hands, so you were hooked that way. You felt like you were already in prison.

"The choices were either to be put in a foster home, stay at home with a zero curfew, or go into a lockup facility for juvenile delinquents. At this time, because it was my first offense, they chose for me to go to a foster home because they felt it was unsafe for me to be at home because of my mom's temper and because of my temper. The fact that all the men were coming in and out of the home—

they felt it was unsafe. I didn't feel right, either. So they took the handcuffs and shackles off me and they sent me with my DSS worker to my first foster home.

"At first I lived with Hispanic people, and that foster home was really crowded," recalled Liz. "There was three little rooms for foster kids, and every room had, like, five or six kids in it. It was the worst place for them to send me to, because the lady didn't care what time I came in or what time I came home. She didn't care what time I got up, as long as I went to school. She didn't care, as long as she got her check. That's what most of the foster homes I was in were like.

"The foster parents get paid to have foster kids there. I felt that the reason why I was there was so they could get a paycheck. A lot of the foster homes were crowded with, like, five foster kids, and when you needed something, most of these foster homes would say they never had any money—when you know they did. You'd see that check come in every week, and they'd have that smile on their face.

"I started hanging out with people ten years older than me, like twenty and twenty-four years old. I got into drugs, alcohol, and stealing. I stole my first car, which was scary because I didn't know how to drive and I worried that the police were going to see that and pull me over and send me to jail.

"After a month I begged to go home, and DSS worked out an agreement between me and my mom. It didn't work out. Two weeks after I moved back home, I ran away again.

"I would run away to people who had things to offer me," said Liz, "not just to some house that had nothing in it. I ran away to people who had food, people who had money to help support me, people who would care for me, people I wished I lived with rather than my mother.

"Every time I ran away, DSS put me in a different foster home. The social workers would try to set goals for me to achieve by certain dates, like achieving a certain amount of days in school. I had a chore chart. I had a checkoff chart. If I earned a certain amount of stars or checks, I'd earn a grab bag. I really didn't have myself focused on any goal, because I really didn't know what I wanted.

"I wasn't stuck in one neighborhood. I went from a poor section of town to rich people. I went to one foster home where it was like one of those fantasy-type houses. Like you would think about it, but you thought it would never come true. It was a real nice house. I had my own room, my own TV, basically my own everything. I could eat whatever I wanted. They had two dining rooms, one for the grown-ups, one for the foster kids. At the time there were only two foster kids, me and this other girl. There was a good-size living room with chandeliers. . . . The kitchen was humongous with a counter in the middle. The bathroom alone was humongous. There was a toilet and you'd walk five steps and then get to the toilet and then another ten steps to the shower. The place was awesome. I felt like I was rich, but I really wasn't. We were in the quiet section of Springfield, which I didn't like, 'cause I didn't know anything about it. I ran away from that home. I don't know why I did it, but I did. That was my problem—I didn't want to have rules. So I totally trashed that house, I just ran. I just forgot about it. I just put it aside. I didn't want to be there no more."

By the time Liz got to this foster home, where the living conditions were relatively good, she was already a veteran of many negative experiences. Her view of herself was so damaged, her self-esteem so fragile, her expectations for her life so shrunken that she could not bear the idea of becoming accustomed to a more comfortable lifestyle that might, without warning, be taken away from her. Unlike an adopted child who would have the security and permanence of a new family, as a foster child, Liz sensed the transience of her situation. She knew that nothing was forever and that she would eventually be back where she started. She felt unworthy and out of place in this house of dreams. Thus, she acted out in a destructive way and instigated her own departure. After this incident, Liz was put on probation. She intensified her gang associations in a desperate search for a sense of belonging that was otherwise absent from her life.

"The reason why I felt comfortable with the gang is that they actually respected me," explained Liz. "They were there for me—at least, I thought they were. They gave me that feeling like I was supposed to be there. I didn't get any of that feeling at home. I'd go home and everyone would be screaming and hollering at me, saying things like 'I hate you!' the minute I walked through the door. I felt like the devil was in my house. But when I was with the gang, it was, like, 'Oh, what's up, how you doing?' There was a general respect for someone. I was more respected in the gang than I was at home."

One of the gang members started giving Liz assignments to go beat up certain girls. Liz would do as she was told. She built up an intimidating reputation as someone to be afraid of. She hated fighting and hurting people. Looking into the frightened, tearful eyes of a girl she had beaten black and blue made Liz feel horribly about herself. That one moment of searing self-loathing was enough to halt her foray into violence.

Liz kept running away from foster homes and cutting school. Between the ages of fourteen and sixteen, she was placed in a lockup detention center on three separate occasions. After being admitted to lockup for the first time, Liz demanded to see a doctor and stated that she wanted to be tested for STDs. She had been having discolored vaginal discharge and feared she had AIDS. She was not HIV-positive but did test positive for gonorrhea. The doctor commended Liz for seeking treatment right away and explained that untreated gonorrhea could increase a person's risk of catching HIV and could also cause PID, an infection of the reproductive organs that sometimes leads to serious, potentially fatal complications during pregnancy. Liz was treated with a single dose of antibiotics. Much to her relief, the infection went away. After serving several terms in lockup, Liz was placed in the Key Program, which was more tightly regulated and regimented than any place she had ever been.

"The Key Program is a place for adolescents eleven and up," said Liz, "who have problems at home and who run away all the time, like I did. It was for people who were considered problem people with gang issues and other stuff like that. It was a really strict place. You shared your room with about three other people. You had to ask permission to go to the bathroom. You had to ask permission to brush your teeth and to get up from your seat. They had control over you. You couldn't do anything unless they said it. It was kind of like a jail. I was there for three or four months. Then they let me out."

Liz was fifteen and a half when she was let out of the Key Program. She was placed in a foster home in Pittsfield. She began dating a local gang member named Ricardo. Eventually she found out he already had three kids and a wife. While Liz was still involved in this relationship, she met a nineteen-year-old named Peter, who treated her with a level of kindness and decency that she was completely unaccustomed to. After years of accepting abuse and disrespect from the adults who had brought her up and the men she had subsequently subjected herself to, Peter was a blast of fresh air, a ray of hope. He empathized with Liz's vulnerability and was able to sense the fragility beneath her tough exterior.

"I first met Liz through my good friend's brother," explained Peter. "My friends would tease me because I was white and Chinese but I hung out with nothing but Puerto Rican or Spanish people. Pittsfield had a Latin dance group. I ended up doing that to do something besides working. One night after dancing, I heard my friend's brother and Liz arguing over their relationship. We all went to the arcade, and he kept bad-mouthing her, not treating her right, not showing her any kind of respect as a female, just none whatsoever. I went up to her while she was playing a video game. She was almost in tears, but she was holding them back, like 'I can't cry, I'm strong.' I rubbed her back and I told her, 'It's okay.' I said I'd bring her home if she wanted to be brought home. She said no and gave me a funny look. I went back and finished playing pool. When it came time to leave, my friend's brother told me, 'Leave her. Don't put her in your car.'

"I'm not like that," said Peter, shaking his head, "I'm not like that at all. I brought Liz home. While I was driving I just kept looking at her, thinking to myself, *Damn, she's a pretty girl!* How could she have a relationship like that? How could a guy not respect her? I believe women should be treated with utmost respect. That's how my grandmother and my mother raised me. When I dropped Liz off, I told her if she needed anybody to talk to, she could give me a call. With me growing up the way I did, I always try to be everybody's big brother. I told her, 'You can always have my shoulder to cry on. My ear is always there to listen to you.' That's how I met Liz."

Peter understood what Liz had gone through. His Asian American father had been raised in a foster home. While Peter was growing up, his parents worked "hell hours" to provide for their six kids. His father had put in eighty hours a week as a general manager at McDonald's, and his mother had worked nights as a security guard for fifteen years.

"My dad would probably work anywhere from eleven o'clock in the morning until midnight. My mother would work from three in the afternoon to seven o'clock the next morning. That was the kinda life that I lived growing up, taking care of my brothers and sisters. It really wasn't much different than being their parent, except I was their older brother."

"When I met Peter, he was a virgin," Liz recalled. "When he told me that, it shocked me. I never had a guy who hadn't been with anybody else. When it comes to a virgin-to-nonvirgin deal, it's usually the guy that's not the virgin and the girl who is. It felt weird to have the role reversed. I felt guilty because I wasn't a virgin, but then I didn't feel so bad because we talked about it and I told him everything about my past. I thought that if I was gonna be with a guy who gave his virginity up for me, it wasn't just a one-night stand—it obviously meant that we'd be together forever—or at least for a long period of time.

"That first night that Peter and I shared together—I think that's the night I got pregnant. We were at my foster home and we were supposed to be watching a movie Peter had rented. It was funny because we watched part of the movie and he kept talking about how he liked me and I kept talking about how I liked him. All of the emotions started happening, and it sort of went from there. I wanted the sex to be more natural, so I wasn't thinking about using condoms and I don't know if Peter was thinking about it, 'cause he didn't ask me and I didn't ask him, either. I didn't say, 'Wait a minute, shouldn't we think about this?' like everybody says you're supposed to. I didn't think before I did it."

Two and a half months later Liz was at a party and she had stomach cramps. She sat hunched over with her arms crossed over her chest. Her friend took a good look at her and shook her head. She told Liz she suspected she was pregnant. The two girls drove to a drugstore in a nearby strip mall. While Liz waited in the parking lot, her friend ran inside and stole a box of home-pregnancy tests. After two pregnancy tests came out positive, Liz went to Peter's job site and broke the news.

Peter was shocked. He stared at Liz, speechless. Becoming a father at such a young age was not part of his plan. He had been hoping not to have a child until he was at least twenty-five. He had wanted his career to be more in order before he started a family.

Peter's parents had divorced several years earlier, and with his father out of the picture, Peter had become the man of the house, responsible for looking after his five younger siblings and his mother. Fatherhood seemed like an impossibly difficult challenge to add to his already full load. All these thoughts swirled through his head as he looked at Liz standing there, gazing at him, awaiting his response.

"I decided to grow up then and there," Peter recalled. "I decided not to be like so many of the men out there these days. When the female tells them they're pregnant, they bounce! They get up and they leave or they tough it out in the beginning and then when they realize how hard it's going to be, they just take off. I decided not to be one of those men.

"Any person can make a child or conceive one," said Peter, "but when it comes down to the nitty-gritty, it takes a man to raise one. The only time I can consider myself a man is when my son is raised. When he's doing well for himself, then I know my job is done."

Liz enrolled in the Teen Parent Program but found it hard to keep up with her schoolwork. "When I was pregnant, I was sick a lot. I was sore a lot. You know . . . typical pregnancy things. It affected my attendance. To try to be in school all the time was hard. I wanted to get my diploma, but it didn't happen. I chose to go for my GED instead, because they don't go based on how many days you've been absent. They go based on how much you've learned."

Peter and Liz rented a walk-up apartment near the center of Pittsfield and started living together. Summer arrived and Liz gave birth to a son, whom she named Pete, after his father.

"Pete's birth gave me a sense of unconditional love," said Peter. "The responsibilities that were bestowed upon me were getting up in the middle of the night, changing his diapers, calming him down

when he was crying, waking his mother up to get ready to breast-feed him, or getting his bottles together. Being a father is basically another full-time job. My twenty-four-hour-a-day job."

Peter had to take little Pete to the emergency room on several occasions. Once Peter found the baby in the kitchen, gagging on Pine-Sol, which was all over his lips. Luckily Peter had stepped into the room moments before the baby could swallow the potentially fatal poison.

During his first summer the baby broke out with hives all over his body and was having trouble breathing. The doctors said it wasn't asthma and concluded that the respiratory difficulties were probably related to the hives. After a month of being sick, the baby recovered.

When Peter's mother and younger siblings were forced to leave

the place where they had been living, Peter graciously allowed them
to move in with him and Liz. This crowded situation was supposed
to be temporary, but it went on for months. The downside was the
total lack of privacy. The upside as Liz and Peter saw it was that
while they worked long, late hours at Kentucky Fried Chicken and
McDonald's, Peter's family members could fill in as built-in live-in
baby-sitters.

For Liz, the problem with being employed at McDonald's and
Kentucky Fried Chicken was that aside from having no benefits or
health care, she had to work nights and there were no child-care facilities in the vicinity that were open late. In the absence of other afford-
able options, Liz and Peter were not at all concerned about leaving the
task of caring for their infant son in the hands of Irene, Peter's eleven-
year-old sister. They felt that Irene was more than up to the task of
watching the baby on her own several nights a week. On the few nights
that Peter's mother and his other siblings weren't working late at
McDonald's, they helped baby-sit. Liz depended on their assistance
because her days and her nights were long and grueling.

"I get up at nine-thirty," she said. "Then I work at KFC from ten
o'clock in the morning until about four in the afternoon. Between
four and six-thirty, I take a shower, clean the apartment, and try to
get ready for my other job. I try to spend as much time as I can
with my son. From seven o'clock on, I'm at my other job at Mc-
Donald's. The end of the night is basically cleaning wherever they
need me to clean. By then I'm really tired and my legs are ready to
give out 'cause I'm on my feet all day. I'm usually done by midnight.
When I get home, I look at everyone sleeping and check to make
sure everything's okay. I'm pretty dead by then. I just want to die

in my bed. That's basically my day, every day except for Sundays and Wednesdays, when I'm off."

Peter was an assistant manager at Kentucky Fried Chicken, in training to be a general manager. He was Liz's boss, which at times added pressure and increased the friction in their already stressful relationship. With Liz working two jobs, Peter worked fewer hours, so it was he rather than she who spent the most time with the baby.

"My day starts whenever the baby wakes up," he said. "When Liz is at work, I feed the baby his lunch or give him his bath, or take a walk. By two o'clock I'm back in the house, showering and getting ready for my job."

Peter was making $500 per week while Liz was bringing home between $165 and $180 per week. Peter accounted for the disparity in their incomes by citing the fact that he had a higher rank at KFC; as an assistant manager he was on salary, whereas Liz was part of the regular crew staff and therefore got paid minimum wage. Peter usually worked from three in the afternoon until midnight, but more often than not his boss phoned him on weekends and on his days off, asking him to fill in for other people. Eager to ascend the ranks to general manager of KFC, Peter almost always said yes to his boss, which annoyed Liz, who wished he would say, "I'm sorry, I can't come in. Today's a day I have to spend with my family."

Like most adolescents, Liz experienced huge swings in her behavior, moods, and emotions. Sometimes she acted immaturely and lost her temper; other times she was wise beyond her years. When people who didn't know Liz looked at her, often they assumed that she was thirteen or fourteen. Sometimes she felt that young inside. Other times she felt much, much older.

"Certain days I'll feel like I'm ninety-five 'cause that's the way my body feels, and then other days I'll feel like I'm twelve because of the way my attitude is. I vary," explained Liz.

In hindsight, Liz wished that she had waited and had her baby when she was financially and emotionally more stable. Her dreams for the future revolved around money, love, and security. Someday Liz wanted to be able to buy a house and get married. In the immediate future, she hoped to save up enough money to buy a white oak bedroom set for her son so that his room could look more like those she had seen displayed in mail-order catalogs.

"My hopes are for us to financially get our act together, you know, where we're not just gonna be broke. I would like to go to college. I don't know what I want to study yet, but I wanna get a degree. I wanna get higher. I don't want to be at these six thirty-five or seven-dollar-per-hour jobs. I want to get a nine- or ten-dollar-per-hour job."

Peter's goal was to become a general manager of a chain restaurant or a hotel. He took his job at KFC seriously, took pride in his work, and saw each day as a step toward a higher position. His identity and sense of self-worth remained rooted in his dedication to work and his devotion to his family.

"I've got two separate lives," he explained. "I live KFC when I'm in the uniform. When I'm in regular clothes, I'm this little guy's dad and Liz's boyfriend. The thing that makes me the most happy is coming home to my family. I like waking up knowing I still have them with me."

"The thing that makes me happiest is being with Peter," said Liz. "Because of the way my past was, I didn't expect my life to be in

such good order. I'm so grateful for Peter and so grateful for my son. It makes me feel good inside to know that I have a family, to know that I have people to be around, to know that they're not just going to up and leave. . . . That trust is really there. That's a good feeling. I'm grateful for what I've done. Waking up in the morning and knowing that you've accomplished a lot more than what you expected yourself to accomplish is great."

chapter four

COLLEEN

"*The other mothers at the Teen Parent Program would be telling me, 'Oh, my baby's doing this, my baby's doing that. . . . ' Jonathan was older than they were and he wasn't doing anything at all with his right arm or leg. His right hand would always be clenched right up to his chest. He couldn't hold his own bottle. He never crawled. He used to just scoot across the floor and drag his feet the whole way. You know your child. I mean, you might not know exactly what they have, but you know when something is wrong. The guilt . . . You always feel it's your fault.*"

COLLEEN GREW UP IN A CATHOLIC HOUSEHOLD. SHE lived with her parents and her elder brother on a quiet tree-lined street in Dalton, a small suburban New England town bordering Pittsfield. Dalton serves as the headquarters for the Crane Paper Company. In addition to its renowned stationery, Crane manufactures the currency paper for the U.S Bureau of Engraving and Printing.

Colleen's father did not work at Crane. He worked alone from a home office adjacent to his dining room, designing machinery on his computer. He printed out his plans and then sent them off to factories. Colleen's mother, Maureen, was a medical assistant in a pediatric unit. Both of Colleen's parents were satisfied with their jobs, but behind the facade of their stable working-class existence, the family lived in turmoil.

"My childhood was hard," said Colleen. "My parents fought a lot because my dad had an alcohol problem and my mom has depression and she's fighting anorexia. Their fighting would just make me so sick. My father—he never wanted to listen to me about his alcoholism. I always felt I had to protect my mom. So, basically, I never really had a childhood. It was all taken away. I never wanted to go out or anything. I just wanted to stay home."

When Colleen was eleven, her grandmother died, leaving Maureen in a state of profound mourning. Her sadness escalated into a full-blown clinical depression.

"My mom being sick was just like this quiet moment in my house," said Colleen. "No one wanted to talk, no one wanted to do anything with each other. We all knew she was quiet. Her attempting suicide—that was really hard. Depression is just something that runs in my family."

More hardship was in store for this already overburdened family. When Colleen was thirteen, her cousin was killed in Florida, the victim of an accidental shooting at a fraternity. Colleen became silent and withdrawn. She could not make up for the loss of her cousin. She could not convince her mother to eat. Nor could she convince her father to stop drinking. Colleen felt powerless. She watched helplessly as her mother suffered in the clutches of deep, black mood swings and was hospitalized several times. Maureen had to be hooked up to IV needles that dripped nourishment into her emaciated body. Colleen plummeted into despair.

Whenever Colleen looked in the mirror, she was filled with self-loathing. She worried that she would never be smart enough, attractive enough, or thin enough to gain the acceptance and respect of others. She became reclusive and spent long hours alone in her bedroom, listening to music and mulling over the problems that were afflicting her family. None of Colleen's teachers reached out to inquire about her quiet, withdrawn, antisocial behavior. Ignored, Colleen retreated further into her shell.

Although she didn't say much at school, Colleen always listened closely to the other kids and kept tabs on what was going on around her. In the seventh grade, she overheard some girls bragging that sex was just the greatest thing they had ever done. Colleen decided that she wanted to find out for herself. She lost her virginity to a boy she befriended at school. Colleen had hoped that the experience would be amazing, magical, loving, and healing. Disappointed, she concluded, "Sex isn't everything it's cracked up to be."

A few months later, Colleen's relationship with her first boyfriend ended. Her next romantic relationship was a secret: at the age of fourteen, she fell in love with a girl from school. Colleen worried about her sexual identity and felt tremendous guilt. She hoped that her passionate interest in girls was just a phase that she'd grow out of.

Colleen started working a full shift after school at Burger King. Work was a welcome distraction from her dark ruminations. Her schedule maximized her time away from home, and when she was on duty, her mind was completely occupied with the task at hand. Meanwhile, at home, Colleen's family problems persisted. She worried that her father was drinking himself into oblivion while her mother was starving herself to death. Whenever her parents fought, Colleen repeatedly tried to intervene in defense of her mother. She continued using every tactic she could think of to get her dad to stop drinking, but all her efforts met with failure. Over and over again, Colleen kept reenacting the drama of confrontation, disappointment, and defeat. Her thwarted desire to play the role of the savior remained strong throughout her adolescence.

Ryan entered Colleen's life on a picturesque winter day. Snowflakes cascaded down from a sky cloaked in thick layers of fog. The streets wore a slick coat of ice. The sidewalks had not yet been shoveled. Colleen trudged through soft snowdrifts on her way home from her driver's ed. A car glided over to the curb. Colleen heard someone call out her name. She stopped and turned around. A girl she knew from school rolled down the window and said hello. Colleen walked over to the car and was introduced to Ryan, who sat in the backseat with some other guys. After sizing Colleen up, Ryan asked for her number. He said half jokingly that he wasn't going home without it.

A few hours later Colleen's phone rang. It was Ryan. The teenagers got to know each other over the course of several long phone calls. As they began spending more and more time together, Ryan opened up to Colleen about his traumatic upbringing.

Colleen recalled Ryan telling her that he had grown up believing that his stepfather was his real father. At the age of nine he found out that this wasn't true, when his mother admitted that she had lied about his paternity and bluntly told him that he would probably never get to meet his biological father. For years Ryan watched in helpless agony as his drug-addicted stepfather abused his mother. Ultimately, Ryan's stepfather was arrested for domestic violence and sent to jail.

Colleen was determined to save Ryan from his own demons. She believed that if she gave Ryan enough love, his childhood wounds would eventually heal. Colleen made excuses whenever Ryan treated her poorly. The harsh truth was that Ryan repeatedly acted in an abusive manner, reinforcing the worst of Colleen's familiar feelings of low self-esteem. In Ryan's presence, Colleen felt helpless, powerless, anxious, and worthless. The pattern of her emotions within the relationship re-created a template that was in many aspects a facsimile of her childhood experience.

The first time Ryan and Colleen had sex, they used a condom but then stopped after Ryan assured Colleen that he knew how to have unprotected sex without getting a girl pregnant. Disregarding the possibility of contracting HIV or other STDs, Colleen gave Ryan her blind trust.

One night Ryan assaulted his mother's boyfriend. This was not Ryan's first violent outburst and proved to be the final straw for his mother. She kicked Ryan out of the house. Colleen asked her mother if Ryan could move in with them temporarily, just until he found a new place to live. Initially, Maureen found Ryan charming. She understood how tempestuous family life could be and was happy to help out this young man who seemed to be one of her lonely daughter's few close friends. Colleen's parents agreed to let Ryan sleep in the den until he made peace with his mother. They offered him meals and did their best to make his stay as comfortable as possible.

Ryan made himself right at home and immediately began to take advantage of the family's hospitality. Late at night, when Colleen's parents were fast asleep upstairs, Ryan would sneak his friends in and party with them into the early hours of the morning. He tried to hide his drug problem from Colleen, who chose to keep quiet and look the other way. She didn't want her parents ever to find out.

Ryan's life revolved around heroin. He made a habit of pocketing cash he saw lying around and stole odds and ends every time he had a chance. As Ryan became more and more desperate for money, his trips to the local pawnshop became more frequent.

For a while, Colleen's parents were unaware of Ryan's nocturnal visitors and hadn't the faintest inkling about the illicit activities that were going on under their roof. Gradually Maureen began to notice that some of her things were out of place; others were mysteriously missing. When confronted, Colleen played dumb and pretended she had no idea what was going on. Unconvinced, Maureen began to monitor Ryan's behavior more closely. At first he had seemed like a nice guy. Now she wasn't so sure.

One evening on the way home from work, Maureen stopped at an ATM and got the cash she needed for her weekly errands. The next morning she woke up early and went grocery shopping. As the cashier rung up her purchases, Maureen reached into her wallet and was greeted with an unpleasant surprise: bare leather, no bills. All her money was gone.

Enraged, Maureen stormed out of the store without her purchases and drove straight to Burger King, where Colleen was working. In a loud, angry voice, Maureen told her daughter about the missing money. Colleen was speechless. A few of her nosy coworkers stared at her, wondering how she would respond. Colleen took a deep breath and told her mother that she had to get back to work.

Disgusted with her daughter and with Ryan, Maureen drove home. Ryan had expected Maureen to be at work, so her stormy entrance took him by surprise. He was caught red-handed in Colleen's bedroom, rummaging through her belongings. Maureen told him in no uncertain terms that he was no longer welcome in her house.

Ryan got defensive and denied Maureen's accusations, but she held fast to her convictions and ordered him to pack his bags. Ryan mumbled that he didn't have anything to pack his stuff in. Maureen handed him a garbage bag.

When Ryan left, he vowed to keep seeing Colleen, no matter what. Maureen subsequently forbade Colleen from seeing Ryan, but to no avail. The teenagers continued to meet regularly.

Colleen's obsession with Ryan intensified. She shut herself off from friends and family and walked around in a daze with a deadened, blank look in her eyes. Ryan was the only thing she focused on or cared about. Like a vacuum, he sucked up all her energy.

Shortly after Colleen's sixteenth birthday, Maureen came home from work to find her daughter lying prostrate on the dining-room table in a state of utter despair. In between wrenching sobs, Colleen told her mother that she didn't want to live anymore. She wanted to die. She said that the family problems were too much to bear and then stammered through tears that Ryan had been cheating on her.

What Colleen withheld from her mother was that when she confronted Ryan about his betrayal, he had responded with verbal and physical abuse, causing her fear, pain, and humiliation. It was not the first time Ryan had been violent and threatening toward her. Colleen was terrified. She was too embarrassed to confide in anyone. Her victimization was her own dark, shameful, secret.

Using a calm, soothing voice, Maureen tried to talk some sense into Colleen, who remained curled up in a fetal position on the dining-room table. Colleen couldn't stop crying. Over and over she repeated the words "I want to die!" Alarmed by Colleen's morbid thoughts, Maureen persuaded her daughter to sit up and gently helped her down from the table. She put Colleen in the car and drove her straight to the emergency room.

"I went into the hospital when I was sixteen," recalled Colleen, "because everything was all adding up: my mom's depression, I knew I was pregnant, and the fact that Ryan had cheated on me. So the nurse took my blood to find out if I was pregnant, and I was. I found out about an hour before my parents found out. We had a meeting with the doctor. My parents weren't too happy, because it was with Ryan's baby, and at that time they weren't really wanting me to have a baby with Ryan, because of other problems that were going on."

After an evaluation, Colleen was admitted to the hospital's psychiatric unit. According to the *Physicians Assistant's Guide,* roughly 26 percent of female suicide attempts presented to a hospital are preceded by abuse. Somehow the abuse element of Colleen's story did not emerge during the evaluation, a fact that would come back to haunt Colleen and her family further down the road.

Colleen's parents did not believe in abortion. In an effort to overcome their reservations about Colleen having Ryan's baby, they turned to God and attributed the pregnancy to His Divine Plan. As the months went by, Colleen and her parents became convinced that the fetus she was carrying was the long-awaited answer to their prayers, a growing, healing force of salvation that would endow their lives with joy, significance, a higher purpose, and the spirit of life.

"I'm Catholic and I just made my confirmation," said Colleen. "My religion set in when I got pregnant. I had the choice of adoption or abortion or keeping the baby. I went to church and they talked

about abortion and how wrong it was. You know all the Bibles—
they all say abortion is against our religion, so I respected that enough
to keep Jonathan. I would just feel so guilty thinking, *Oh, you know,
I killed a child.* People say it's just a seed, but it's really not. It's a
human being that hasn't fully grown yet. I didn't want to worry about
my religion and the jeopardy I was putting myself in. So abortion
wasn't my choice.

"When I was younger, I had a lot of doubts about my religion,"
confessed Colleen. "Because of the way my life was going, I kind of
didn't think there was a God. There were the problems with my
parents, I wasn't smart enough, I wasn't pretty enough. God had
certain people die in my family. Then finally when I was a few months
pregnant, I felt Jonathan moving in me, and that made me realize
that there was a God."

After being released from the psychiatric ward, Colleen transferred into the Teen Parent Program. She noticed a marked difference
in Ryan's behavior toward her. He was not happy about the news
that he was going to be a father.

"When he found out I was pregnant, everything went downhill,"
said Colleen. "Ryan's drug problem went out of control."

Over the next few months, Ryan was repeatedly arrested on
various charges, including larceny and shoplifting. One day, while on
probation, he got into a massive fight with Colleen. Maureen's eyes
filled with tears as she recounted the incident.

"Colleen called me at work one day. She was crying hysterically.
Ryan had assaulted her. I called the police and when I came home,
there were three police cruisers outside. They were interviewing
Colleen and her friend, who had witnessed the attack. Apparently,

Ryan had gotten angry and thrown a phone at Colleen. Then he had kicked her in the stomach, not once but several times. The police were very worried about Colleen. They were especially worried about the baby, since she was several months pregnant at the time."

Ryan fled. The cops put out a warrant for his arrest. Several squad cars were sent out to scour the neighborhood. Later in the day the cops found their suspect. They immediately snapped handcuffs around Ryan's wrists and hauled him off to jail.

Like so many abused women, Colleen was trapped in a web of fear and ambivalence. She decided not to press charges. The state of Massachusetts was less forgiving. Ryan was sentenced to a year in jail.

As Colleen's pregnancy advanced, her father weaned himself off alcohol. Over the past few years he had cut back significantly on his drinking. The forthcoming baby was his main incentive to stop completely. With Ryan behind bars, he knew that Colleen would need all the help she could get from both him and his wife. By the time the baby was born, Colleen's father was sober. Maureen had gained some weight. Colleen was no longer depressed and suicidal.

"Giving birth to Jonathan was the happiest moment of my life," she said. "I gave birth naturally, four and a half hours of labor. I loved him from the first moment I saw him. Jonathan is my world. I thank God every day for my son. He brought everyone in my family together. I feel like God sent him down here to make me happy."

Soon after Colleen brought Jonathan home from the hospital, she resumed her studies at the Teen Parent Program. When Colleen was

in tutoring sessions, her tiny baby spent his day in a crib in the nursery, one floor below her classroom. During meals and recess Colleen
visited her son and fed him. When Jonathan was done feeding, Colleen held him on her lap, fidgeting with him incessantly: tugging at
his shirt, diapers, and socks; smoothing his hair down with the palm
of her hand; shifting him from one side of her lap to the other. Colleen's hands were hardly ever still. In contrast to his mother, Jonathan was incredibly immobile. Most of the time he stared straight
ahead with his right fist clenched tightly by his chest and his body
slightly slumped over into the crook of his mother's arm.

At the end of each school day, Colleen drove home to her parents' house, where she peeled off her clothes and took a brief shower.
After putting on her uncomfortable uniform and pulling her hair back

into a tight bun, she waved good-bye to her parents, planted a kiss on Jonathan's forehead, got back into her car, and drove ten minutes to Burger King. On her feet for six hours straight, Colleen stuffed bags for the drive-through, worked the register, and sorted through change as car after car came and went, the faces of the customers a complete blur, their voices amplified and distorted through the speakers as they shouted out their orders, one after another in what sometimes seemed like a never-ending, monotonous cycle.

"It's really hard going to school, going to work, and raising a baby," Colleen lamented. "I know that I'm only seventeen and people do look at me as, like, you know, a teenage mom, so they think we're all on welfare or whatever, but I'm not. I work every day. I only have Sundays off. I don't see Jonathan a lot, and when I'm at school, he's taken care of by the day care. I go to work at four and get off at nine, so it's really hard finding time for him."

Three days a week, Colleen took Jonathan to visit his father in jail. Jonathan's first sight of his father was through the strong glass barrier that separates prisoners from everyone else. Colleen described their weekly mother-father-son ritual:

"Visiting hours start at two o'clock. You have to go into a cagelike room to check in. Then you sit down at tables and he comes out and there's a counter between you. He can hold the baby for five minutes and then he has to give him back. And usually we're getting along, but just sometimes you argue about things, like him being in there. It just gets really hard to think that I'm sitting out here eleven months waiting for him. He loves Jonathan, I can see that, but I don't know if he'll change."

Colleen deluded herself with comforting fantasies of how great things would be when Ryan got out of jail, completely disassociating herself from memories of the physical and verbal abuse she had suffered before Ryan's incarceration. She remained optimistic that Ryan would get off drugs and turn over a new leaf. But even while incarcerated, Ryan managed to have drugs smuggled in to him.

"Jail was like a vacation for Ryan," said Colleen. "He still did drugs and he had free rent and free food to eat every night."

Undeterred by being locked up, Ryan worked hard to maintain psychological control over Colleen. He continued his pattern of abusive, manipulative, sadistic behavior, sending wonderful letters that never failed to raise Colleen's hopes, followed by cruel, obscene letters full of horrible threats and accusations. Often when Colleen showed up for visiting hours, Ryan showered her with insulting, degrading comments and accused her of cheating on him, using the crudest terms he could think of.

In the wake of these incidents, which left her in tears, Colleen became more and more enmeshed in the relationship, in part because, like so many daughters of alcoholics, she experienced love intertwined with erratic behavior, denial, disappointment, anger, and shame. Because her father had finally become sober after a lifelong struggle, Colleen believed that Ryan, too, could and would eventually conquer his drug addiction. She attributed Ryan's bad behavior to the influence of drugs and held on to her belief that apart from the drugs, Ryan was essentially good and loving.

Colleen went to elaborate lengths to convince herself that the cruel Ryan wasn't "the real" Ryan. To counteract her devastation and loneliness, she escaped into a world of fantasy. Here, Ryan loved her passionately and unequivocally and was the man of her dreams, not the incarcerated brute who had kicked her in the stomach when she was pregnant. In her dream world, Colleen was beautiful and beloved, not abused and disrespected.

As the months went by, Colleen fell deeper and deeper into an abyss of idealization and delusion. Gradually, fantasy and reality merged completely. In the same way that Ryan depended on heroin, Colleen fed off her fantasies of a fairy-tale romance and relied on them to transport her far away from an acutely painful reality.

While Ryan was in jail, Colleen began attending Carol Gilligan and Normi Noel's writing workshops at the Teen Parent Program. In these seminars, Colleen nourished her sugarcoated fantasies by writing dramatic, impassioned letters to Ryan, which she read aloud to her classmates.

Dear Ryan,

I would like to thank you for our beautiful son. I see the sun every morning, but it never shines because we're not together. I always look forward to the days I see you. I'm mad that you have totally vanished out of my life, but the day that you return to me my sun will shine. I will feel safe again. We can be the family we should have been a long time ago. You are my best friend, my lover, and most of all, my baby's father. Thank you so much. I love you until the day I pass on to my next life. I could never imagine my life without you.

Love always,
Colleen

When asked to explain why she was so convinced that Ryan would be a good father once he got out of jail, Colleen said, "Ryan knows how important it is for a child to have a father because of everything he went through not knowing his real father." She then paused for a moment, realizing that besides this one idea, she couldn't come up with any good reason or solid evidence that might even faintly suggest that Ryan would be an adequate—let alone "good"— father. At that point, Colleen confronted reality.

"If Ryan and I don't end up together, then fine," she concluded dejectedly, "but I don't want Jonathan not to have a good mom and a dad." Colleen took a deep breath. "One thing I regret is that maybe he won't."

When Colleen navigated the depths of her despair, she occasionally heard a thin voice rising up from deep within her, struggling to be heard.

"If I listened to the little girl in me, she would say not to take this crap from Ryan," Colleen confessed. "She would say that I should move on. She would say that I can leave Ryan. She would tell me that I won't be alone forever. She would say that one day I'll find someone else."

Despite all the conflicts and the strong, obvious negatives, Colleen's amorous investment in her troubled relationship with Ryan remained disturbingly unwavering. When Ryan got out on parole, she told her parents that she wanted to take the baby and move in with him. Colleen's parents were against the idea. They thought that Colleen and the baby should continue living at home.

Colleen argued that Ryan had reformed his old ways. She told her parents in no uncertain terms that they were not to interfere with her wish to raise her baby in the presence of his biological father. They had no choice but to let Colleen do as she pleased. The situation was beyond their control.

For Colleen, setting up a household with Ryan was a rite of passage. She put her pride on the line, determined to prove that she was a mature, self-sufficient, independent adult and a competent caretaker, capable of living in her own household with her boyfriend and baby.

"The day Ryan got out of jail, we got engaged," said Colleen. "Then two weeks after we moved in together, he started doing heroin again. It started off once a week and then became an everyday thing. Ryan on heroin was like . . . he'd be quiet at times—or he'd be so nice to me. He could be this wonderful person, but yet it was the drug that was making him that happy. When he was down from the drugs, it was just awful. He was mean, terrible. He would say, 'Get me money, do *whatever* you have to!'

"He'd get so mad at me if I didn't give him any money for the drugs. He'd say I didn't love him and call me names. . . . Horrible verbal abuse. When I would get mad and want to leave, it would turn into physical abuse. The physical abuse at our apartment was really bad. The cops were called on us. I never pressed charges 'cause I knew he'd just keep doing it anyway.

"Ryan would hit me on my body but not on my face, so when the police came, they couldn't see the bruises. I would be crying, but I had to pretend that nothing was going on, that we were fighting, just arguing. I think I was more scared of my life than anything."

Like many abusers, Ryan worked hard to make Colleen feel as though she deserved to be punished. Using manipulative mind games, he brainwashed Colleen and distorted reality to the point where she believed that she was provoking him to abuse her. Ryan persuaded Colleen that his violence was a justifiable reaction to her negligence and that he had every right to be enraged by her failures as a girlfriend and as a mother to their son.

Colleen internalized Ryan's accusations and felt stupid, inferior, and powerless in his presence. When questioned by the police, Colleen denied being abused because she was frightened that Ryan would be arrested. Colleen knew that ultimately Ryan would blame her and hold her responsible for his jail time. She worried that as soon as he got out, he would retaliate by beating her even more severely. She feared he might attack her family. As devastating as the abuse itself were the paralyzing terror and the blanket of silence that enshrouded her.

Colleen's parents had no idea what was going within the four walls of the young couple's apartment. Whenever they called to ask how she and Jonathan and Ryan were doing, Colleen always told them that everything was just fine. Meanwhile, Ryan hovered menacingly in the background, hanging on her every word. Colleen always had to have an excuse prepared in case her parents asked to see her and the baby. Perhaps Colleen's parents should have been more suspicious, given Ryan's history, but they themselves were no strangers to fighting, addiction, and its companion, denial. When Colleen insisted that everything was "fine," her mother and father chose to believe her.

Ryan kept the apartment stocked with a rotating supply of stolen

TVs, VCRs, and car stereos. When he was low on cash, he bartered these items for heroin. During the day, he stayed home with Jonathan while Colleen worked double shifts at Burger King in order to pay the rent. Every minute she was away, Colleen was gripped by the fear of coming home from work and finding her son dead or injured on account of Ryan's drug-induced negligence.

After several months filled with fighting and repeated episodes of domestic violence, Colleen's fear began to outweigh her tolerance. It took time for her to come to terms with the fact that her efforts to be autonomous had failed miserably. She was reluctant to relinquish her dreamlike hold on the idealized, romantic adult life she had aspired to. It was humiliating to acknowledge her feelings of worthlessness and dependence after having rebelled so strongly to win freedom and independence. That her parents had been right about Ryan all along was a bitter pill to swallow, but to her credit, concerned about her own survival and determined to get her baby out of harm's way, Colleen put her pride aside and asked her parents if she could move back home.

"Just because a teenager has had a child and is shouldering the responsibility, that doesn't mean that she's an adult," explained Maureen. "Teenagers don't have the mental capacity and the experience that adults have to make their decisions. They are new at it and they do need the support of their mothers, fathers, family, and friends. Colleen was very fortunate that she had all that. When she found out that she did indeed make a mistake, we were all here for her."

Colleen's parents were relieved to have their daughter and their grandson back under their roof but were worried about Colleen, who appeared to be severely traumatized by events she refused to discuss.

Maureen decided not to push her daughter. She realized that when Colleen was ready, she would talk about what was bothering her. Meanwhile, both parents did their best to make Colleen and Jonathan feel safe, comfortable, and loved.

Colleen's self-esteem was in shreds. Recovery was a painstakingly slow process. Gradually she established a threshold of trust and began to open up to her mother about the devastating abuse she had suffered. Maureen was shocked.

"While Colleen was living with Ryan, she never mentioned anything to her father or myself about the daily beatings that she was getting. After she moved back home with us, she finally told me everything that had happened. I asked her one question. I said, 'Colleen, why? Why did you take it from him?' She said, because she was afraid, afraid for herself, for me, for her father, and for the baby. She said that she thought the abuse was all her fault. For months after she moved back home, I had to keep reassuring her. I had to keep telling her, 'It's not your fault. It's not your fault.' "

Ryan's troubles with the police induced him to leave Pittsfield. After crossing the Massachusetts state line, he continued south, finally stopping in Florida. He never sent any child-support payments. Ryan occasionally called Colleen long-distance and harassed her. Maureen advised her to hang up on him the moment the conversation took an ugly turn. Colleen followed her mother's advice. Eventually, she stopped taking Ryan's calls.

With the help of her therapist, the support of her family, and her own hard work, Colleen was gradually able to understand her self-destructive pattern of embracing the dual roles of rescuer and care-taker. When Colleen looked back at the past, instead of blaming herself for not being good enough or loving enough, she began to hold Ryan responsible for all his actions. Colleen finally accepted that Ryan wasn't separate from the drugs; when the drugs were in his system, they were part of him.

"I guess I was just naive about Ryan," she said in retrospect. "I didn't realize that people were telling me the truth about his drug addiction and about how mean he is. I didn't want to believe it, because I saw a different side of him. I saw, like, two different sides: the really nice part of him and the really mean side. The mean side just didn't mix with me. That's why we're not together right now. And I don't see myself going back with him, either. Yeah, I did love him at one point, but the love that I did have for him is not in me anymore. I have no desire to even speak to him at this time because I have so much anger—that's about all I have for him.

"If a teenage girl were to ask me what she should do if her boyfriend has a drug problem, I would give her the following advice: He won't change. If drug addicts want to change, they have to change for themselves. They're not gonna change for you—they're not gonna change for your child. That fact is a pretty hard thing to accept. People told me all the time, 'You need to get out of this relationship.' I regret not listening to them sooner, but I had to learn for myself."

Relieved of the burden and stress of Ryan's dark presence in her life, Colleen blossomed with the passing of each month. She lost a great deal of extra weight she had wanted to shed for some time. Her acne all but disappeared. She stopped speaking in a flat monotone. Her eyes regained their luster. She found herself able to laugh again.

After graduating from the Teen Parent Program, Colleen left her job at Burger King and got a job making grinders at Angelina's sub shop. After a few months there, she quit and got a job at Wal-Mart as a supervisor and customer service manager.

"I take care of customers," she explained. "If they need a certain item or a price check, I help them out. I also supervise my cashiers. If they have a problem with a customer, I take care of them. I help them answer any questions that they have."

At Wal-Mart, Colleen made three hundred dollars per week. This was just enough money to cover her car payments as well as toys and supplies for Jonathan. Colleen was proud that she was doing everything within her power to make ends meet.

"I've never been on welfare or any kind of assistance," she said. "If I'm capable of working, then I'm gonna work. I'm not out to get free money. I have family to help me watch Jonathan."

In addition to her job at Wal-Mart, Colleen enrolled in several classes at Berkshire Community College. She was studying to be a respiratory therapist but soon became unhappy with her jam-packed schedule.

"My time with Jonathan was very limited," she explained. "I was going to school every day and working every day. I was only seeing my son for about an hour, and during that hour he was taking his nap. So I decided to put school off for a little while. It may be a bad decision, but it's the decision that I've made."

Colleen's decision was strongly influenced by her concern about her son, who appeared to be lagging alarmingly behind in his development.

"The other mothers at the Teen Parent Program would be telling me, 'Oh, my baby's doing this, my baby's doing that. . . .' Jonathan was older than they were, and he wasn't doing anything at all with his right arm or leg. His right hand would always be clenched right up to his chest. He couldn't hold his own bottle. He never crawled. He used to just scoot across the floor and drag his feet the whole way. You know your child. I mean, you might not know exactly what they have, but you know when something is wrong. You always feel it's your fault."

Although Colleen had a bad feeling that something was wrong, for months she was too afraid to take Jonathan to the doctor to see exactly what the problem was. Encouraged for nearly a year by staff members at the Teen Parent Program, Colleen finally mustered up the courage to overcome her terror and denial. She gave up her fantasy that Jonathan's symptoms would miraculously disappear and went to her local pediatrician, seeking a diagnosis.

"It took me three months to get a referral to a neurologist," said Colleen. "The doctor kept putting me off, which made me angry. Finally I walked into his office crying and told him that I wanted a referral. I got one, and that made me happy because I felt like I accomplished something. I overpowered a doctor by telling him that there was something wrong with my son. I just had this instinct about it."

A neurologist at Bay State Hospital in Springfield examined Jonathan and administered an MRI, after which he immediately diagnosed Jonathan with two serious medical disorders: cerebral palsy, caused by defects in the brain and spinal column, and polymicrogyria, a rare brain disorder.

When Colleen looked up *polymicrogyria* on the Internet, she found the following description of how it can affect those who suffer from it: "Most children with polymicrogyria, but not all, have some degree of global developmental disabilities or delays, seizures, feeding difficulties, respiratory problems, motor dysfunction and mental retardation. It is difficult to make a predictable prognosis for children with the diagnosis of PMG because each child is very unique in their presentation of this disorder."

Maureen cringed as she recalled the moment when the doctor

came out and said that her grandson was mentally retarded. "We use the word disability," she explained. "That's a much kinder word. It doesn't put such a label on a child."

Children with cerebral palsy have a hard time controlling movement and posture. The doctor told Colleen that Jonathan would need a leg brace in order to walk. The doctor warned Colleen that because the left side of Jonathan's brain was underdeveloped, there was a high chance that his cognitive and verbal abilities would be permanently and significantly impaired.

"I was wicked upset when Jonathan was diagnosed," recalled Colleen. "The guilt . . . When something's wrong with your child, you always feel it's your fault."

Many of the causes for cerebral palsy remain unknown, but known reasons include injuries during pregnancy or birth that cause prolonged oxygen deprivation, leading to a stroke in utero; an infection in the mother during pregnancy that spreads to the baby and the uterus; chromosomal abnormalities; and meningitis during infancy or childhood.

After looking at the results of Jonathan's MRI and a battery of other tests, the neurologist asked Colleen if she had experienced any severe trauma during her pregnancy, such as a fall, an illness, or an infection of any kind. Colleen answered with a firm no. Maureen challenged her daughter's claim and could not shake her gnawing suspicion that Jonathan's cerebral palsy was a direct result of the trauma that was inflicted when Ryan kicked Colleen in the stomach several months into her pregnancy.

Colleen was determined not to give up on her son just because he was disabled, so she restructured her entire life around his need for special attention and intensive medical care. As part of an early-intervention program, a pediatric worker began coming to Colleen's house once a week to do exercises with Jonathan. At first, Colleen had no idea how she could possibly afford these kinds of treatments. She was assured that doctors' bills, medication, physical therapy, and eventually leg braces would all be covered by Social Security and medical insurance, both of which offered special benefits for disabled children.

Colleen and her family rallied around the baby and showered him with affection and support. The adorable red-haired toddler loved all the attention. He frequently wore a huge smile on his face. He made eye contact with the adults around him and played with his huge pile of toys. He had no fear of strangers and gradually became bold enough to attempt to balance upright on his own. When Jonathan was about eighteen months old, much to everyone's surprise, he started taking tentative steps, holding on to railings, tables, and the arms of chairs for support. Then one afternoon, according to Maureen, Jonathan let go of the table and "just took off by himself and started to walk across the room. Every time that he would walk across the room, all of us would clap. My husband and I would clap. We'd say, 'You did a good job.' And Jonathan thought this was great. He realized that the more he did this, the more we would clap. To see this child walk, and to think that he was never gonna walk without a brace . . . It just filled us with so much happiness. It's almost like a miracle. We prayed and prayed that he would do this. He's still got a way to go yet. He's kinda behind on his speech, but we're working on that with pediatric development."

Colleen was delighted with Jonathan's progress but was careful not to elevate her hopes to unrealistic heights. "So far, my son walked without a brace and he's learning to do things with just one hand," she said, "but he is going to need a leg brace eventually. We'll be getting that for him soon."

From time to time, Colleen mourned the death of her dream of a strong, intelligent, healthy, athletic child. Occasionally her thoughts would be dominated by worries about how Jonathan's life would be affected by his multiple disabilities. Despite moments of bottomless pain and sorrow, Colleen and her parents refused to allow themselves to be paralyzed by anger, regret, and disappointment. Instead, they maintained the highest expectations for Jonathan. They focused on the best possible prognosis and tried not to think about the worst possible outcome.

Colleen kept her heart set on eventually being able to mainstream Jonathan into a school with children who were not disabled. She and her parents believed in Jonathan, and every day they encouraged him to defy the dire predictions of his doctors. They didn't treat him like a damaged child, nor did they protect him as if he were a piece of glass that they feared might shatter upon the slightest impact. Not wanting Jonathan to feel stigmatized or rejected by his own family, they interacted and played with him as if there were no limitations on his abilities. This approach proved to be very beneficial for the child. Rather than withdrawing and dislocating like some handicapped children do, Jonathan began to develop a playful sense of self-confidence.

Many handicapped children often appear more disabled than they really are because they internalize the pity and horror of people around them and ultimately evolve into receptacles for shock, grief, disgust, and disappointment. Like sponges, these children soak up the negativity around them, adding intense emotional handicaps, such as self-pity and self-hatred to existing organic handicaps. Colleen and her family were determined not to let that happen to Jonathan. They provided him with support, admiration, and positive reinforcement. When it came to caring for the little red-haired boy, there was never a shortage of love.

Colleen had started to keep a journal when Jonathan was diagnosed. She was very proud of her writing. Articulating her thoughts and feelings on paper gave them weight and durability. In her journal she wrote about her mother and her son, and she wrote about the new object of her affections, an artistic young woman. Colleen's love for this woman was deep. It inspired her to write several romantic poems. The two women found an apartment in Pittsfield and began living together and sharing the responsibility of raising Colleen's son.

Colleen found the courage to open up to her parents about her bisexuality. Although they were upset at first, both her mother and father ultimately accepted her choice of lifestyle and continued to love her and their grandson unconditionally.

In her journal, Colleen wrote:

> In my dreams I never would have imagined my life this way. I would want nothing to be wrong with my son. Could it be that my dreams are not meant to be? Could I work harder at my dreams? Is it possible? Will anyone really know why this was brought upon us? Do I blame myself? In some ways, yes. I don't understand why life is the way it is. Why can't people accept what they are and accept what others are like? Will kids realize that Jonathan has a disability? Will they be able to look beyond that? I could sit here and blame myself, but I'm not going to anymore. Jonathan will be brought up strong enough to the point that no matter what someone may say or do to him, he will know that his life is important.
>
> I am a young mother trying to be stronger for her son.

chapter five

SHAYLA & C.J.

"When I was sixteen years old, I really wanted to have a baby because all my friends had babies. I wanted a baby so I'd have a friend twenty-four hours a day, and because I thought they were really cute. I sort of planned it because I didn't take any birth control, so I knew it was going to happen."

SHAYLA GREW UP BELIEVING THAT SOMEDAY HER GOOD looks would be her ticket out of Pittsfield. She fantasized about being a model and practiced strutting down an imaginary catwalk like the tall, skinny girls she saw on TV. Shayla also dreamt about being a cheerleader for the Dallas Cowboys. She pictured herself wearing their official uniform: knee-high white cowboy boots, short white shorts, a navel-baring shirt knotted at the sternum, and a crystal-studded, star-spangled vest that sparkled in the sunlight.

On winter afternoons when temperatures hovered close to zero, Shayla could often be found curled up on the sofa, poring over the latest edition of the sizzling-hot Dallas Cowboys Cheerleaders swimsuit calendar. Impressed and intrigued, she flipped through photographs of scantily clad, nubile young cheerleaders frolicking on the sandy shores of some distant tropical paradise. With their perfect bodies, pearly teeth, and gigantic smiles, these cheerleaders were magnets for the adoration of millions. Shayla longed for a similar level of attention, approval, affirmation, and appreciation and wondered what it would feel like to perform in Texas Stadium in front of television cameras and thousands of fans.

By the age of sixteen, Shayla was pregnant, and instead of cheer-

ing for heroes at Texas Stadium, she was making them at the local
Subway. That summer the heat was stifling, but the humidity didn't
deter any of the hungry customers who crowded into the sandwich
shop, forming a lunchtime line that snaked around in a semicircle.
Behind the counter, Shayla pulled a steaming loaf of bread out of the
oven, pausing to wipe the sweat off her brow before satisfying a
customer's demand for bologna with extra cheese, lettuce, mayon-
naise, mustard, pickles, salt and pepper. Her body ached from exhaustion. Her feet were swollen. She felt faint. She wondered if her
friends were swimming down at the lake at that very moment.

Shayla had once thought that someday she would be able to invent
a life as lavish as those she saw depicted on her TV screen, but as
each month passed, the worlds of the characters she admired on *Sex
and the City* seemed more and more distant and inaccessible. Wal-
Mart didn't carry anything even closely resembling the Jimmy Choo
shoes on Carrie Bradshaw's feet, and Pittsfield had no equivalent of
Bungalow 8, the hot spot Carrie frequented with her friends. The
food court at the local mall just didn't compare, and though Shayla
could place her hand flat against the television screen, there was
always that unsurpassable glass barrier.

Mired in a state of frustration and despair, Shayla redirected the
mental energy she had once devoted to her own goals toward her
relationship with her nineteen-year-old boyfriend, C.J. From the outset, Shayla's relationship with C.J. had been laced with tension. She
attributed some of the stress and fighting to the fact that they both
lacked parental role models and therefore had no positive examples
to emulate. Perpetuating the familiar was automatic. Shayla noticed

herself repeating patterns of behavior she had witnessed growing up as the daughter of teen parents.

When Shayla was born, her mother, Kelly, was fifteen and her father, Alan, was seventeen. Kelly and Alan went through numerous separations and subsequent reconciliations. They never married. Kelly got a job working with the elderly in a home care program, and Alan worked in a home for delinquent boys and took classes at the community college.

Shayla suffered at the center of her parents' explosive relationship. Some nights she cowered in her room, her hands pressed hard against her ears, muffling the sounds of screaming and yelling and "stuff being broken." When things got really rough, Shayla was shuttled off to the home of her maternal grandparents.

Shayla's grandmother worked in the produce department at Stop & Shop, and her grandfather had retired from GE. Now working as a carpenter, he made extra money building furniture for people in the neighborhood. Their home was a haven compared with the chaos Shayla faced living with her parents.

When Shayla was six, her little sister, Ashley, was born. Soon afterward, Alan was arrested on drug-related charges and sentenced to two years in prison. While incarcerated, he completed a special-educational program that helped him qualify for a scholarship at a state college. The fact that his college tuition was completely funded shocked and upset Kelly, who had to struggle to raise their two daughters while getting a GED and working three jobs without any help from the state. Kelly found it unjust that the father of her two children got more opportunities as a result of going to prison than she got as a young mother forced to juggle all her responsibilities.

Neither Kelly nor the girls visited Alan in prison. When he was released, he was a stranger. "He was a different man when he came home," said Kelly, "harder to deal with and harder to understand." Alan had converted to Islam in prison. He went out of his way to impose his newly adopted religion on his family. Behind bars, his beliefs, rules, and rituals had been enthusiastically shared by a host of other inmates. At home, his entreaties were met with steadfast resistance.

Alan cracked down on the girls. He insisted on keeping Shayla cooped up in the house even on sunny days when most kids in the neighborhood were outside playing. Alan made sure that his daughter understood that her education was his number one priority. When Shayla finished her homework early, he assigned her extra reading. Boys were completely off-limits.

Alan was adamant about disciplining his daughters. Shayla feared the belt whenever she disobeyed him. Anticipating punishment, Shayla's judgment was often clouded by feelings of panic, dread, and gnawing anxiety. She had trouble making decisions, especially under pressure, and grew up questioning her ability to do the right thing. Too often her fear of failure prevented her from taking on new challenges.

Soon after entering middle school, Shayla began cheerleading for the football, soccer, and basketball teams. She adored the dance, the music, and the acrobatics. With her long brown legs kicking higher than those of the girls beside her, Shayla effortlessly exuded the grace and agility that came naturally to her. After her fifteenth birthday, Shayla's dedication to cheerleading wavered. Science, once her favorite subject, suddenly lost its allure. She began to devote most of her attention to her appearance, and to boys.

These pronounced shifts in Shayla's priorities coincided with her parents' decision to permanently end their relationship. Shayla's father moved away to another town to attend college and medical school. Shayla and her little sister stayed behind with their mother in Pittsfield.

"Before her dad left home to go to UMass, Shayla had been an A student and a cheerleader," recalled Kelly. "She wanted to go to college. But after her dad left the home, I could see her start to change. When her father stopped coming back and forth to pick the kids up for weekends and started breaking promises, I could see Shayla start going after all the wrong things. She started dating. She was very secretive and for a while she was seeing lots of different guys. Her first year of high school, she met C.J. He was her idea of a 'bad boy,' I guess: tattooed, a rock-and-roller type, really rough around the edges. Shayla's father was always telling her, 'Don't you ever date any white boys!' Knowing how her dad felt about her dating white guys, I think Shayla's relationship with C.J. was her way of striking out at him.

"I think Shayla's anger wasn't so much because of what her father had said to her—it was the abandonment. Her father broke so many promises. He used to call her and say, 'I'm gonna pick you up, be ready! We'll go out to dinner, we'll do this, we'll do that. . . .' Then he'd be a no-show. Shayla would put herself out there time and time again, and her father just kept on disappointing her. It got to a point, I think, when she just really wanted to get back at him."

As Shayla got closer to C.J., he gradually opened up to her about his difficult childhood. When angry and upset, C.J. sometimes resorted to violent outbursts as a means of self-expression. On one occasion, his mother called the police and asked to have her son forcibly removed from the family home. She claimed that he was a disruptive presence. Outside the home, C.J. exhibited threatening behavior toward his ex-girlfriend and her new boyfriend, prompting police to serve him with a trespass notice for violating a restraining order the ex-girlfriend had obtained against him.

Shayla was fully aware of C.J.'s short temper, lack of self-control, depression, drinking problem, and violent streak. Whereas some young women might have been deterred from pursuing a romance, Shayla dismissed such behavior, convinced that it was part of C.J.'s past, not part of the future she was going to build with him. The two teenagers bonded over the inner darkness they sometimes felt. During late-night conversations, they shared their dreams, fears, and insecurities. After several months of dating, their relationship became more intimate.

"C.J. was the first person I had sex with," said Shayla. "We were together for a couple of months before I had sex with him. It was really embarrassing. It was like little-kid sex. It was bad. I mean, it wasn't bad . . . it was different. It was kinda weird. We weren't open with our bodies. It was a pretty middle-school type of thing. We didn't plan it. It just happened."

Kelly expressed her disapproval of the relationship. Shayla found her mother intrusive and chose to ignore her. In Shayla's mind, certain topics were completely off limits to her mother. Sex was one of them. Shayla was determined to guard her idealized vision of her relationship with C.J., even if that meant hiding troubling aspects of their turbulent romance.

C.J. tended to be possessive and controlling. He was verbally abusive, especially when he drank. He soon learned that in Shayla, he had met his match. She quickly proved herself more than capable of dishing out her share of insults and profanity. But beneath her tough exterior, Shayla's self-esteem was achingly low. She craved love more than anything and was willing to go to great lengths to transform C.J.'s abusive behavior into something that felt more like affection. Terrible clashes were followed by passionate reconciliations. After one altercation, the two teenagers got their tongues pierced.

They began sporting matching tongue studs as a sign of their commitment to each other.

C.J. dropped out of high school and began working at a small flooring company run by his mother. He went from client to client, installing tiles, carpets, and linoleum floors. His goal was to save up enough money to realize one of his biggest dreams: owning a tattoo parlor. C.J.'s other big dream was to become a father—the father he had never had—and Shayla was eager to become a mother. Together, the two teenagers made a conscious decision to become teen parents. Shayla began trying to conceive.

"I felt that if I had a baby, it would change things," she said. "I thought it would make my life a lot better, not only in my relationship with C.J. but with my friends. I thought it would bring my popularity up because people would be like 'Hey, she's got a baby, and that's cool.' "

For Shayla, gaining the admiration of her friends was paramount. Her peer group exerted enormous influence and set standards for acceptance at a time when she, like many adolescents, was at her most vulnerable, insecure, and malleable. Because Shayla feared rejection and was desperate to belong, she tended to go with the flow and was easily influenced by others. When the first few girls in her class started to have babies, they enjoyed their fifteen minutes of fame. Shayla wanted hers, too.

The skewed values of Shayla and her peers reflected the widespread lack of role models, support, guidance, and resources either at home or in school and the community at large. Shayla had neither a solid sense of herself nor a robust vision of her future. She felt what she described as "a void" deepening within her. Rather than looking ahead to a future filled with choices, transitions, and different opportunities, she looked around and saw a lot of poor, unhappy, frustrated people, struggling and stagnating, so she adjusted her expectations, lowering the bar to avoid disappointment and the all-too-real possibility of failure.

"I love to learn," she said. "I always wanted to go to college but I never sat down and said, 'I want to try to get good grades because I need good grades to get into a nice college.' I don't like to make long-term plans, because they always seem to get broken. They always do."

In the absence of clearly defined goals, Shayla began to rely exclusively on her peers for a sense of direction. She copied their behavior and adjusted her standards to match theirs. Buddies since kindergarten, Shayla and her best friend, Sheri, had sleepovers, partied together, got into trouble together, and stayed out late together, drinking and missing curfew. The two girls seemed to be on parallel roads, egging each other on, sharing experiences, breaking rules, and commiserating when their boyfriends cheated on them. One afternoon Sheri called Shayla and announced that she was pregnant. Shayla could hear the mixture of fear and elation in her friend's voice. Sheri now had something definitive and real to look forward to, something that would be completely hers. It wasn't long before all that was standing between Shayla and teen motherhood was nine months.

Too frightened to tell her mother that she was pregnant, Shayla sought help from her grandparents. Initially, she didn't confide in them and just said that she couldn't bear living at home anymore because she and her mother were always fighting.

Shayla's grandparents were concerned about her. They welcomed her into the sanctuary of their immaculate home. In their custody, Shayla felt safe with her secret. Life with her grandparents was calm and predictable. Her grandmother hosted barbecues every Sunday and invited all her relatives. Her grandfather devoted a good portion of his spare time to keeping his spacious backyard in tip-top shape. Intent on making the half acre of grassy space a fun environment for his grandchildren, he hung a tire from a thick rope and tied the rope to the strongest branch of a giant elm tree. When Shayla's little sister came to visit, she loved spinning around and around on the tire, tilting her head back to catch glimpses of greens, blues, browns, and yellows blurring together into a kaleidoscope of brilliant color.

As Shayla sat on the back deck, watching her little sister carousing in the yard, her own childhood seemed far away. As she looked at her sister's skinny body and flat chest, she touched her own rounding stomach that no one apart from C.J. knew about.

"My reactions to Shayla telling me she was pregnant were very good," C.J. recalled. "I was happy, smiling, you know, my life started all over again. I didn't have a father. I didn't have a very good childhood. I wanted to have a child so I could give him a good childhood and teach him to be a better man than I could be, 'cause I didn't have a father to teach me. I was raised by my mother, and by my brother's father. And it's just . . . there was always an emptiness."

Shayla described similar feelings of worthlessness. At a very young age, partially as a result of frequently being punished by her father, Shayla had started to believe that she was a "bad" person. She blamed herself for every mistake she made and often felt that she couldn't do anything right. With a fractured sense of logic, she believed that somehow having a baby would resolve all her problems and erase her self-doubt because at least in the baby's eyes she would be a "good" person. She craved the intense unconditional love that only a speechless, dependent infant was capable of giving.

Shayla's pregnancy was the perfect antidote to her fear of abandonment. She wanted to believe that C.J. would never leave her the way her father had, but if he did, having his baby ensured that she would hold on to at least a part of him. By making a conscious decision to get pregnant at age sixteen, Shayla actively turned the tables on her father, so that instead of her being disappointed in him, he was disappointed in her. She succeeded in creating a situation that allowed her to take an active rather than a passive role in the dissolution of the father-daughter relationship.

"My dad warned me my whole life not to get pregnant because it was so hard," she explained, "but I'm the type of person that does whatever I want to do because I have to learn on my own. So when I got pregnant, he didn't accept me at all. He totally disowned me, and to this day he doesn't want anything to do with me. He thinks I don't deserve to have a father, because I didn't listen to him. He was supposed to be there to protect me, and I went ahead and did it anyway, so it's my own fault."

So, instead of being overwhelmed with boundless sadness, Shayla could accept blame, take responsibility, and point to a concrete explanation of why her father was no longer in her life. This justification lent Shayla an illusion of power over her father's abandonment. It was easier for her to bear the thought that her father had disappeared from her life because she had disobeyed him by getting pregnant than to think that he just simply didn't give a damn.

A small part of Shayla had dared hope that her pregnancy, an act of blatant defiance, would attract her father's attention and reawaken his capacity to give unconditional love—if not to her, then to her baby. This hope was dashed the moment Shayla called him to share the news.

"Her father basically told her, 'You no longer exist,' " Kelly recalled. "He just dismissed her. He hung up on her, and she's never talked to him since."

"My mother couldn't handle the news, either," said Shayla. "She was bawling. It was hard for her to take. She talked to my grandfather and my grandmother. They said, 'Kelly, we went through this same thing with you. We're not gonna turn our backs on Shayla. You just need to understand that she's gonna have a baby.' It was really hard for my mom to understand. She wanted me to have an abortion."

Shayla's fantasy of having a baby had been wonderful, but almost immediately after getting pregnant, she became ambivalent about the grave reality of her predicament. Overwhelmed by the extremely negative reactions of her parents, she began to reconsider her decision to become a teen mother. After a few weeks of deliberation and heartache, Shayla made a doctor's appointment to find out about the option of having an abortion, allegedly in an effort to appease her mother. She got to the hospital and was examined by a doctor. C.J. followed Shayla to the hospital, and while she was having her ultrasound to see how far advanced her pregnancy was, he came in and said, "No! You're not getting an abortion!"

Shayla decided not to terminate the pregnancy. She didn't feel comfortable going against C.J.'s wishes, and when it came down to making the decision, she realized that, like C.J., she wanted the baby, despite her mother's incessant warnings about how hard it would be to raise the child. Incredibly conflicted over her decision and debilitated from repeatedly arguing with C.J., Shayla enrolled in the Teen Parent Program. She was frequently absent because of stress, exhaustion, illness, and crippling depression. Her grades suffered.

Members of the staff were fully aware of the difficulties Shayla was facing. They made a concerted effort to prevent her from dropping out of school. If Shayla was late in the morning, Helen, the wonderful and dedicated headmistress, would get in her car, drive to Shayla's house, drag her out of bed if necessary, and make sure that she made it to her tutoring sessions. B.J., the social worker in residence, drove Shayla and the other pregnant teenagers to their doctors' appointments, wanting to be sure that they didn't miss out on prenatal care. Even in her incapacitated state, Shayla could see that the staff at the Teen Parent Program really cared about her. These unfalteringly committed individuals gave Shayla the strength and support she needed to continue with her studies.

During the first few months of her pregnancy, Shayla had dropped out of gym class at Pittsfield High School, citing medical problems as her excuse. As a substitute assignment, her gym teacher asked her to write an essay on the subject of women in sports. Shayla never finished the essay because a few days before it was due, she was rushed to the hospital.

"Shayla went into false labor six times," recalled Kelly. "Her son was underdeveloped. She almost lost him several times during the pregnancy. I think it was due to all the stress and all the arguing with C.J."

Shayla winced as she recounted the excruciating agony she endured her last trimester. "When I was about five months pregnant, I found out I had kidney stones. I was in the hospital two or three times a week because the kidney stones would bring on preterm labor. So from the time I was five months pregnant to the time I delivered my son, I was in the hospital in unbearable pain, on medication and IVs to keep the fluids in me. I couldn't really eat or drink anything, because everything I was eating was coming back up. The doctors said the complications were caused by a calcium buildup from my prenatal vitamins, which happened because I wasn't really a milk drinker and I didn't really have a lot of dairy products, so my body wasn't used to processing the calcium. They told me to start putting calcium in my regular diet."

Having completed all her required academic work, Shayla was eagerly looking forward to graduating with her class at Pittsfield High School. During the many long hours she spent in the hospital, the thought of this exciting day was like a light at the end of a long, dark tunnel. Sadly, however, she was denied her diploma because her gym teacher flunked her for failing to turn in her "Women in Sports" paper, leaving her one credit short. He refused to accept the complications with Shayla's pregnancy as a medical excuse, citing her for "not completing the assignment" and for "having a bad attitude."

Both Shayla and her mother pleaded with the principal for leniency, but to no avail. Brutally disappointed, Shayla deeply resented that her diploma had been denied her on the basis of such a small technicality. She was furious about having to enroll in yet another semester of the Teen Parent Program, where she had to take more classes in preparation for her GED. Shayla made a promise to herself: First she would get her GED as soon as possible. Then she would enroll in a course at cosmetology school. If she couldn't be a model, at least maybe she could be a model's hairdresser. She hoped that once she got licensed, she'd be able to do hair for the fashion shows they had several times a year down at the Berkshire Mall. But before she could even think about doing any of that, she had a baby to deliver.

Shayla gave birth to a son, whom she named Jaiden. This baby was living proof of her power to conjure up a human being who, by nature of his infantile dependence, would be "a friend twenty-four hours a day." Back when she had first gotten pregnant, Shayla had only thought about how great it would be to have a baby. She hadn't given any thought to the painful, draining birthing process and its aftermath and was shocked to discover the rigorous aspects of this experience, which the women she knew had kept to themselves.

"After you have your baby, there's so much trauma that goes on in your body," Shayla explained. "You really don't want to be touched. When your milk comes in, your breasts start leaking. They're, like, rock hard. It's really uncomfortable. You don't want nobody to touch you. For a while, sex wasn't really an option."

C.J. had thought that the baby's birth would transform him into the ideal father he had always dreamed of but had never known. In theory, C.J. "wanted" to be a good father, but in practice he left Shayla with the bulk of parental duties. C.J. had expected that fatherhood would make him feel stronger, more confident, and more capable. Instead, when it came to caring for his son, he felt terribly inadequate whenever he failed to live up to Shayla's and his own expectations.

"In terms of responsibility for the baby, I'd have to say that

Shayla takes care of him most of the time," admitted C.J. "Because I'm either working all week or . . ." His voice trailed off as he fumbled for an excuse. "Or . . . I'm usually doing something."

Listening to C.J., Shayla rolled her eyes, knowing all too well that his all-important "something" was usually partying, lifting weights, or playing video games with his friends.

Shayla made it clear that she wanted C.J. to take on a more equal share of child-care responsibilities, both financially and in terms of parenting. C.J. found this arrangement unacceptable. He had no qualms about asserting his extremely rigid, old-fashioned views of gender roles. He told Shayla that a woman's place was in the home, cooking, cleaning, doing laundry, and taking care of the children, while her man was out working and spending time with his friends. To drive his point home, C.J. added, "That's what women are supposed to do and that's what the man does, and if you don't like it, that's tough."

Furious and frustrated, Shayla resorted to relentlessly nagging C.J. to do things like changing the baby's diapers. When that tactic got her nowhere, she started yelling at the top of her lungs. When pestered, C.J. would retaliate with vicious rounds of verbal abuse that left Shayla feeling withered, crushed, despondent, disgusted, underappreciated, and even more enraged.

After a few miserable months of living with Shayla and the baby, C.J. moved out. He got a couple of his buddies together and rented an apartment. One of C.J.'s best friends was an obese youth nicknamed Pills, after the Pillsbury Doughboy. This young man was a self-cutter who mutilated his own skin on a regular basis, leaving scars and open sores. C.J.'s other friend had enormous tattoos all over his back and arms. These guys all partied hard and kept late hours. Their apartment was a filthy maze of beer cans and dirty laundry. C.J. made no secret of the problems he was having with his baby's mother.

"If it were up to Shayla, our son would be dead," said C.J. "He'd be dead, he wouldn't be here right now." C.J. paused and looked over at his buddies, who sat beside him on the couch, nodding in silent acquiescence. C.J. took a moment to reflect. "You know," he said, "not to be bad or nothin', but maybe I should have just let her do it. If it was gonna be all this hard to be a freakin' parent, then I should have."

Shayla was uncomfortable around C.J.'s friends. She did not feel safe leaving her son alone with his father in this unpredictable environment. C.J. resented Shayla for not trusting him. They had hideous fights about how to parent Jaiden. When Jaiden cried, Shayla would always want to pick him up. C.J. argued that if Shayla picked Jaiden up every time he cried, he'd never become independent. The last thing C.J. wanted was a son who was a spoiled, sissy crybaby and a mama's boy. Loud altercations repeatedly escalated into fights, ending with Shayla storming out, taking the baby with her.

Seeing C.J. living in a pigsty, spending his time playing video games with his dazed and hungover friends, did not exactly inspire Shayla's confidence in his ability to be a responsible caretaker. She did not want her son exposed to that seedy environment. Fed up with listening to C.J. hurl insults at her, she stopped taking Jaiden to visit his father. C.J. was livid.

"Everybody thinks I'm such a bad father because I never see Jaiden," he raged. "I never see him because Shayla never brings him over here! If I could take him and raise him all by myself, I'd do it in a heartbeat. I'd take him for weeks—I'd take him for weekends. . . . I could do it all by myself. I know I could."

C.J.'s frustration was very real, as was his genuine desire to be a good father. Although he may have had the best intentions, they bore no relationship to the practical reality of his immediate environment and lifestyle. C.J. rarely went out of his way to visit the baby at Shayla's mother's or her grandmother's house, both of which were nearby. He accused Shayla of restricting access to their son. As Jaiden's father, C.J. felt he was entitled to authority and respect. He was resentful of the control Shayla had over their son. His anger grew as he felt more and more trapped in this unsatisfactory relationship.

"If I break up with Shayla, then she's gonna use the kid to get back at me," he lamented. "She's gonna say, 'No. You can't see him.' Or she's gonna say, 'You can see him, but only when your mother's around for supervision.' If I needed supervision, I wouldn't have had him! If I didn't have a baby with Shayla, I wouldn't be with her right now. I really wouldn't. There ain't no point in us being together if we can't get along."

As the baby got older, Shayla and C.J. tried living together again. The problems between them intensified.

"C.J. definitely has a problem with alcohol," Shayla explained. "When he starts drinking and he's around his friends, he's fine. But when he starts drinking and he's around me, he just flies off the handle. He doesn't know how to control himself."

After several brushes with the police, C.J. was put on probation for offenses that included drunk driving. A few days after Christmas, C.J.'s explosive behavior got him in trouble with the law again. This time it was on a charge of domestic assault and battery.

"Me and C.J. got into a huge fight," said Shayla. "I asked him to do something, and he criticized the way that I raise Jaiden. I went over to him and I decked him; I punched him right in his face. He grabbed me and was shaking me, calling me all types of names, telling me, 'I can't believe you just did that!' He said, 'I'm done with you! I'm leaving! We're not going to be together no more!'

"Every time he said that, I took it to heart," said Shayla, "so I started beating him up and he started shaking me around. The cops came. I was sitting there, crying, saying, 'C.J. hit me in my ear—I can't hear!' I was making myself be the abused one that night. I just wanted attention.

"I was going through a bad time and I wanted everybody to hate him, so I said a lot of things that weren't true. I just said a whole lot of things and never really understood what the outcome would be. And, yeah, he shouldn't have even been putting his hands on me, but people don't understand. I mean, I went over there and I decked him right in his face. If anybody had any marks, it was him. He had scratches all down his neck and his chest."

Shayla's contradictory account of events encompassed accusations, denials, self-recrimination, repression, and confession. She portrayed herself in a derogatory light and made it sound as if she had instigated and manipulated the entire incident. By sharing responsibility for the violence, Shayla was able to protect her love for C.J. and her positive feelings toward him, which the reality of being abused by him would have undermined.

In the picture Shayla painted of that night, the truth remained slippery. In her mind, the roles of victim and aggressor swung back and forth like a pendulum. Shayla had trouble distinguishing one from the other. She blamed herself and she blamed C.J. Her distorted, jumbled thinking served an important purpose: it offered a solid defense against the inherent disappointment and devastation of fully acknowledging that the man she loved and had a child with was damaging and hurtful toward her, compromising her equilibrium and the well-being of their child. When the police arrived on the scene, they evaluated the situation and made an immediate judgment call: they took C.J. to jail, where he was booked and fingerprinted. Shayla was taken to the hospital.

After depositing C.J. in the local jail, the policeman who made the arrest went to Berkshire Medical Center to see how Shayla was doing. He spoke with her and her grandmother. Shayla agreed to file a report. She took out a restraining order against C.J. and was given a domestic-abuse card.

"I told my family that C.J. kicked me in the ear, but the thing was, we were wrestling and I hit my ear. I thought he hit me. . . . I don't know. . . . I know he didn't come out and punch me," said Shayla, still trying to protect C.J. and her lingering romantic feelings for him. "I can't really remember what happened that night," Shayla said, her eyes going completely blank. "I block that stuff out. I don't know. . . . I can't explain."

"I don't know" and "I can't explain" were much more efficient shields than "I know" and "I can explain." In order to justify her love and her overriding self-destructive desire to reunite with C.J., Shayla needed to see reality through her own distorted lens. She wanted to live in complete denial about the abusive nature of her relationship with C.J.

Shayla longed for C.J. to live up to her idealized image of him as her lover and her baby's father. She preferred to focus exclusively on the parts of C.J. she loved, and to pretend that the negatives didn't exist. Shayla attempted to warp reality just enough to bend C.J. into a shape that would fit into her cookie-cutter dream of a stable, intact family. Maintaining the fantasy of a happy future together became more difficult in the aftermath of C.J.'s arrest.

"Because of that night we fought, my family believes that C.J. hit me," said Shayla. "They don't want nothing to do with me and him together, which makes things a lot harder for me now because we want to work things out. We're trying to be a family now. I can't share that with my family, because they have such a strong hate toward C.J. because of all the pain that he put me through.

"All the times that I cried when I was pregnant—I was all upset and having to go to the hospital because of stress. . . . My family witnessed that. They seen how many times I cried and how angry I got when C.J. did things to me. C.J. really took a toll on me, and my family noticed that. They noticed that a lot. They put a temporary restraining order on the house. His mom bailed him out of jail, and he started living with her."

A few months later, the police were called to the residence of Shayla's grandmother, who at the time was baby-sitting for Jaiden. C.J. had tried to kick in her front door, with the intention of taking the baby. By the time the police got to the house, C.J. had fled. The police searched for him all over Pittsfield; when they finally found him, they served him with a trespass notice.

"Even though Shayla didn't want to press charges, the state did," Kelly recalled. "They took over the case and C.J. ended up leaving the state of Massachusetts to get away from the police and the court."

Fearing prosecution, C.J. took what little money he had, packed his bags, and drove out of town. He had been threatening to leave for a while. Shayla had never believed that he would actually go through with it.

"When I first left Pittsfield, I was on my way to California to be an actor," C.J. explained. "I wanted to try something new, but I stopped in Arizona to see my brother and I ended up just staying there. I got my GED and I'm going to school to be an accountant, then hopefully I'm going to go to a four-year college. I'm doing everything just for my son. That's the whole reason I came out West: to make myself a better father for Jaiden. Before I left, things were real bad between me and Shayla. Everything was always her way or the highway. So I finally packed up and hit the road. Shayla needed a reality check, and I needed to get out of Pittsfield.

"Lately things have been okay over the phone, but it's long-distance. Shayla says she's changed, but I'll see. I just want her to grow up. We had an immature boyfriend-girlfriend relationship. I want trust. I don't want to fight about every little thing. All she used to say was 'You can't do this, you can't do that,' like I was her kid or something. I hope maybe now she's starting to realize that we don't own each other, we just love each other.

"In Pittsfield, I was just doing the same thing every day, hangin' out, partying, makin' no money, so I decided to punish myself by taking my family away. When I left Shayla and Jaiden, I said to myself, 'You don't deserve them. You gotta do something to win them back.'

"I've matured these past months. Now I'm not partying no more, I got more responsibility. I really don't do the bad things I used to do. I don't want to get back to my old ways. I don't have any friends over. No partying. No distractions. I just work and go to school. If I do good enough, maybe I'll earn my family back."

When she heard that, Kelly, Shayla's mother, was incredulous.

"Earn his family back? To this day, C.J. has never paid one dime for no Pampers, no formula, no clothing, nothing."

According to Kelly, it would be virtually impossible for law enforcement to do anything about the fact that C.J. was a deadbeat dad, given that he was out of state and didn't have a steady job.

"If C.J. worked, they could do something," explained Kelly, "but C.J. doesn't work. This past year, I doubt he kept a job for more than two weeks. C.J. doesn't know how to continue. He starts something, decides it's not for him, then says, 'I'm done,' and quits. He doesn't realize that this is not something you can do when you have a son."

Shayla consistently attended her classes at cosmetology school and got licensed. Without any help from C.J., she supported herself and Jaiden with the one hundred dollars a week she got from working in a hair salon at the Berkshire Mall, plus the money she received from welfare, which totaled roughly four hundred dollars per month. Although Shayla was grateful for the money she so desperately needed, she hated being dependent on the system and wished that she could earn enough money to break free from all its rules, regulations, inquiries, and constraints.

"If you get a job while you're on welfare, you have to report every paycheck stub," said Shayla. "You have to get a letter from your employer saying that you work there. You have to report any kind of income you have—your bank accounts, whether you have a car, whether you have money on the side, if you make tips. . . . You have to get a letter from your day-care provider so that in return they can give you a voucher for day care, because you can't pay for full-time day care on your own because it's really expensive.

"It's hard because I was sixteen years old and trying to have a baby somewhat on my own. But welfare is just not letting yourself be independent because you have them in your face 24/7. They want to know everything about everything you do. They get really personal and ask questions like 'When did you have sex? What day? What time? Did you have sex with multiple people?' You have to put up with a lot of hassle and a lot of stress. They're so involved in your life, and you don't even get that much money.

"You have to report your child's doctor's appointments and hand in his immunization charts, and if you're missing one little piece of information, they cut you off. If you're not there for your appointment with the social worker, then your money doesn't come in. If your money doesn't come in, you're not getting diapers and you're not getting food." Shayla sighed. "I've had repeated times where my welfare was cut off."

Shayla and Jaiden moved into subsidized housing on April Lane. They lived right across the street from Shayla's best friend, Sheri, and Amy, whom she knew from the Teen Parent Program. Shayla couldn't afford to buy a car and had to rely on the Job Access Program, which provided her with transportation to and from the workplace. On her way to work, Shayla usually dropped Jaiden off at day care.

"When I first started working after Jaiden was born, I put him into a home day care because I wanted him in a smaller setting where there weren't so many kids around where he could get enough attention. I noticed a lot of times when I picked Jaiden up from day care he had bruises on him, like this one time he had a black eye. But I never asked any questions because he's a hyper kid. He does jump around a lot and fall down and stuff, so I never really put two and two together.

"But now people are saying the lady who ran that day care died of a drug overdose. It bothers me because a lot of times things weren't always a hundred percent, and I never put two and two together. How do I know she wasn't a hostile person? How do I know she wasn't spanking my kid or neglecting my kid?

"A few times when I took Jaiden home from day care, he was acting strange. He was different, more drawn away from people, more sad. When I used to discipline him, he'd come over and kick me back and yell in my face, 'No, Mommy, you don't tell me!' Then when I yelled at him, he'd curl up in a ball and say, 'I'm so sorry, Mommy.' I look back and I see all of these things that I should have asked questions about. But how was I supposed to know that the lady who ran that day care was on drugs?"

Shayla switched Jaiden to a new day-care facility and did her best to reduce the amount of time he spent there. Whenever possible, she preferred to leave him with her grandmother, and on her days off she kept him at home with her. Shayla found that taking care of Jaiden was much more exhausting and stressful than her job.

———

Jaiden grew into an extremely demanding, hyper, energetic, and adventurous toddler. He was constantly asking questions. Shayla found that he never wanted to sit still and was always pestering her to play with him and always wanting to run around outside. Since he couldn't play outdoors unsupervised, often she would have to stop whatever she was doing and take him out—or listen to him throw a tantrum if he didn't get his way. Shayla rarely had a moment of peace and quiet. She longed to sleep late on Sunday mornings and resented never being able to enjoy that luxury.

"On days when I'm not working, Jaiden wakes up at eight and he's a total terror until he takes his nap at noon. He likes to stick stuff in outlets, stuff like that. If he touches something that could hurt him, I usually just say no and talk him through it. He likes to tell me no all the time, and he likes to bang his toys around. Sometimes he breaks lamps and dishes. Lately, he's been hitting and spitting and saying 'bullshit' a lot. I try to discipline him by saying no in a loud, firm voice, and if he keeps on hitting me, I slap his hand. If he's really having one of his days when he's not listening, then I spank him. Then he starts to understand.

"I definitely think that if you were brought up being spanked, then that's how you bring your child up. I don't feel being spanked had a bad influence on me. I don't think that I was abused or anything like that. I just think that it was enough that I knew my limits. That's the way I intend to raise Jaiden."

Though Shayla blamed her son's acting-out on the terrible situation at his former day care, her mother offered a different theory about the origins of her grandson's aggressive behavioral problems.

"I think Jaiden started hitting people when he seen his father hitting his mother," said Kelly. "Now that's his way of greeting you. You open your arms to him and he hits you. That's his way of his saying hi to his mom now. He doesn't know how to love her; he just wants to hit her. We can't seem to break those habits. So, you can see, the damage has already been done."

As Shayla struggled to teach her son right from wrong, C.J. remained in Arizona and had no contact with them other than by telephone. Gradually Jaiden's behavior began to improve. Shayla was proud to see him coming home from day care singing songs and reciting the alphabet. At night she often took him across the street to play with her friend Sheri's daughter, Leeah.

While the kids entertained themselves, Sheri and Shayla cooked dinner together and watched television. They enjoyed each other's company and took solace in being able to talk frankly about what they were going through. Before they had become mothers, their conversations had centered on lipstick colors, unrequited crushes, the latest awesome song on the radio, grueling homework assignments, nasty teachers, petty arguments with other girls, fights with their mothers, and agonizing decisions about which outfit to wear to so-and-so's party on Friday night. Now all those concerns seemed trivial. On languid summer nights, as Jaiden and Leeah prattled in the background, Sheri and Shayla's conversations centered on two subjects: raising their children and the challenges of maintaining their relationships with their boyfriends.

Lonely in C.J.'s absence, Shayla spent a tremendous amount of mental energy obsessing over how to get him back. The distance between Pittsfield and Arizona and C.J.'s extended absence both served as safeguards, enabling Shayla to sink into a quicksand of idealized romantic fantasies about how great things would be when they saw each other again after such a long separation.

Sheri gently gave Shayla a reality check. She reminded her how rough things had been with C.J. and suggested that she consider dating other guys. Shayla refused to even consider dating someone new. Convinced that C.J. would come back for her and Jaiden, she held on tight to her hope that they would soon be reunited as one happy family. When months went by and it didn't happen, Shayla came up with a plan. She decided to hunt down C.J. in Arizona. She envisioned one of two outcomes: either C.J. would come back to Pittsfield or he would ask her and Jaiden to live with him in Phoenix.

One payday, Shayla realized to her delight that she had finally earned enough money to make the trip to Arizona. She grabbed her week of vacation and proudly bought two Greyhound bus tickets to Phoenix. Having never ventured far from Pittsfield, Shayla was apprehensive about making such a long journey all alone with her toddler, but she was propelled by her intense desire to see C.J.

Aboard the bus, Shayla and Jaiden stared out the window at long stretches of seemingly endless highways. By the third day, they were both impatient and exhausted. Fearing a temper tantrum, Shayla held Jaiden in her lap, stroking his forehead, doing her best to keep him calm. To her surprise, the little boy behaved well during the entire bus ride, as if somehow he sensed that the trip was vital to his mother.

Finally, mother and son arrived at their destination, their exhaustion mixed with excitement. C.J. met them at the station. Within minutes, he told Shayla that he wished she had not come.

During her short stay in Phoenix, Shayla telephoned Sheri long-distance four times, sobbing uncontrollably. Through her tears she told Sheri that C.J. was being really mean to her. He wanted her to go home, and he told her that though he wanted to be friends for the sake of the baby, he didn't want to continue any kind of romantic relationship. Shayla made a similarly desperate call to her grandmother, who immediately purchased two airplane tickets, eager to get her granddaughter and great-grandson home quickly and safely.

For the first time in both their lives, Shayla and Jaiden got on an airplane. As the plane took off and climbed toward the sky, Shayla stared out the window, mesmerized by the view. She had always dreamed of flying to some faraway place where she could build a new life for herself, but instead, a few hours after the plane's wheels bumped down on the runway, she was back in Pittsfield, sitting on the sofa in her apartment on April Lane, watching TV.

Shayla was devastated. She couldn't accept what had happened in Arizona, so she began reinventing the events of the disastrous trip, transforming the upsetting facts into a fairy tale. When family and friends asked how the visit went, Shayla pretended that it had been a blast and that everything with C.J. was just fine and dandy. She told people how gorgeous C.J.'s apartment was. These stories wore thin a few days later when C.J.'s phone in Arizona got disconnected and he was kicked out of his gorgeous apartment for not paying rent.

Despite these developments, Shayla continued to conjure up images of a rosy, romantic future with C.J., while sinking deeper into depression. She lived in a state of denial, caught up in a web of unrealistic ideas and longings, unwilling to confront her disappointment, despair, and terrifying uncertainty about her future. In addition to Jaiden, the one thing that kept Shayla going was her job at Hair Express. She found the atmosphere at the mall socially stimulating and enjoyed the distinction of being regarded a professional hairdresser. She managed to cross the six-month threshold, marking the longest period she had consistently held one job.

Then without warning, Shayla was abruptly fired after being accused of handling a customer rudely and unprofessionally. Shayla insisted that the charges weren't true, but her boss chose to believe her coworker's account. She told Shayla in no uncertain terms that she was no longer welcome at the salon.

"I was really, really upset," said Shayla, shivering at the memory of those bitterly cold winter months. "I had picked out all types of stuff to get Jaiden for Christmas and I couldn't get that stuff, because my boss fired me over something that I didn't even do."

Shayla did her best to bounce back. She landed another job at Filene's. She quickly moved on to a resort, where she worked in housekeeping, cleaning rooms for ten dollars an hour. When that didn't work out, Shayla asked Sheri if she could help her get a job cleaning rooms at the bed-and-breakfast where she worked. Sheri

spoke to her boss, and Shayla was hired. For a few months the two friends worked side by side, doing laundry, vacuuming floors, dusting tables, scrubbing toilets, and changing sheets. Shayla often thought of C.J. and wondered what he was up to in Arizona. She told Sheri that she hoped C.J. was "growing up" and "getting his act together." Sheri was skeptical and encouraged Shayla to consider dating other guys.

C.J.'s prolonged absence combined with her own life experience as a single mother gave Shayla some necessary distance from her high-school years as well as a new perspective on all that had transpired since then. With the enhanced self-awareness, Shayla reflected on her decision to get pregnant at such a young age. Looking back on her younger self, Shayla saw "a very immature sixteen-year-old." She acknowledged that her relationship with C.J. had been overburdened with problems from day one. Having a baby hadn't magically resolved these issues, as she had hoped—instead, it had complicated them.

"I thought having a baby would work out all corners of my life, but it really hasn't," said Shayla. "It stressed my life out and it made everything much more difficult."

"I think we should have waited," agreed C.J., "because there's a lot more to life than just hurrying up. I feel like I'm already, I don't know, thirty or forty. I feel like I'm grown up and there's not much left to do in the world."

As Shayla matured, she got used to being a single mother. She realized she was capable of dealing with the challenge of raising her son.

"Six months ago, if you had asked me if I was prepared to be on

my own, I would've told you straight up, 'No!' " said Shayla. "I would have said that because I was so dependent on C.J. But now I'm starting to grow up and I realize, it's true: I am definitely prepared. Nothing really matters but Jaiden. My whole focus goes toward him. I'm just gonna work on making things right for him. If C.J. decides that we can be a family and things are gonna work out so that Jaiden is happy, that's fine. But Jaiden comes first."

Shayla finally got over C.J. and started dating Ian, whom she had known since elementary school. Ian had recently gotten out of jail and needed a place to stay, so he moved in with Shayla and Jaiden. Ian already had a daughter with another teen mother. He complained to Shayla that his ex-girlfriend wouldn't let him see the child and had taken out a restraining order against him. After Shayla found several items missing from her apartment, she kicked Ian out.

When things didn't work out in Arizona, C.J. returned to Pittsfield. He had to keep a low profile because there was still a warrant out for his arrest. Shayla gave C.J. a chance to prove that he had changed. He quickly failed to persuade her.

"At first, we were gonna try to be together," said Shayla, "but after five years putting up with all the arguing and fighting, I decided I didn't want to be with him, so he moved back in with his mom. He takes Jaiden once a week. We get along as friends for Jaiden's sake.

"C.J. used to make me feel really insecure about myself. He used to tell me all the time that he was the only one who wanted me and that I was ugly to everybody else. All that crap wasn't true. I thought me and C.J. were gonna be together for . . . I wouldn't say forever, but I'd say for a long time. I thought we'd stick it out—but I wasn't happy with him. Jaiden knew I wasn't happy. He could tell. I couldn't take care of him being all sad and depressed every day. I take care of him a lot better now because I'm a happier person."

Soon after breaking up with C.J., Shayla began dating Jay. He was white, tattooed, and roughly the same height and physical type as C.J. He had dropped out of high school in tenth grade and worked as a butcher at a grocery store. He and his friends all wore their pants down super low so that their boxer shorts stuck out jailhouse-style, between their long T-shirts and their belt buckles.

At eighteen, Jay was younger than Shayla. He was content to let her be the dominant one in the relationship. On his days off he hung out at Shayla's apartment, watching TV, or wandered around the neighborhood with his buddies.

"Jay treats me with respect and makes me feel a lot better than C.J. made me feel," said Shayla. "I really like him a lot and he really, really likes me a lot. Jaiden loves him to death. He doesn't look at him like he's his father because he knows who his dad is, but they're getting along real well."

Three months into their relationship, Shayla got pregnant. She offered contradictory explanations for how and why this second pregnancy occurred. Sometimes she made it sound as though she and Jay had planned the pregnancy, other times she indicated that she had been taking the Depo-Provera shot and had combined it with muscle-relaxing medication, which she claimed had caused this method of contraception to fail. In either case, once she was pregnant, she decided to carry the baby to term.

Jaiden was already three years old. He was becoming independent, and Shayla missed having a baby in the house. Also motivating Shayla to have the second child was her feeling that with Jaiden, she had missed out on the relaxing, wonderful, bonding moments a mother and infant were supposed to have together. Two weeks after Jaiden was born, she had rushed back to school. After a long day at school she had worked at Friendly's, and then there had been all the stress with C.J. Shayla felt that Jaiden's infancy had gone by way too fast, and she longed for the chance to mother an infant all over again, this time the right way. She wanted to stay home with her second baby without any other demands on her time and energy. She also desperately wanted a baby girl. Jay was pretty relaxed about the idea of becoming a father. Many of his friends had kids, and he felt ready to do the same thing.

"At first, my mom and my grams were a little upset about me

being pregnant again," said Shayla, "but within the same day they were fine about it. I already have to wake up in the morning with Jaiden. I'll have to wake up in the morning with the baby. I give Jaiden a bath. I'll give the baby a bath. It's the same thing. I'm a little nervous because I don't know how Jaiden will react to a baby coming home. I worry about if he's gonna be jealous, but other than that, I'm fine about it."

Shayla knew that she would need more money when the second baby arrived. She and Sheri enrolled in a computer class at the Mildred Elly Business School. They learned how to enter data and how to make spreadsheets in Excel. Shayla hoped that her newly acquired skills would help her get a better job.

As her pregnancy continued, Shayla became determined to make C.J. pay child support for Jaiden. Whenever she broached the subject with him, he would verbally attack her and refuse to pay. Absolutely furious that Shayla was carrying Jay's baby, C.J. was eager to make life hell for both of them. Although fear of the warrant for his arrest made him circumspect about where he went and with whom, it didn't stop him from using the telephone as a weapon.

"I was three or four months pregnant, and Jay was working full-time. I was home and C.J. would call me all day and he'd threaten. . . . He'd call me a bad person because I had a new boyfriend and I was starting a new family, and he'd harass Jay and threaten to beat him up and strangle him and stuff. . . . I told him, if you keep calling my house, harassing me, I'm going to call the police on you."

C.J. disregarded Shayla's warning. When the phone rang again, Shayla picked up, hung up on C.J., and called the police. She told them exactly where to find their man.

"C.J. was arrested immediately, and he went to jail," recalled Shayla. "He had to serve four months in a correctional institution, and he had to do a month of rehab for his alcohol and drug abuse because he was smoking marijuana and he drank uncontrollably."

Jaiden didn't visit his father behind bars. "C.J. wanted him to come," said Shayla, "but I don't think they allow children in that jail anymore."

C.J. was surprised to find that the months he spent in jail did him a lot of good. Most of the other prisoners in the local jail were incarcerated on charges related to drugs, stealing, domestic violence, alcohol-related brawls, or drunk-driving incidents. Behind bars, C.J. worked out, ate three regular meals, and put on thirty pounds. He started reading the Bible, searching for the meaning and purpose of his life. The months flew by. C.J. got sober, got rest, and matured. Jail was his rite of passage into manhood.

When C.J. was released from jail, another court date awaited him. Shayla, six months pregnant, faced him in front of a judge and demanded child support. The judge made it clear that if C.J. didn't get a job and support his son, he'd go straight back to jail. Soon after, Shayla received the first of what would be regular child-support payments. They were small at first but gradually increased when C.J. got a better job painting houses.

All the stress of these traumatic, emotional events took a toll on Shayla's pregnancy. One afternoon while she was attending her computer class, she went into labor. She panicked. It was way too early. Shayla's voice trembled as she called Jay. He rushed over, picked her up, and took her to the local hospital. The doctors there made arrangements for her to be transported to a bigger hospital in Springfield.

"When I first started going into labor, I was only twenty-four weeks pregnant, and in Pittsfield they can't take you into labor if you're before thirty-four weeks, so I had to go to Springfield, which is about an hour and a half away by ambulance. The doctor gave me some medication through an IV, and it stopped my labor. I stayed in the hospital for a week and a half to be monitored so that they could make sure that the labor was stopped. Then they sent me home on total bed rest. They told me to take sponge baths because they didn't want me standing up in the shower. But I had a three year old at home and I had a house to take care of, so I couldn't stay on total bed rest. I was up walkin' around, and that put me back into labor at thirty-two weeks. They brought me into Springfield for an emergency C-section because the baby was in breach position. The umbilical cord was wrapped around his neck, so they were really worried about his breathing."

Shayla gave birth prematurely to Caleb, a baby boy who weighed only three pounds. He spent the first week of his life hooked up to life-support machines in the intensive care unit for newborns at the hospital in Springfield. After only five days, he was taken back to Pittsfield by ambulance. The infant spent another three weeks in an incubator at a hospital there. Shayla, Jay, and Jaiden visited every day. Jaiden was extremely worried about his little brother being in what he referred to as "that little box."

"After almost four weeks in the incubator, the doctor said Caleb had gained enough weight," said Shayla, "so we brought him home. He seemed absolutely fine until Jay woke up at two in the morning to feed him and suddenly he just stopped breathing and started coughing up blood."

Jay called out for Shayla. She leapt out of bed, alarmed by the sheer terror in his trembling voice. After one glimpse at the baby, Shayla switched into full gear.

"I snatched the baby. I was trying to get him to breathe," said Shayla. "I was shaking him a little bit, shaking his little arms to get him going, and he kept breathing very faintly but he had a lot of mucus stuck in his throat. So it was like three in the morning. I wrapped him up in a blanket, and it was freezing outside. I put him in the car. My whole windshield was glazed thick with ice, so I couldn't see. I had to roll my window down and look out the driver's side window all the way to the hospital.

"When I got to the emergency room, I was frantic. I said to the nurse, 'You need to help my baby out! He's not breathing!'

"The doctors were so worried about taking Caleb's temperature, and they were just poking at him. That frustrated me a lot because it was really serious to me, and they were saying, 'Well, we have to take his temperature, we have to do this, we have to do that. . . .'

"To me it was like 'He's not breathing! Can't you help him out a little bit?' It was really frustrating. Although he made it through the night, I wanted to switch him to a better hospital, so we went to Bay State in Springfield. As soon as I got him down there, they told me exactly what he had and within five minutes they took care of him."

Caleb was diagnosed with respiratory syncytial virus (RSV), a common condition that affects nearly all adults and children in the form of a common cold. The doctor told Shayla that premature babies such as Caleb were at much higher risk of developing an acute, potentially fatal form of the contagious virus, which strikes mostly during autumn, winter, and early spring. Caleb remained in the hospital in Springfield for two weeks. While he was being treated for his illness, the hospital allowed Shayla and Jay to stay a block away at the Ronald McDonald House, a residential facility that offered rooms free of charge to parents of hospitalized children.

"You could live there for two days or two months," explained Shayla. "It's absolutely free. They offer you a kitchen. They have a huge basement playroom in case you have any other children you have to bring with you. It was really nice. The hospital was right down the street, so me and Jay would walk there. The baby's feedings were, like, every three hours, so every single night we'd switch, every other feeding, so that we could go up there and sit with him and feed him. We stayed there for hours."

After several weeks, the doctors pronounced Caleb healthy enough to leave the hospital, ending the long ordeal. Shayla spent six months at home taking care of him. This time around, the welfare caseworker was much more understanding and tolerant. Shayla was pleasantly surprised to learn that as an adult in possession of her GED, she was governed by a different set of rules. She managed to get through Caleb's infancy without ever having her welfare cut off, which had been a constant worry when Jaiden was younger. Shayla cherished the time she spent with Caleb. It was a luxury to be able to be a mother for six months without having to worry about work and school.

While holding and feeding her baby, Shayla spent hours watching MTV. She particularly liked the reality shows. Her favorite show was called *MADE,* which took real teenagers who had a dream and gave them the means to realize that dream.

"They had two shows," recalled Shayla, "one where a girl got to become a model and one where she got to become a professional cheerleader. That really interested me because I want to be either one of those things. The one that I liked the most was about a girl who became a model. I think her name was Nadia, and she didn't look that special. She just looked like a normal black girl, and when I was watching the show, when I was looking at her doing the shopping and getting her makeup done, I thought it was something I could do. She just looked like an average person, and I know I could do the same thing. They set her up with a coach who taught her how to walk and how to be a model, and while she was being trained, they set her up with a place to live in New York City and they helped her get a job as a waitress at The Coffee Shop. Her coach took her to all the different modeling agencies until she finally got a contract. She went to, like, twenty agencies and got offered a contract by six of them.

"It was easier for that girl than it would be for me," said Shayla, "because she was in college and didn't have any kids, so she could just move to New York for two months while she was being trained. She could just quit school and quit her job and just up and leave— but for me, I wouldn't be able to do the same thing because I have two kids.

"But I was just wondering if there's some way that I'd still be able to be on that show. If MTV says the rules are that you have to dedicate all your time twenty-four hours a day to training and going after your dream, then it would be something I wouldn't be able to

do. But I know that a lot of the girls who are Dallas Cowboys Cheerleaders have kids. So they must be able to do both. They make their schedules for dance classes and their exercising fit in with being a mom. It just seems like when you're a singer, or you become a model or a cheerleader—people start when they're like sixteen and actually get into it by the time they're twenty. I'm gonna be trying to start something when I'm twenty-one or twenty-two," Shayla lamented.

C.J. and Shayla went back to court to define the terms of his rights as Jaiden's father. Jaiden was now four years old, and Shayla had

matured to a point where she recognized that it was important for him to have a relationship with C.J. Her son often asked about his dad. Shayla decided to put her negative feelings aside and do what was best for the child.

"I started to allow C.J. to visit Jaiden for an hour a week under outside supervision," she explained. "During these supervised visits Jaiden really got to know his dad. They started spending a lot of time together."

After a few months of supervised visits, C.J. was allowed to take his son by himself on weekends. He had rented a studio apartment on a quiet residential block, eager to provide a peaceful, positive environment for his son. Continuing the search for purpose and meaning in his life that had begun while he was incarcerated, C.J. read a book that made a huge impact on him. It was titled *SQ: Connecting with Your Spiritual Intelligence,* and was cowritten by Danah Zohar, a professor at Oxford University, and Dr. Ian Marshall, a psychiatrist and psychotherapist. Their ideas offered C.J. a new way of appreciating himself and gave him a sense of value and direction, helping him begin to fill the inner void he had described so vividly when reflecting on his life at about the time he and Shayla had conceived Jaiden. C.J. began doing yoga every morning, copying the movements from a class taught on television. He mellowed out, got a steady job as a waiter at a local restaurant, and held on to it. Jaiden's overall behavior improved significantly as he spent more time with his dad, adhering to a consistent, predictable schedule.

"C.J. told me that he's not angry anymore about the whole situation," said Shayla, "but when he first went to jail, he was so mad at me for calling the cops. Now he thanks me, because he's a lot more mature now, so he's happy with the outcome. Going to jail helped C.J. grow up. It helped him learn to take care of Jaiden responsibly, the way he's supposed to."

When Caleb was seven months old, Shayla got a part-time job in telemarketing. At malls across the country, people were given the opportunity to enter a raffle to win a Jeep. On the raffle ticket they had to put down their telephone numbers in case they won. These phone numbers were then assigned to Shayla. She was instructed to try to sell these people time-share vacation homes. Irritated at being bothered and having no idea how she got their home numbers, people

usually spoke to her rudely and then hung up on her. Shayla hated the job and eventually quit.

Jay was also temporarily out of work. He and Shayla sat home together with the two kids, watching television. Their phone was cut off because they didn't pay the bill. People who wanted to get in touch with them had to go to their apartment in person.

"My relationship with Jay is a lot different than what I had with C.J.," said Shayla. "Jay and I get along. We like a lot of the same things. I don't really go out that much. I'm kinda a homebody. I like to stay at home and keep to myself, and Jay doesn't mind that. He doesn't mind sitting at home with me, watching a movie. He's not the type of person who needs to be out all the time. One of the big problems I had with C.J. was that he never liked to stay home and help. Now, whenever I need any help, Jay is right there. He's there all the time. It's a lot easier to get along with him and have a better relationship when he's always here. He doesn't give me a hard time about having to get up in the middle of the night with the baby. He just sucks it up and he does it."

Jay adopted a pit bull puppy from a friend who didn't want the dog anymore. He named the dog Tigger. Shayla hated having the dog in the house with the two kids. The dog kept getting out and jumping over the fence. It tore open garbage bags and whatever else it could sink its teeth into. Shayla wanted to get rid of the dog, but Jay wanted to keep him. Jaiden grew very attached to the dog. The little boy often tried to hug Tigger, but usually the pit bull just growled and scared him away.

When Jaiden was four, Shayla noticed that his upper front teeth were growing abnormally sharp, yellow, and rotten. The doctor diagnosed him with "milk rot," a dental condition that occurs when infants and toddlers sleep with bottles in their mouth, leaving milk or, worse, high-sugar juices or soda in contact with the teeth for extended periods of time, causing decay. Jaiden had to have his front teeth pulled and his back teeth filed down.

As the baby got older, Shayla needed to get a full-time job. In an effort to help her out with the two kids, her grandmother took a course offered by an organization called Resources for Child Care. Upon completion, she received accreditation as a home day-care provider. With this certification, she could take care of her great-grandchildren and get paid for it with vouchers that she could trade in for cash.

Now that Shayla didn't have to structure her work hours around the hours of a day-care center, she could work longer hours and had more options and flexibility in terms of shifts. There was an opening at Dunkin' Donuts a block away from where she lived. Shayla was hired. The branch where Shayla worked was always busy, frequented by a broad array of characters, ranging from tourists to locals to homeless vagrants who wandered in, clutching a few coins in their hands, begging for a cup of coffee.

Shayla liked the hustle and bustle and the fast turnover. She became friendly with her coworkers. The pace, the energy, and the camaraderie stimulated her and made the hours go by faster.

On most days, Shayla wore her hair pulled straight back in a simple ponytail. The hair extensions she had once been so enamored with sat unused in a drawer. Shayla wore glasses all the time and rarely wore makeup. When she wasn't in her uniform for work, usually she hung around in jeans, T-shirts, and baggy sweatpants. Her days of dressing glamorously and daydreaming about modeling bikinis were long gone.

Shayla's younger sister, Ashley, was now in junior high. She and her friends sometimes passed by Dunkin' Donuts when Shayla was working her shift. Witnessing her elder sister's struggles, Ashley did what she could to help out with her nephews. She doted on Jaiden and took tremendous delight in playing with the baby. Whereas Shayla was always exhausted, Ashley had boundless energy and could easily keep the baby engaged and entertained when Shayla nodded off for a nap. Shayla saw how much her sister enjoyed spending time with the baby and made sure that Ashley participated in the drudgery of childrearing as well as its pleasures.

"My sister and I are two very different people," said Shayla pointedly. "She sees how hard it is to have a baby because I give her things to do. I don't think she'll end up like I did. She's into a totally different direction.

"Right now my little sister sees a lot of stuff on TV and in the movies with the young girls doing a whole bunch of things," said Shayla, "and that kind of inspires her. She's fourteen, and she's seeing all these girls on TV actually doing something and not just sitting around, having a boyfriend or having a kid. So she actually is inspired to do something else. Like on MTV, there was one show called *Sorority Life,* and it was just them following these college girls who wanted to be in a sorority. You follow them partying and hanging out and trying to get their homework done, just stuff that happens in their real lives. My sister watches that and she's like 'Oh, I want to go to college. . . . I can't wait to go to college!' "

Ashley was a talented cheerleader. She devoted most of her energy to rigorous practice sessions and participated in competitions. At night and on weekends, when she was bored at home, she would visit Shayla and the kids, often dressed in short miniskirts that showed off her unbelievably long legs. An array of camisoles and colorful tank tops accentuated her lacy bras and her developing cleavage.

"That's exactly what Shayla used to look like," said Sheri nostalgically as she watched Ashley walk down the street and disappear around the corner.

chapter six

SHERI

"*You just didn't know what was gonna happen at my mom's. You just took it minute by minute. You didn't know if there was gonna be a fight. You didn't know who was gonna show up or at what time. There were always people there who I didn't like. My mom's friends were lowlifes. They didn't have nothing goin' for 'em. I don't know exactly what kind of drugs they were into, but I didn't want to be a part of that.*"

SHERI'S MOTHER, PAT, WAS FIFTEEN THE FIRST TIME SHE got pregnant. She lost the baby not long after being beaten up by her boyfriend and was unable to put the guilt and bereavement behind her. Every year on what would have been her baby's birthday, Pat's spirits plummeted and she entered a state of profound mourning.

At the age of seventeen, Pat was pregnant again. She dropped out of high school and married her new boyfriend, Greg, who already had a two-year-old son. Pat gave birth to a baby boy and devoted the remainder of her teenage years to raising this child and her stepson. Several years later, Sheri was born.

"Sheri's dad was an alcoholic," Pat recalled, "and when he'd have his hangovers, he'd be verbally abusive and he'd make me go out and mow the lawn, pregnant. The lawn mower would break down and he would tell me where the parts were to repair it. He wasn't a very loving husband. He did a lot of running around. In fact, when I went into labor with Sheri, he unplugged his phone. So I had Sheri all by myself that night."

As a toddler, Sheri witnessed wild fights between her parents. Fists flew, plates were shattered, furniture was broken, and liquor bottles were smashed. By the time Sheri was three years old, she had a large, wide, half-moon-shaped scar on one of her cheeks but no memory of how the injury occurred. Her mother told her she had fallen while running, carrying a glass of water. According to Pat, the glass had shattered and one of the fragments slashed Sheri in the face, leaving a deeply etched mark that measured nearly two inches. The injury nearly cost the child one of her eyes and required several operations. Finally, when Sheri was a teenager, plastic surgery resulted in a dramatic improvement, but even as the scar on her face faded, the internal scars she incurred growing up remained raw.

"While I was pregnant with Sheri's little sister, Nadine, my husband just got up and left," Pat recalled. "He never gave us any child support. . . . He was gone for ten years, without a trace."

Sheri, nearly four, waited and waited for some word of her daddy's whereabouts—an address, a phone number, a letter, a birthday card, a message—but there was nothing. By the time Nadine was born, Sheri and her elder brother had adjusted to their father's absence. They no longer expected him to show up at the front door, begging Pat to take him back, as he had done so many times before.

Four years later, when Sheri was seven and Nadine three, Pat married her boyfriend, Steve, a truck driver. Nadine grew up mistaking Steve for her biological father. Pat and Steve's marriage was strained by financial hardship and loud arguments. Pat was frequently tired, irritable, depressed, and strung out. She chain-smoked nonstop and suffered from recurring anxiety attacks. Because of a severe cocaine addiction and an eating disorder, Pat was dangerously underweight and incredibly volatile.

"My mom's mood—it was always changing," Sheri recalled. "One minute she'd be nice and caring and loving, and the next she'd be kind of on the edge. There was times when I felt like she didn't want me around. I would sometimes ask myself, 'Why am I even here? Should I be doing something different for my mom to want me here?' " Sheri took a deep breath and shook her head. "I shouldn't have had to feel like that," she said.

Echoing her elder sister's perceptions, Nadine explained, "My mom has many different personalities. She can be really nice. One minute she'll be laughing, next minute she'll be throwing things at you, next minute she'll be crying, and the next minute she'll be going psycho, just screaming and breaking things. Her moods change like that!" Nadine said, snapping her fingers to illustrate the rapid shifts.

As the girls were growing up, Pat and Steve were each arrested more than a dozen times on charges related to drugs, assault and battery, and disturbing the peace.

"Cops were always showing up," said Nadine. "Watching that every day—fighting, drugs, drinking, drug dealers coming in and out—it got a little crazy. It was hard. I dealt with a lot of abuse," she said quietly, raising her finger to touch her forehead. "It ruined me up here—and everywhere else.

"When I was about five years old, there was fighting," recalled Nadine. "Pans were flying and I got hit with hot grease. I went to school and they wound up seeing that I was burned from grease and I wound up telling them what had happened and the cops wound up coming and taking us away. Sheri and I got put in a foster home because of the drugs."

After a few months, the girls were returned to the custody of their mother and stepfather. Pat took Sheri out of school for several months, which resulted in her having to repeat a grade. One afternoon when Sheri was seven years old, she and another little girl were dropped off at the house of a family friend. Sheri had never met this man who was supposed to "baby-sit" for the day while her mother and aunt were both at work. As soon as Sheri's aunt drove away, the man locked the two girls in the bathroom, where they were surrounded by sex toys, lewd photographs, and S&M costumes. They were held hostage for several hours.

When he finally let the girls out, the man forced them to watch pornographic videotapes featuring children performing sexual acts on various adults. One of the children they saw was a six-year-old boy they knew. Sheri was terrified. She and her friend were asked to dress up in costumes. They refused. Trembling, Sheri kept quiet and watched the videos, praying that her aunt would come to pick her up.

In the late afternoon, Sheri's aunt arrived to retrieve the girls. As soon as she got home, Sheri told her mother everything that had happened. Pat took her to the police station. A report was filed. A week later the police raided the man's house. He was found dead in his garage. He had committed suicide.

Sheri was haunted by this death. She felt guilty, sensing that people blamed her for the suicide. She worried that by telling her mother what had happened, she had caused this man to kill himself. From that point on, when bad things happened behind closed doors, Sheri embraced silence. To this little girl, silence seemed much safer than causing someone's death.

One night Sheri and her little sister were awakened by sounds of yelling and screaming. They opened their eyes and saw strangers standing in their bedroom. They were urged to get dressed and pack their suitcases. Frightened, Sheri went downstairs and asked her mother and stepfather what was going on. She was told that she was being taken to a foster home. No further explanation was given.

"Sheri and I went in and out of a few foster homes together, but we didn't stay long," recalled Nadine. "We just wound up going in and out of them and then back to my mom's."

Sheri and Nadine loved their mother in spite of her shortcomings. Each time the Department of Social Services intervened and put them into foster care, Pat blamed the girls "for causing trouble." From a safe distance, the girls worried about betraying their mother by telling the truth about some of the things that went on inside the four walls of their small wood cabin. They felt immensely ambivalent about being separated from their mother, and thus had great difficulty settling in to the foster homes where they were placed. Deep down, they didn't want new families to take them in—they just wanted their own family to be different.

"A lot of foster parents, they're really mean people," Nadine said. "They're not nice at all, and you can tell for a fact they're just doing it for the money. If you try to talk to them, pretty much all they say to you is 'Go to bed' or 'It's time to eat' or 'It's time for you to do a bath.' They don't sit down and really talk to you. They just tell you what to do and then say good night or good-bye."

As a result of these failed foster care placements and the girls' intense ambivalence, Pat was given many second chances to take care of her children. She knew that her daughters loved her. Not wanting them to be taken away from her for good, she made a conscious effort.

"I went to the adult learning center and got my high school diploma," Pat recalled. "Then I got a housecleaning job at an inn. That didn't last too long, so I got my hairdressing license and did hairdressing for a couple of years. Then I needed benefits, so I went to got my certified nurse's assistant license. It was hard living on welfare like we did all those years. It was a long, hard struggle."

When Sheri turned sixteen, she was eligible for her working papers. Her aunt worked as a housekeeper at Canyon Ranch, a world-class spa and resort located in Lenox, fifteen minutes from Pittsfield. She helped Sheri get a job there.

"I worked long hours and cleaned lots of rooms," Sheri remembered. "After school I'd go in from three o'clock until nine, almost every day, because I needed the money." The rooms at Canyon Ranch were usually empty when Sheri cleaned them. The hours she spent at work passed quietly. No one bothered her. She had been cleaning her mom's house for as long as she could remember, so the skills she needed came naturally. Sheri found the atmosphere of the resort soothing compared with her frazzled family life. Between going to work and school, her goal was to spend as little time at home as humanly possible.

At sixteen, Sheri was old enough to distance herself somewhat from the chaos at home. She chose to steer clear of substance abuse and devoted her time and energy to her job and to maintaining her close relationship with her boyfriend, Jon, whom she had met at school. With his calm voice and quiet, relaxed manner, Jon became Sheri's anchor.

Nadine had no anchor. At twelve, she was sensitive, vulnerable, and very impressionable. Trapped with her mother and stepfather, she was at sea in a culture of violence, crime, and addiction.

"I first partied when I was eleven," she recalled. "Already back then, I had a problem with alcohol."

The existing stress in the household was exacerbated when Sheri and Nadine's stepfather, Steve, took a leave of absence from work because of a back injury. At the same time, their elder brother was recovering from surgery following a car accident. With the two men incapacitated and hanging around the house all day, the burden of supporting the family fell squarely on Pat's shoulders.

In order to pay the bills and keep food on the table, Pat, then employed as a nursing assistant, had to increase her workload to fifty or sixty hours per week. Most days, she arrived at work exhausted, pale, weak; by then she was emaciated. It was all she could do to summon up the strength to push the elderly around in their wheelchairs. During the limited hours she spent at home, Pat divided most of her time between sleeping and arguing with her husband. She had to curtail her partying habits because she couldn't afford to lose her job. She had very little patience with her children.

Most days when Sheri came home from school, Steve was waiting to greet her. Sheri had very little privacy, and as the tension between her and her stepfather escalated, she felt safer and more at ease outside the home, working or hanging out with friends. Faced with Sheri's emerging femininity and youthfulness, Pat was intensely competitive and envious. She accused Sheri of acting inappropriately and of being provocative at home. She screamed, shouted, intimidated, and grounded Sheri—but all her efforts to rein her eldest daughter in failed miserably.

Seeking attention, Sheri tested her mother by disobeying rules and staying out past her curfew. Any reaction was better than nothing. Any show of emotion, including anger, was seen as a sign that her mother did indeed care about her. Instead of asking Sheri what was bothering her and trying to create a safe line of communication, when faced with Sheri's blatant defiance and lack of respect, Pat became more and more explosive. Pat had more than enough problems of her own and couldn't tolerate Sheri's adding to them.

Sheri had an equally hard time tolerating her mother's behavior. She saw the example Pat set in the house with her own friends, partying into the early hours of the morning, and couldn't understand how she could then turn around and forbid her daughter from doing whatever she wanted. Sheri was too embarrassed to bring friends home, because her mother and stepfather were usually drinking, fighting, and doing drugs.

Sheri continued acting out and spent less and less time at home. Her reluctance to stay home was due to much more than simple teenage rebellion. She didn't like being around her stepfather. Pat refused to acknowledge what made life at home so unbearable for both her daughters.

"When I was in eighth grade at Reid Middle School, I wound up talking to a counselor about the situation in my household," said Nadine. "DSS wound up coming for a meeting, and my mom said I was lying about everything, and I knew I wasn't. So one day I flipped out and screamed and yelled at my stepdad, 'Get the fuck outta my house!' He wound up leaving, but then my mom took him back and threw my sister out."

Sheri confided in Jon, who by then had been her steady boyfriend for three years. She told him that a string of bitter fights had made life at home impossible for her and her mother. Jon had witnessed the friction and upheaval in Sheri's household. He couldn't stand seeing his girlfriend so miserable all the time, so he asked his parents to let Sheri come live with them.

Aware of Sheri's toxic home environment, Jon's parents agreed to allow her to move in to their home. Several days later, Sheri arrived at their front door, suitcase in hand. She stayed with Jon and his family for six months while Nadine remained with her mother and stepfather.

"The fighting in our household was out of control," said Pat. "I thought Sheri would run away. I didn't want to see her out on the streets. I didn't want to see anything happen to her. That's why I agreed for her to go to Jon's house and stay with him and his parents. They had a very nice home. They were very good people.

"I was kinda afraid that maybe Sheri would get pregnant," Pat confessed. "The thought crossed my mind several times. I took her to the doctor, and it was her decision to take the Pill or practice safe sex."

Sheri went on the Pill. She was Jon's first serious girlfriend, so it was a special time for them.

"When I was living with Jon's family, it was great," Sheri recalled. "They made me feel really comfortable. I loved it. I really did. Jon's parents made me feel like they cared more about me. They cared more about my feelings. They just made me feel good. They made me feel like they were my parents. My mom, on the other hand . . . I mean, I don't know . . . see, it was different. It was hectic at my mom's. At Jon's parents house it was nice and calm."

Sheri enjoyed being a guest in Jon's home, but as the months passed and the winter holiday season approached, she felt guilty about being estranged from her family. She knew that she couldn't impose on Jon's family forever. Not wanting to wear out their goodwill toward her, she moved back to her mother's house.

"It's just not the same around Christmas without your own family," she explained.

The small two-bedroom wood cabin with its thin walls and low ceilings was exactly how Sheri had left it six months before. Nadine was thrilled to have her elder sister back. She quickly cleared her stuff out of Sheri's half of their room. Upon settling in, Sheri did her best to make peace with her mother.

"When I moved back in, things got a lot better," Sheri said, " 'cause my mom was glad I was home, and I was glad. We sat down and talked, and I told her what was really bothering me. I said, 'Mom, I don't like the friends of yours that come in and out of the house. They come here at two o'clock in the morning. . . . I don't like that. That's not a home to me.' My mom said, 'I do want you back, and things will change.' "

A tired grin spread across Sheri's face as she shook her head, all too familiar with her mother's broken promises. Deep down, she knew it was just a matter of time before her mother and stepfather reverted back to their old ways.

One afternoon the following spring, Nadine, now thirteen, came home from school and found the house deserted. She knocked on her parents' bedroom door. There was no answer. She knocked again.

Silence. Pat and Steve had told the kids that they were planning a trip, but Nadine hadn't expected them to leave so soon. She wandered into the kitchen and saw that the sink was stacked with dirty dishes. A crumpled note lay on the counter. Pat had scrawled a quick message in black ink:

We'll see you sometime. . . . We're in Florida.
Love, Mom and Dad

"They took off on us," Nadine explained. "It was me and Sheri and our brother. While my parents were away, Jon wound up sleeping over a lot, and that's when Sheri got pregnant. When my parents came back from Florida, a lot happened. More drugs were coming in. It was real bad."

Sheri first realized she might be pregnant when she missed her period. She took a home-pregnancy test, which came out negative. Wanting to make sure that she wasn't pregnant, Sheri took another test, just in case the previous result had been false. The second pregnancy test came out negative. Sheri didn't consider the possibility that maybe she wasn't administering the home pregnancy test correctly. She was relieved about the negative results—until she missed another period.

Sheri woke up with morning sickness. She dragged herself out of bed, staggered to the bathroom, and vomited. Still worried that she might be pregnant and confused about why the home-pregnancy tests kept coming up negative, Sheri decided to confide in her mother. Pat took her to the see a doctor, who determined that Sheri was indeed nine weeks pregnant.

Sheri was shocked. She had been taking birth control pills regu-larly—well, almost. Going back and forth between her mother's house and Jon's house, she had misplaced a packet of pills and hadn't gotten around to replacing them for four days.

"And in those four days, I got pregnant," she explained.

Sheri was seventeen: the thought of having a baby at that point in her life was overwhelming and terrifying. She didn't feel ready. Tears streamed down her face as her skinny legs dangled over the edge of the doctor's examining table. Across the room, Pat was crying tears of joy.

"I was happy," Pat recalled. "We were gonna have a new life in the family, and I was gonna be a grandma! I can't believe I had such an excited feeling about that. I told Sheri that there was nothing we could do to change things, so we might as well accept the facts and be happy and make the best of what was to come."

In Pat's experience, destiny was something one surrendered to and survived, as opposed to something one tried to shape or control. Having been a teen mother herself, Pat knew the ropes. She didn't feel it necessary to discuss abortion or adoption, nor did she address any hopes, plans, or opportunities Sheri might have had other than motherhood.

"I'm Catholic," Pat declared, "and I don't believe in abortion. We've made it, struggling all our lives. What's one more mouth to feed? I knew we'd make it. We'd do whatever we had to, to make it."

Sheri's stepfather had a dramatically different reaction.

"When Sheri got pregnant, my husband was very upset," said Pat. "He wanted Sheri to finish high school. He thought her having a baby so young would interfere with her future. His opinions created a lot of problems in the home."

Pat and her husband continued to fight bitterly over Sheri's pregnancy. Pat remained stubborn and unyielding when it came to discussing options other than Sheri's giving birth and raising the baby herself. The violence in the house escalated.

"My dad took a picnic bench and put it through my ma's car window. That really shocked me," said Nadine, "so I went to school and I called DSS on myself this time. I said, 'Listen . . . I can't be at home.' "

The Department of Social Services sent a social worker to talk to Nadine's parents. Pat and her husband assured the worker that everything was just fine. Nadine's complaints were dismissed.

The next morning, while looking through a calendar, Pat told Nadine that she thought Sheri's baby would be born close to February 28, the day that would have been the birthday of Shannon Marie, the fetus Pat had lost, years earlier at the age of fifteen. Pat became intensely focused on how closely Sheri's predicament resembled her own experience at a younger age. The sense that Sheri was heading down a familiar, well-trodden path made Pat feel much more validated than she would have felt if Sheri had rejected her lifestyle. The line that separated Pat's identity from Sheri's was blurred so that one bled into the other. At a certain point, Pat's image of her daughter became a self-fulfilling prophecy.

"I kinda wasn't surprised when Sheri told me that she was pregnant," Pat finally admitted. "I kinda thought that that would happen, 'cause I was a teen mom.' "

Although Pat was pleased about the news that she was going to be a grandmother, Jon had mixed feelings about Sheri's pregnancy and his becoming a teen father. Still a junior in high school, Jon was an extremely laid-back, quiet fellow with modest ambitions. A slacker when it came to schoolwork, Jon's favorite pastime was shooting hoops and hanging out with his friends. Several nights a week he worked in the kitchen of a local restaurant. Enmeshed in his life as a regular teenager, Jon was afraid to even contemplate shouldering the responsibility of caring for a child and providing for a family. From the outset, Sheri was honest, open, and direct about her condition.

"I told Jon right away, as soon as I found out. I said, 'Jon, I'm pregnant.'

"He started crying. He hugged me. He said, 'Everything will be fine. I'll be there for you, Sheri. We're gonna raise this baby together.' "

Throughout Sheri's pregnancy, Jon remained at Pittsfield High School. His day-to-day life remained much the same as it had been before, but Sheri's life was turned upside down. When she transferred into the Teen Parent Program, many of her so-called friends from her old school stopped calling her up to see if she wanted to hang out. She got the impression that they had written her off, assuming that she wanted to be left alone to deal with the pregnancy in complete privacy.

Nothing could have been further from the truth. Sheri longed for the support of her friends, more so than ever, but most of them were self-absorbed and busy with their own lives. It seemed Sheri had gone from being popular to being forgotten overnight.

Soon after entering her second trimester, Sheri suffered from severe abdominal pain. She was rushed to the emergency room, where the doctors diagnosed her with acute appendicitis and announced that they had to remove her appendix immediately. Before she went under the knife, she was warned that there was a chance that she could lose the baby. Terrified, she went into surgery. The operation went smoothly and Sheri didn't have a miscarriage. However, her problems were far from over. While she was recovering from the surgery, her phone rang. It was Jon.

"Sheri, I think we should just be friends," he said. When Sheri asked why, he replied, "Because I don't want to be with you. I'll take care of my baby, I'll take on that responsibility—but I don't want to be with you."

Sheri, now five months pregnant, was totally crushed. But worse was to follow when she discovered that Jon was spreading rumors about her. He accused Sheri of cheating on him and convinced his parents that he wasn't the father of her unborn baby. When Sheri invited Jon and his family to the baby shower, they refused to go. They said they had no business there because the baby wasn't Jon's.

Sheri was sure both that the baby was Jon's and that he knew that abandoning his pregnant girlfriend for selfish reasons would make him look like a bad guy. Thus he had come up with a convenient lie that allowed him to turn the tables and blame Sheri for wrongdoing while at the same time exonerating himself. She was devastated that someone she had loved was capable of hurting her so deeply and so dishonestly with no regard for her reputation or dignity. Jon stopped taking her calls.

"When Jon broke up with me, it was like the world was on my

shoulders," Sheri recalled. "I had to deal with it. I cried all the time. I never heard from him. . . ."

Jon's lack of communication and his denial of their relationship was particularly heartbreaking to Sheri because it created a scenario that replicated her father's abandonment of her at the age of three, when he disappeared without warning, offering no explanation.

The closer Sheri got to giving birth, the more desperate she became for Jon to acknowledge paternity. When Jon refused to even discuss the issue, Sheri cried for hours at the thought of her baby growing up as she herself had, without a biological father. Sheri suffered severe depression but emerged from it determined to do everything in her power to reverse the circumstances.

"When I was eight months pregnant, I called Jon and said, 'We have to work things out. We have to be a family.' "

Jon was unresponsive. Sheri kept calling him, emphasizing how important it was for them to get back together, if only for the sake of the child. Jon would just listen without saying much. Then he would say he had to go. What little communication they had was always on his terms.

When Sheri went into labor, she called Jon, who finally broke down and cried. Realizing that his false accusations would soon be exposed, he raced over to the hospital, arriving just in time to see Sheri give birth to a baby girl. Sheri named her daughter Leeah. She was not surprised to see that the newborn looked exactly like Jon. A paternity test showed that Jon was definitely the baby's father.

At Jon's suggestion, they went for counseling, where Sheri made it clear that despite how badly Jon had treated her when she was pregnant, she was willing to bury her anger. She was prepared to make any sacrifice necessary to keep him involved in her daughter's life.

"As a child, I would wake up every day and know that my real dad was not there or around," she said. "I don't want Leeah to feel the same way that I felt. I want her to wake up and be able to be happy and know that both parents are there for her."

Although Sheri and Jon got back together after the baby was born, they decided not to live together. Jon continued living with his parents, and Sheri remained living with her mother, her stepfather, and Nadine. Jon visited Sheri and the baby regularly and tried to make amends. Sheri was thrilled. They began the slow process of trying to repair their fractured relationship.

"Jon apologizes every day for what he did to me when I was

pregnant and for how he hurt me," Sheri reported. "I mean, he looks at the baby every day, and he even apologizes to her. It's so funny, but he does. He's a great dad. He's the best dad. I couldn't ask for a better dad for Leeah."

After Leeah's birth, Sheri quickly returned to the Teen Parent Program, desperate for companionship, mentorship, advice, and some familiar faces. When Leeah was a few months old, Sheri confided in Jon about how cut off she was feeling from the world and began an effort to get back into the loop with some of her old friends. Together, Sheri and Jon made a pact to keep doing most of the things that teenagers without babies did. Sheri was ecstatic when Jon asked her to the prom. She rushed to the mall and purchased an elegant black gown.

On the afternoon of the prom, Sheri went to the hairdresser and had her hair styled in a chignon, studded with baby's breath held in place by bobby pins. After carefully applying her makeup, Sheri asked her mother for help zipping up the sexy tight-fitting dress, which flattered every inch of her slender frame. A wistful look crossed Pat's face as she watched her daughter posing in front of the mirror, studying her reflection and examining how the dress looked from every possible angle.

"I didn't get to go to my prom," she sighed. "I was home with the kids and married." Pat tried to smile but her eyes filled with tears, which she quickly brushed away, not wanting to ruin Sheri's big night.

Out on the back deck, Sheri paced back and forth nervously as she waited for Jon to come pick her up. She was unhappy with how her hair looked, but it was too late to do anything about it other than worry. Her mother and stepfather came out to check on her.

"Do I look okay?" Sheri asked them, trembling with insecurity.

"You look like a movie star," her stepfather reassured her. "Can you walk like one?"

"No."

"Can you act like one?" Pat asked.

"Probably not," Sheri murmured sheepishly.

"Well, have fun," Sheri's stepfather said, grinning from ear to ear. Sheri grimaced and squirmed as he took her in his arms and gave her an affectionate hug and kissed her good-bye as Pat watched, a few feet away, leaning against the railing of the back porch, smoking a cigarette.

Nadine came out to the deck to let Sheri know that Jon had arrived. The family walked around to the front of the house, and everyone watched as Jon presented Sheri with her corsage. Pat proceeded to take pictures of the beautifully dressed young couple and their daughter. Sheri handed Leeah to her mother and got into Jon's car. Nadine and Steve wished the couple well and went inside. Pat remained on the sidewalk, holding the baby, following the car with her eyes until it disappeared around the corner. Suddenly the street seemed quiet and very empty. Pat carried the baby back into the small wood cabin. The screen door slammed shut. Inside, Pat finally let out the tears she had struggled all afternoon to contain.

The prom was without question *the* social event of the year for the entire town of Pittsfield. Every year families, friends, and teachers lined up outside the entrance of the building where the prom was held, creating a human corridor that stretched across the entire length of the huge parking lot. Flashbulbs popped relentlessly as Sheri, Jon, and their peers paraded down the red carpet, the emphasis on looking the part of the perfect couple. The onlookers acted out the role of the paparazzi, making sure that these teenagers had their fifteen minutes of fame, or at least the illusion of it.

In imitation of the Hollywood celebrities they saw on TV and in magazines, the boys wore tuxedos and sunglasses and the girls wore gowns that were as tight, skimpy, and glamorous as possible. The Goth kids were the exception: white-faced, heavily made-up, garbed in black from head to toe, and carrying the occasional riding crop, this striking group looked ready to party with vampires.

For a few hours Sheri and Jon were able to lose themselves in the myth of carefree adolescent romance. On the dance floor, Sheri and Jon's physical contact appeared inhibited, stiff, and somewhat reserved. This was most apparent during the slow dances. Sheri later acknowledged this discomfort and attributed it to their need for time to slowly rebuild the trust in their relationship.

"We have a little bit of trust now, but it's not like it was in the beginning, when we had all the trust in the world. Our trust will come back, it just takes time, that's all."

As Sheri voiced these thoughts, she sounded more like a jaded forty-year-old than a romantic teenager. In fact, Sheri was somewhere in between these two extremes: less optimistic than she should have been at her young age but unusually and precociously pragmatic and realistic about the need for compromise, particularly when it came to maintaining her relationship with Jon. Sheri understood the stark difference between her dreams and the reality of having to settle for less in order to keep her baby's father involved in her life.

As Sheri and Jon left the prom early, music spilled into the night. Couples stood outside, leaning against the railing of the ramp, smoking, making out, and lingering in the cool breeze before returning to the crush of the dance floor. Drivers sat in stretch limos talking among themselves in the parking lot. As Sheri and Jon walked toward Jon's car, one of their friends yelled, "Sheri, Jon, hey! Where are you guys going? To a motel?"

Sheri shook her head and kept walking.

A few weeks after the prom, Sheri and Jon brought Leeah to their high school graduation ceremony. Leeah stood out in Sheri's arms, her pink hat and matching pink outfit, a stark contrast to the purple and white gowns worn by graduating seniors. Prior to the ceremony, many of Sheri's old friends gathered around the couple to admire the baby for the first time. One girl looked at Leeah and then at Jon, and then back at Leeah, comparing the baby's features with those of her father.

"Oh my God!" she squealed. "She looks *just* like him!"

Sheri nodded and exchanged a knowing look with Jon. Music began to play. The seniors lined up in single file. Sheri followed her fellow students into the auditorium and took her seat next to Jon. When her name was called, she marched onto the stage and received her diploma and a white rose from the mayor of Pittsfield. As Sheri returned to her seat, she looked around the theater filled with hundreds of students and their families. Her eyes were shining.

"I'm so proud I did it," Sheri said. "Without the Teen Parent Program, I never would have gotten this far."

"We never had a Parent Teen Program," retorted Pat. "So there was no going back to school for me."

Right after graduation, Pat made it very clear that she no longer wanted Sheri and the baby living under her roof.

"There was a lot . . . a lot of stress in the family," Pat explained. "I was working a tremendous amount of hours, basically taking care of the whole household, and that gave me awful anxiety. I couldn't eat. I lost an awful lot of weight and became very ill through the whole ordeal. Especially when it was prom time. I was overwhelmed. I think I was overwhelmed with the whole situation.

"It's not that I didn't want Leeah in my house, or that I didn't love Leeah, or that I wasn't happy about her being born . . . it was just, with the stress and everything—I got ill—and the fighting between my husband and myself was just ridiculous. I felt it would be better if Sheri got her own place with Leeah so that she could be more relaxed, so that she wouldn't have to hear us fighting all the time. I felt it wasn't healthy for a baby to be around so much anxiety."

After months of witnessing the decline of her mother's mental and physical health, as well as the constant drug-related traffic within the house, Sheri was eager to find her own apartment—a small, quiet place where she and Leeah could live in peace. She found a two-bedroom duplex apartment in the same low-income housing project on April Lane where Amy and Bernard and her best friend, Shayla, lived. When Sheri packed her bags and said good-bye to her family, fifteen-year-old Nadine had to face Pat and her stepfather alone. Before long, she was back in foster care.

"The foster home I was sent to was really bad," she said. "I couldn't use the phone. I couldn't watch TV. I felt like I was behind bars all day, every day. I was there for about a month. Then I went back home, and it was like a repeat of my life, you know what I mean? Going in and out, and back and forth for the same reasons— but they still let me go back home, which is what I don't understand."

By then, Nadine knew the drill as well as she knew the alphabet. When things went terribly wrong at home, she could complain to the counselor at school, who would promptly issue a report to the Department of Social Services, causing social workers to confront her mother, who would inevitably claim her daughter was lying, at which point either they would dismiss the case and leave Nadine to her own devices or they would attempt to temporarily remove her from the home and place her in a foster home where she didn't feel comfortable. Nobody took the time to get to know her well enough to make an appropriate foster care placement. She was passed from counseling to DSS to foster care like a baton changing hands in a relay race. There was no continuity or permanent support. Sometimes Nadine would run away and stay with a friend or neighbor, but she never got very far; inevitably, the cycle would end up where it started—at Pat's house. Shortly before her sixteenth birthday, Nadine dropped out of school—this time for good.

"School just wasn't working out for me," said Nadine. "I wasn't getting up. I wasn't going to bed at the right hours. It just got real tough."

Nadine would visit Sheri at her apartment on April Lane. Sheri was grateful to see her sister's familiar face, but as she listened to Nadine's tale of woe, she felt immensely relieved to be out of her mother's house once and for all. Nevertheless, living all alone with the baby without any help whatsoever was proving to be an intensely lonely, isolating experience. The April Lane housing project was located several miles away from town and the nearest shopping mall, so there was really no place for Sheri to go without a car, other than the swing set in the communal yard behind her apartment and the mailbox in the parking lot.

"I didn't have no car or no day care or no baby-sitter," Sheri explained. "I wanted to go back to work, but I really couldn't."

For the first year of Leeah's life, Sheri relied on the monthly $485 welfare check to help pay the rent. Rent alone was $418 per month. The rest of the money went toward food, clothing, diapers, toys, and other supplies for the baby.

Jon received a promotion and became a cook at the restaurant where he had worked steadily for several years. He frequently visited Sheri and Leeah but continued living at his mother's house. Sheri accepted this arrangement with Jon but found it difficult to be alone in a room for hours on end with no one to talk to but her baby. Frustrated, bored, and craving human companionship, Sheri sank into a state of gloomy depression. She registered for an educational program in accounting but dropped out after just two weeks because she wasn't interested in the subject.

When winter came with its short days and slivers of sunlight collapsing into darkness undercut by freezing cold, Sheri spent day after day inside her apartment with the baby. She began to go stir-crazy. At times when Leeah would cry, it was a struggle for Sheri to stay calm, but she soon realized that if she lost her temper or burst into tears herself, it only made Leeah more upset.

Sheri became anxious as her "free" time on welfare started to run out. She knew she had to find a job or enroll in school or a vocational training program but she didn't want to rely on the welfare-to-work transportation service. Sheri wanted to be able to come and go whenever she pleased and she wanted privacy and flexibility in case there was an emergency with her daughter, but she simply couldn't afford to buy a car.

When Sheri's elder brother received a settlement from an insurance claim he had made three years earlier after being injured in a car accident, the money was enough to buy three used cars: one for himself, one for Pat, and one for Sheri. Having a car changed Sheri's life. With the help of her aunt, she immediately got a job in housekeeping at a small bed-and-breakfast, a twenty-minute drive from her April Lane apartment.

As soon as Sheri started working during the day, Jon began to share the responsibility of taking care of Leeah. Because he worked the night shift at the restaurant, he was free during the day while Sheri was at work. Their schedules complemented each other, and as a result, both parents were able to spend large chunks of time with their daughter. This new arrangement brought Sheri and Jon closer. Jon started staying at Sheri's place several nights a week. They began talking about living together full-time.

Pat insisted that her daughter's life was a dream compared with what she had to go through. "When I was on welfare, it was harder for me," she said, raising her eyebrows so that the lines in her forehead became more pronounced. "I had three kids. I had no transportation. I had no education at all. It was very difficult for me to find day care or employment to support three children. We were living in foundations and places nowhere near as nice as where Sheri lives. So, the difference between me and Sheri is . . . I don't know . . . she's just so far advanced from where I was at her age."

Though Sheri's life may have been somewhat easier than her mother's, it was by no means easy.

"Leeah wakes me and Jon up between eight and nine in the morning," Sheri said, describing a typical day. "We go downstairs and change her diaper. I give her a glass of milk and some vitamins, and then I make her breakfast. While Leeah's eating her breakfast, she watches her cartoons and I clean the house and do the dishes. Then me and Leeah go upstairs and wake Jon up so I can get ready for work. While I'm in the shower, Jon watches Leeah. Then I go to work at the bed-and-breakfast in Lee where I work as a housekeeper.

"I get to work at about ten. I make sure all the laundry is done. I make sure the sheets and towels are folded up and put away. There are ten rooms. Like room one maybe gets a 'turnover.' That means the guests are checking out, so we have to do the whole room— change the bed, clean the bathroom, dust, and just make sure that it looks really nice. Then sometimes we have a 'change,' which means to just change the bed and put fresh towels in, 'cause the guests are staying another night. Or we have a 'make.' That means that we don't change the bed. We just give the guests fresh towels and make sure the room's nice and neat when they come back. It's an all right job. I make about ten dollars an hour. It's good pay. I don't really mind doing that kind of work right now because my pay is pretty good, but I know I don't want to do it forever.

"Jon pays thirty dollars for child support a week, but I only see fifty dollars a month because I'm on welfare, so they take the other half. My rent right now is four hundred and thirty-five dollars a month. I pay all my own utilities. It gets high, so I need to work every day.

"While I'm at work, Jon watches Leeah and takes her outside. Before lunch Leeah takes a nap for about an hour. When Leeah wakes up from her nap, Jon feeds her lunch. After lunch, Jon plays with Leeah until I get home. When I get home from work at two o'clock, Jon goes to work at the restaurant. Me and Leeah drop him off. Then we visit my mom, go for a ride, or get an ice cream.

"After that I come home, and most of the time Shayla comes over with her son, Jaiden, and we let the two kids play together. At five o'clock I make dinner for me and Leeah. While I'm making dinner, Leeah is running around the house. We sit down and eat. Me and Leeah always eat dinner together.

"After dinner, Leeah takes a bath. While she is in the bath, I sit in the bathroom with her until she's done. After her bath we come back downstairs and I clean up the after-dinner mess. After that me and Leeah sit down and watch TV and just relax. By that time she's tired and I'm beat.

"We usually watch movies on Lifetime. I love Lifetime. Leeah goes to bed between eight-thirty and nine. Then I come back downstairs and make myself a cup of tea and I just watch TV. After Leeah's asleep, I have nothing else to do. I watch the nine o'clock movie and go to bed at eleven, when the movie ends. Jon gets home around midnight."

Sheri's routine remained constant throughout the second year of Leeah's life. During this period, the biggest change in her life involved

Pat, who finally separated from her husband. Living on her own, Pat gained forty pounds and cut down on her chain-smoking.

"I'm much more relaxed now," Pat said. "Right now I'm doing an introduction to basic computers, learning the keyboard. I'm on the Internet, which is fun. I like the computer. It's interesting. I want an office job. I know it's gonna take me a little time, but I know I'll do it. I'll do it."

"My mom is doing really good for herself," remarked Sheri, who then admitted, "I never thought I would see this day. It makes me so happy to see my mom like this. I'm glad Leeah gets to see her like this, too."

In sharp contrast to Pat's round cheeks and new curves, Sheri's face was gaunt. Her arms and legs were like toothpicks and when she looked in the mirror, her hungry eyes and protruding bones reminded her of how her mother used to look. The resemblance wasn't just physical—the roles of mother and daughter had effectively been reversed.

While Sheri embraced her identity as a mother and assumed the adult responsibilities that such a role entailed, Pat attempted to resume her life where she had left off at age seventeen, when she first got pregnant. Pat saw an office job as a step up from the more menial labor she had done in the past. Initially, she was excited to have the chance to obtain the skills she needed to be considered for this type of work.

Nearing forty, Pat had to start at the bottom rung. Her skill level, even after weeks of computer training, was lower than that of many teenagers straight out of high school. Pat soon realized that in the job market, even for entry-level positions, she would have to compete against some kids and young adults who had grown up in the Internet age, for whom computers were second nature. Despite these harsh realities, Pat swallowed her pride and continued her classes. After years of what she perceived to be self-sacrifice, she was content finally to be able to do something for herself.

Sheri, on the other hand, was leading a completely selfless existence. Her life was structured around Jon and her daughter, yet she dared dream of a future that was very different from her mother's life. In Sheri's fantasy, enduring love, strong family values, and financial stability were central themes.

"What would make me happiest is me and Jon getting married, hopefully soon," Sheri said. "I've asked him if he wants to get married

and he said yes, but we know we can't get married right now. We both want a big wedding, we want a lot of people there, and we can't afford it. We figure if we save up, in about four years we can have a nice big wedding.

"I would love to grow old with Jon. I would love to buy a new car, buy a house, and be able to give Leeah whatever she needs and more. Within a couple of years, I would love to have another baby, when we can afford it, when we don't need welfare.

"Jon told me he wants to be with me forever. I feel the same way about him. He and Leeah are my life."

Pat had a less romantic outlook when it came to predicting what lay ahead for Sheri. "I think that Sheri's future is gonna be going back to cosmetology and being a hairdresser," she said. "I think that's really what her dream is. As a matter of fact, we talked about it the other day. She gave me a haircut. She definitely wants to get back in the profession. I can see Sheri getting her cosmetology license and staying in town."

Sheri agreed that she would probably remain in Pittsfield, but she definitely did not see herself becoming a hairdresser. Her close friend, Shayla, had completed the full-year cosmetology course required for entry-level certification as a hairdresser, but as Sheri pointed out, Shayla had already been fired from Hair Express and wasn't able to find another opening in a hair salon. A few months later, when Shayla's new job at a chain store didn't work out, she asked Sheri for help getting a housekeeping job. For a while, the two friends cleaned rooms together at the same bed-and-breakfast. Judging from Shayla's experience, Sheri didn't see the point in wasting a year of hard work on a cosmetology course if when all was said and done, she was likely to end up right back where she started, cleaning rooms.

Sheri's goal was to get off welfare. She was prepared to do what she had to in order to get by. She saw her job not as a way of finding fulfillment, satisfaction, and happiness, but as a necessary step she had to take in order to provide the essentials for herself and her daughter. Her first priority was to make sure that Leeah was given the opportunities that she had missed out on. Sheri was thrilled when Jon's father gave Leeah an old computer. Eager to know enough to at least teach Leeah something about computers, and hopefully to get a better job, Sheri enrolled in a computer course at the local Mildred Elly Business School. She learned how to enter data using the program Excel.

In order to make time for school, Sheri had to adjust her hours at the bed-and-breakfast, where she had worked steadily for two years. Without warning, her boss replaced her with "a girl who was more available." Sheri was disappointed, but she couldn't afford to be picky. She immediately found a new job cleaning rooms at a sprawling hotel in Lee, which was more than four times the size of where she used to work. Her new position required her to clean rooms for forty hours each week. Working on weekends and holidays was mandatory. Sheri was forced to withdraw from her computer class mid-session.

"I know I should be in school," she explained, "but I'm not, because I need to work."

At this hotel, Sheri was one of many employees. She felt anonymous, interchangeable, and unappreciated. She had one thirty-minute lunch break in the middle of her eight-hour workday. The housekeeping staff wasn't invited to eat food prepared in the hotel kitchen, and there was no staff dining room where prepared meals were available. Half an hour was barely enough time for Sheri to drive into town, get something to eat, and drive back, so usually she brought food from home, a sandwich wrapped in tinfoil or a container of cold ravioli.

Sheri saved more than a thousand dollars. The more money she made, the closer she came to being able to realize her dreams for herself, Jon, and Leeah. Soon after Leeah's third birthday, Sheri's welfare counselor told her that she made too much money to continue on welfare. Sheri regarded her independence from the system as a marker of success and a rite of passage. She considered getting off welfare to be her biggest achievement in her adult life.

Armed with new confidence and strengthened self-esteem, Sheri set out to find a job that she would enjoy more than being a house-keeper. She no longer wanted to work weekends and holidays, be-cause day cares were closed then and it was much more difficult and expensive to find baby-sitters who were available. Sheri longed for a regular nine-to-five job in a stimulating environment where she would have a chance to meet some new, interesting people.

In response to an ad in the newspaper, Sheri dropped off her résumé at a local bank. When she called a week later to schedule an interview, her call was not returned. She phoned the bank several times to inquire about the status of her job application but never received any response.

Cleaning rooms forty hours a week was physically exhausting, and Sheri was dangerously thin. She thought about trying to get a job as a waitress at the end of the summer when all the college kids who worked in the fancier restaurants went back to school. When September approached, Sheri changed her mind, deciding that she didn't want to commute to the neighboring towns where those upscale restaurants were located. She preferred to be closer to her daughter and wanted to work weekdays, as opposed to nights and weekends.

Sheri asked for a job at Leeah's day care. During her interview with the woman who ran the center, she admitted that she didn't have any formal credentials but stressed that she had plenty of experience raising her own daughter. To her surprise, Sheri was given a job taking care of infants in the day care's nursery. She was delighted. The pay was a bit less than it had been at her previous job, but she got benefits and the hours were longer and more consistent.

Sheri was thrilled to be working in the same building where her daughter spent her days, right down the hall in the toddlers' room. At her previous jobs, Sheri had always been preoccupied and concerned about whether or not Leeah was safe and being cared for properly. It was extremely comforting to be able to check up on Leeah anytime she wanted.

This job at Leeah's day care improved Sheri's life dramatically. The hours were decent, her coworkers respected her and treated her like a human being, she had weekends and holidays off, and she could see her daughter as often as she liked.

"I finally have a life," said Sheri, her voice brimming with pride.

Though Sheri maintained her momentum, her mother's energy waned. Her positive attitude toward finding a new job that "had something to do with computers" was short-lived. Frustrated with her lack of progress and no longer wanting to put in the effort, Pat quit school and remained unemployed. She took up with a new boyfriend and succumbed to her old addictions.

Nadine was sixteen and still living at home after another failed foster care placement. Her stepfather was finally out of the picture, but now she had to contend with her mother's new boyfriend, who had a criminal record and a history of drug abuse.

"My mom was in the other room, drunk, passed out on the floor," Nadine recalled. "I was in my room sleeping, and her boyfriend came into my room and wound up leaving me a hickey. When I felt him, I ran into my mom's room and I woke her up."

"You better get out of my house," Pat drawled in a daze.

Nadine stared at her mother, incredulous.

"Get out now!" hollered Pat. "Go find your own boyfriend!"

"I wound up having to leave there at four o'clock in the morning. I went to a neighbor's house up the street and slept there. The next day my mom wound up blaming it on me. Telling me I just wanted him, and that ain't even true. I don't need to go out with her boyfriends. I can find my own."

Nadine found a tough white guy named Brad.

"Brad was twenty-five when I met him. I was sixteen, just turning seventeen. We met down by Pontoosuc Lake. We started hanging out. He had his own apartment, so I started staying with him. He seemed really nice. I was going through a lot with my mom, and he helped me, he was really there for me. I could talk to him about anything, and he'd just sit down and listen to me. I felt like he was the only person I had at that time."

Brad had already fathered a son with another teenage girl. He made quick cash dealing drugs, and when he wasn't dealing, he was using. His vicious rottweiler dog accompanied him wherever he went. On command, the dog was trained to inflict maximum damage on his victims. Most people knew better than to mess with Brad.

"About five months into our relationship, Brad just snapped," Nadine recalled. "He beat me every day. I got so scared that sometimes I wouldn't even get out of bed. I was too scared to leave.

"Brad's rottweiler got put to sleep for tearing skin off legs of cops in Lenox, but then he got another mean dog. One day when I ran out the front door, Brad pointed to me and said, 'Get her!' The dog went wild. I got away, but he ate the curtains.

"I was always puking. I was always sick. I was always stressing. I didn't know if I was gonna live."

Following one of Brad's beatings, a friend of Nadine's called the cops. They came and picked up Nadine and dropped her off at her mother's house. Nadine limped in to her mom's living room, wearing sunglasses and a baggy sweatshirt. Sheri and Leeah had stopped by for a visit. They were outside on the back porch with Pat. Nadine could hear them talking, but depressed and exhausted, she didn't feel like joining them. Without telling anybody that she was home, Nadine slumped over on a faded beige sofa, unable to think of anything outside of her own pain. As she recalled, "Leeah came in and said, 'Take those sunglasses off, Aunt Nadine.' I said no, and she took them off me and I had two black eyes. She started crying—she didn't know what it was. She was shocked. I told her it was makeup. She kept crying and she said, 'Aunt Nadine, please, go wash your face, 'cause it's everywhere.'

"I had bruises all over my arms. That's why I had a sweatshirt on. My mom came in and said, 'Let me see, because I know you have more bruises than that.' I was bruised from my eyes to my legs. That's when my mom and sister found out what Brad was doing to me."

A week later, Nadine returned to Brad and suffered more abuse. He continued to violently assault her and eventually he was arrested and sent to jail. By the time Brad went behind bars, Nadine knew that she was pregnant with his baby. She tried to figure out exactly when the baby had been conceived.

"I was on the Pill and I missed three days and that's how I wound up getting pregnant. Brad flushed my pills down the toilet, but I thought I misplaced them. But when we broke up, he wound up telling me, 'I flushed your pills. . . . I cut the condom, and I hope you're pregnant.' I guess he thought if he got me pregnant, I'd stay," she murmured.

The doctor asked Nadine if she would consider having an abortion, in light of the horrible circumstances and the violent beatings she had endured during the first month of pregnancy. Nadine's mind filled with thoughts of her mother and her unborn sister. Instead of distancing herself and viewing her mother in a critical light, Nadine identified with her and adopted her views on abortion.

She looked the doctor in the eye and said, "I'm having the baby."

Soon after Brad's arrest, Colleen's ex-boyfriend, Ryan, was partying with Pat and her friends. He went into the kitchen for a drink and saw a photograph of Nadine adorning a magnet stuck to Pat's refrigerator.

"Your daughter is so pretty," he said. "When can I meet her?"

Pat explained that Nadine had been in a violent relationship for months and had suffered terrible abuse. Ryan decided to wait at Pat's house until Nadine came home. He told Pat that he already had a disabled son with Colleen, a teen mother who had attended the Teen Parent Program with Sheri. He didn't tell Pat that his relationship with Colleen had collapsed when she could no longer tolerate his heroin binges and violent abuse. After a stint in jail and a sojourn in Florida to avoid a warrant for his arrest, Ryan was back in Pittsfield, eager to find a new girlfriend who would meet his needs. He stayed in Pat's living room for several days, until Nadine, who had been staying at a friend's house, finally showed up.

Nadine and Ryan formed an intense, obsessive, codependent relationship. Most people mistakenly assumed that the baby Nadine was carrying was Ryan's. As Nadine's pregnancy progressed, she witnessed her mother's deterioration.

"My mom was abusing her psych meds and drinking while she was on them, so she wound up going into seizures. She'd start flopping everywhere and foaming. . . . Her tongue was going back in her throat. It got to the point where we couldn't stop it and had to call an ambulance."

Nadine went into early labor during her first trimester, and again when she was six months pregnant. Both times she was rushed to the hospital, where they gave her medication to stop the contractions. Nadine kept quiet about her traumatic home situation and did not tell her doctor about the crippling depression that was slowing down her thinking and enhancing her fear that her life was hopeless.

Nadine spent most of her last trimester hanging out with Ryan, who was still heavily involved with drugs. She worried constantly about the fact that soon after her baby was born, Brad would be out of jail. Extremely troubled and upset throughout her pregnancy, Nadine made a big mistake. Toward the end of her pregnancy, she did cocaine. The stimulant immediately put her into labor.

"At the hospital I hemorrhaged in labor and they thought something was weird because I hemorrhaged really bad. Real bad. Blood clots the size of watermelons were coming outta me. They almost had to put more blood into me. And my water was a funny color. It was a brownish green because the baby pooped inside me because the drugs got him worked up. They knew something was weird about that."

Nadine gave birth and named her son Dylan. The hospital immediately contacted the Department of Social Services. As the umbilical cord was cut, Nadine felt dread rather than relief. She feared that she wouldn't be allowed to keep her baby.

Sheri was in the delivery room when her nephew was born. She watched helplessly in horror as the doctors discovered drugs in his system. Her sister was forbidden to leave the hospital. The doctors kept a close watch over the baby to make sure that he had adequate medical support as he went through the difficult symptoms associated with cocaine withdrawal. Nadine was told that her baby would have to be placed in foster care until she could prove to DSS that she was fit to be a mother.

"That's when I flipped out," recalled Nadine. "I threw things. I broke the phone. I told them my baby wasn't going home with them. They told me when I find a good environment for my son—then I'll get him back. The cocaine did show up in his system, so I was screwed."

The Department of Social Services took custody of the baby when he was one day old. It was devastating for the entire family. Sheri considered trying to get permission to have the baby and her sister live with her but realized that with work and her own daughter, it would just be too much for her. Sheri and Nadine were allowed to visit Dylan. They were impressed by how big and grand the baby's foster home was compared with where they lived, and were relieved that the baby was being well looked after.

"I became good friends with my son's foster parent," Nadine said. "Really good friends. She's the one who got me through all of this. If it wasn't for her, I don't know what I would've done. When we went to court, I told the judge the truth—I didn't lie. I told them that I hated my lifestyle . . . hated it. I said that I didn't want my son having the life or the environment that we had when we were younger. I told the judge how I never wanted my life like that, and how I always, always wanted it to change."

Nadine's pleas for a second chance were ultimately successful. After nearly two months, it was decided that Nadine would be allowed to have her son back, but only if she moved to Redfield House, a high-security subsidized housing project for single mothers and their children. This residence had its own nursery, day care, and playground on site, as well as a trained professional staff on hand to advise the young women on issues related to health care, safety, welfare, and childrearing issues. Many residents were coregistered at the Teen

Parent Program, which was located within walking distance from Redfield House. In order to get her son back, Nadine had to agree to frequent randomly administered drug tests.

Every area of Nadine's life was tightly supervised by the Department of Social Services. She had to agree to begin treatment with a psychiatrist, who put her on Zoloft for her depression. She had to attend counseling regularly. Social workers and investigators routinely visited the apartment to check up on her and the baby. There was tight security at the front door of Redfield House. The guard asked Nadine for a photograph of Brad. He was out of jail, and just in case he happened to show up, the guard wanted to know what he looked like so that he could be prepared. All Nadine's visitors had to be approved by the social worker in charge of her case and were closely monitored.

"My mom can see my son," said Nadine, "but it has to be visitation rights with DSS at the Y. She has to get drug-screened and she told me she don't think she's gonna be able to see him because she knows she can't pass 'em. That hurts me—knowing that she ain't there for me when I need her because the drugs are more important."

Nadine paused. Her baby was crying. She rocked him gently and tried to soothe him.

"I've been involved with DSS since I was born," she said. "At first I was really mad that I had to work with them when I had my son, but now it's not bad with them being in my life. They help you a lot. They're really getting me on the right road I need to be on with my son."

After all Nadine's terrible experiences as a child with counselors who couldn't seem to get her out of the room fast enough, she was understandably wary about trusting a new counselor. Like Sheri, Nadine had learned from experience that remaining silent was much safer than voicing the truth. She struggled to come to terms with her fears about talking about her problems.

"Last time I got involved with counseling, I wound up getting taken away from my ma," she said. "So now I know what to say and what not to say. But my son—I don't want him to get taken away if I say the wrong thing."

Nadine was assigned to a counselor who seemed legitimately concerned and dedicated to helping her. As Nadine realized that this counselor might actually stick around for a while instead of passing her on to someone else, she began to look forward to her weekly sessions.

"My counselor—she just sits there and I tell her everything so I don't blow up. I tell her what bothers me . . . just stupid shit like that. She's, like, in her late thirties or early forties. She just talks to me and tries to help me through my problems.

"They want me to take Zoloft and keep going on it until I prove better with my depression, because I cry a lot and I stress out a lot. They referred me to go see a—I can't say it . . ." Nadine fumbled with the syllables. "A psy-chi-a-trist. Because of my past, when I was younger and the fact that I did try cocaine, they're gonna work with me to get off it and make sure I don't go back."

As Pat deteriorated even further, Sheri and Nadine's estranged biological father, Greg, reappeared in Pittsfield and did what he could to help both girls, in an effort to make up for all the lost years.

"Since I had my son and he got taken away from me, my real

dad, Greg, he's been really helping me out a lot, because I'm not getting any income. Nothing," said Nadine. "So my dad's been supplying me with baby diapers and wipes. He brings me to all my appointments when it's cold and I can't walk. He's there. He's the only one I really talk to now besides my sister."

It was agonizing for Sheri and Nadine to see their mother self-destructing. At times, Sheri cut off all but the most basic, essential communication. The relationship became too emotionally taxing, and Sheri needed to stay strong for her own daughter. She had chosen a drug-free life for herself and didn't want Leeah exposed to her grandmother's world. Like Sheri, Nadine also felt that in order to protect herself and her son, it was necessary to disengage emotionally from the strong ties that bound her to her mother.

"I can't deal with my mom no more," said Nadine. "I just can't watch it. I can't do it no more. I don't think she's gonna make it. Nope. My mom is very, very sick. The doctors say that she's doing really bad. She has meningitis and she has pneumonia. Every other day she's puking blood. Sometimes she can't even get out of bed. And she's only forty-five years old. She's not even old. Her bones ache. They're killing her. She can't walk. She has very bad arthritis. Her body is just shutting down.

"I've been trying to help her for eighteen years now, and I know when she goes, I'm gonna . . . I'm gonna flip, really. But there's nothing I can do now. I have a baby of my own now. I just worry about him. My mom's forty-something years old. She should know better. I don't want her to go, but everybody goes sooner or later, and I think her time is almost here. Ain't nothing I can do about that."

Under all the stress of dealing with her mother and her sister's troubles, Sheri continued losing weight at an alarming rate. Her head began to look too big for her frail body. Referring to Sheri's arm, which was blocking the TV screen, Leeah, now three and a half and very talkative, leaned over and said, "Mommy, can you move your bone?"

Sheri wanted to gain weight. She drank special milkshakes that were supposed to help people put on weight, but worried about the cost of these drinks—six bucks for a pack of six. Eventually she stopped buying them. Sheri grew smaller and smaller.

The one part of her life that Sheri was content with was her relationship with Jon. She was extremely grateful that he was there for her and Leeah. He was her rock of stability, and besides her daughter, he was the one person who made her feel valued and appreciated. Sheri was saving up money and working hard to build a solid future with Jon. Her intact family was the center of all her hopes and dreams. She was excited about the possibility of getting married in the very near future.

One night while Sheri was home alone with Leeah, her phone rang. It was Jon on the line, calling from the restaurant where he worked.

He told Sheri he wasn't coming home. Ever.

"I'm not happy," he said.

The fact that Jon was unhappy was news to Sheri. When Jon

came by to pack up his things, he refused to discuss his abrupt decision to break off their seven-year relationship.

"I would respect Jon more if he would've came to me and sat down and said, 'Listen, Sheri, these are the things bothering me; if they don't change, I'm gonna have to leave.' I'd respect him more for talking it through instead of just getting up and walking out. Which is exactly what he did. It's funny, because the week before Jon left, he wanted to have another baby with me. We were even trying. And then a week later he leaves. When I call him and ask him to explain why he wasn't happy, he says, 'I don't want to talk about this right now.'

"See, I was Jon's first girlfriend and I think he wants to go see what's out there. I wish he would just tell me, but he can't. And the restaurant business does not help. He sees all these young people with no kids, no responsibility, going out every night, doing what they want, not answering to anybody, and I think that's what he wants right now.

"I did ask him, I said, 'Don't you want to come home to your family?'

"He said, 'I would love to come home to my family, but I can't.'

"That's all he says. . . . He don't explain why he can't. . . . So I've got to figure it out for myself. I just wish he would sit down and talk to me. You know . . . And just say . . . you know, Sheri, this is what I want, this is what I don't want. If he would just let me know. . . .

"I think Jon just wants me to hang on, so that if he does plan on coming back, I'll be there. I don't even want to go out and find another boyfriend and date—at least not right now. I still hope he's coming back. I mean, if it comes down to it and months down the road I definitely know he's not coming back, I'll go out—but not right now. Right now it's just me and Leeah. Hopefully Jon will come back soon because I'm not gonna sit around and wait forever. I'm not gonna be alone forever.

"If Jon were to come back right now, I wouldn't take him back right away. He'd have to go to counseling with me. He'd have to sit down and talk to me. He'd have to prove to me that he wants to be with me and Leeah.

"Right now I don't receive any child support. Jon said that his employers are taking it out of his checks, but I still have not received child-support checks. I don't know if he's lying, or what. I tried to call the child-support unit, but I can't get through to them. They have an 800 number, but you can't talk to a representative unless you punch in your PIN number and I don't have one. I guess I'll have to go to the courthouse.

"Since Jon moved out, he don't see Leeah very often, not nearly as much as I'd like him to see her. They had a really close relationship, but now it just seems like they're separating quick. I want their relationship to be close and I know Leeah does, too, but I think Jon's just pulling away from a lot of things and not thinking.

"Leeah's hurt that Jon just got up and left. You know, how do you explain to a three-year-old that Daddy's not gonna be here no more? It's hard. A couple of nights ago I walked out of the room and she called me back in and said, 'Mommy, you're not gonna leave, right?'

"I just lost it. My daughter shouldn't have to feel like that."

Nadine tried her best to be supportive of her elder sister. She wanted Sheri to get Jon out of her system so that she could move on with her life, but Sheri just couldn't let go. She started stalking Jon, and when she found him and his new girlfriend making out in a parking lot, she took her umbrella and scratched up their car, then dragged the girl out of the car by her hair and started punching her.

"Sheri's just so hurt, she don't know how to react to it," said Nadine. "This girl knew Jon had a family. The girl knew that he had a kid. She knew that they were together for seven years 'cause Sheri used to go to school with her. But I think that Sheri was Jon's first. And I think Jon just wants to experiment. He's still young. She's still young. Yes, they might have a kid together, but there's more men out there—she don't need to be chasing this one down."

Sheri finally convinced Jon to come to her apartment and talk things over. Once Jon was there, Sheri told him over and over again how much she and Leeah loved him and needed him. Reluctantly he agreed to move back in with Sheri and said he was willing to give their relationship another try. Sheri forced him to call his girlfriend and break up with her. Wanting to make sure that there were no mis-understandings, Sheri listened in on the phone as Jon told his girl-friend that their relationship was over and made it clear that he had decided to go back to his family.

Jon played house with Sheri. He read to Leeah, fed her, gave her baths, tucked her into bed at night, and sat with her until she fell asleep. For three straight days Sheri's apartment was a portrait of domestic bliss. Then Jon left and moved into his new girlfriend's apartment.

"Sheri's crushed," said Nadine. "She cries to me every night. Leeah's always talking about her dad to her mom, saying 'When's he coming home? Why ain't he home? I miss him!' She keeps thinking her daddy's coming home to pick her up, but he ain't."

Sheri broke down, immobilized by acute depression. She missed a week of work and kept Leeah at home with her. She lost her job at the day-care center, the one job she had loved so much.

Nadine wasn't able to stick to the program at Redfield House. She took the baby off the premises after hours and continued seeing her boyfriend, Ryan, who was eventually sent back to jail. DSS removed Dylan from Nadine's custody and put him into another foster home. This time around, his foster mother was interested in possibly adopting him. Nadine checked herself into rehab, determined to try again to reclaim custody of her son.

"I'm only eighteen and it's just been . . . it's just been too much," she said. "Drugs, alcohol, abuse; it's just been goin' down generation to generation. I wish I had been in a foster home my whole life." Nadine paused, full of emotion. A moment later she swore, "I'm gonna get my son back. I've got to get him back."

While Nadine was in rehab, Sheri got back on her feet. She got a job at Rent-A-Wreck. Sheri was bored stiff at this job. She had to sit in a tiny office all day. Business was slow. She was lucky if she leased three used cars in a day. After several weeks she quit.

Sheri found a new job at a shop at the mall. Finally she gave up on Jon and began dating one of his relatives, Ian, who had briefly lived with her best friend, Shayla. Times were tough, but Sheri remained steadfast in her commitment to steer clear of drugs.

"Believe it or not, I've never touched drugs," she said. "I don't see my life going that way, because I don't want my daughter to see the things I've seen or to live the life I've lived."

chapter seven

JESSICA

"I had so much going for me before I got pregnant. I was doing everything. I was doing great. I was getting really good grades. I was someone to look up to."

JESSICA DREADED THE LONG INTERSTATE DRIVE FROM Pittsfield to the drop zone. She much preferred spending weekends hanging out with her friends. Jessica begged her mother, Doris, and her stepfather, Bill, to let her stay home alone while they went skydiving.

Bill's mother lived in a small apartment at the front of their house. The old lady agreed to poke her head in every now and then to check up on Jessica. With this safeguard in place, Bill and Doris had no qualms about letting their fifteen-year-old spend weekends in Pittsfield while they went out of town. They trusted Jessica and thought she was exceptionally mature and reliable for her age.

Bill endearingly referred to Jessica by her childhood nickname, the Little Princess, because unlike most teenagers he and Doris knew, Jessica showed no outward signs of rebellion. The Jessica that Bill and Doris saw every day was charming and good-humored. She hung out with a crowd of respectable, well-behaved kids, took school seriously, got good grades, earned her own money at an after-school job, and didn't even have a boyfriend. She planned on going away to college and was smart enough to understand that a good education could be a key that opened many doors.

Although Jessica lived with her mother and stepfather, she remained extremely close to her biological father, Robert, who lived in an old mill in Pittsfield, where he worked as an artist and sign painter. Like Doris and Bill, Robert had high hopes for his beautiful daughter. Jessica longed to live up to his expectations.

Jessica's mother and father had married as teenagers. They had Jessica a year later and divorced when she was two years old. Robert remained in Pittsfield and saw Jessica a few days a week. He and the little girl developed a close bond. Jessica was his sunshine, the one bright light that made his life worth living.

When Jessica was seven, her father was sentenced to a year in jail on charges of marijuana possession. Robert didn't want to lose touch with Jessica and was adamant about having Doris bring her to visiting hours. While holed up in his cell, Robert spent a great deal of time drawing. He gave the pictures he made to his daughter as gifts. After each visit, Jessica took her father's artwork home and hung it on the wall by her bed. Whenever she missed him, looking at his pictures gave her tremendous comfort.

When Robert got out of jail, he found an old, abandoned, ramshackle school bus. He fixed it up and began living there. When Jessica went to see him, he took her on hikes and to the lake. He taught her to appreciate the beauty of nature and to have respect for all forms of life. Together they rescued injured dogs and scooped up birds with broken wings. During their frequent visits to the vet, they made every effort to save these suffering animals.

Jessica enjoyed the visits, but as she grew older she began to worry about her father's dramatic mood swings. She was troubled by the fact that he often seemed sad. Robert struggled against depression but refused to speak to Jessica about the violent abuse that had indelibly marred his childhood. He was determined that the trauma he had experienced as a child would not repeat itself. He longed to protect Jessica from the pain that he, his mother, and his eight siblings had endured. He was convinced that silence regarding that subject was the best way to shield his daughter from the agonizing truth.

From snatches of conversations that Jessica overheard throughout her childhood, she guessed that her father's secrets had something to do with her paternal grandparents, but for years their absence remained an unexplained gap in her life. One day when Jessica was ten years old, she saw her grandparents featured as fugitives on the television program *America's Most Wanted*. Jessica watched the show in the company of her mother and stepfather, who assumed that the disturbing content went way over their little girl's head and therefore did not discuss it with her. Although Jessica was indeed young and too scared to ask questions, she understood much more than Bill and Doris gave her credit for.

"The story was about how my grandfather used to sexually abuse my aunts and how he abused my uncles, and how my grandma didn't do anything about it," explained Jessica. "He and my grandma went running from the law and changed their names."

John Walsh, the host of *America's Most Wanted*, reported the story of how Jessica's grandmother and grandfather had slipped under the radar and evaded justice. Back when Jessica was a toddler, her two eldest aunts had finally summoned up the courage to break the silence that had enshrouded their family's tangled web of physical, sexual, and emotional abuse. At the time they pressed charges against their father, Jessica's aunts were young adults. They had moved out of the family home but were certain that their father was continuing to beat and rape their three younger sisters the same way he had for years beaten and raped them. Their mother had always known about the violent abuse and had also been subjected to it. Nevertheless, she allowed herself to continue being victimized and did nothing to protect her children from their father.

Longing to save their family members from more torture, Jessica's aunts finally reported the abuse. Their younger siblings were taken out of school and into safety by a social worker and were later placed in foster homes. Jessica's grandparents were arrested and put on trial.

Newspapers in Pittsfield and Springfield covered the case. Jessica's aunts went through the painful process of testifying in public against their own father. Then a day before the verdict was to be announced, Jessica's grandparents abruptly vanished without a trace. For more than ten long years, they lived hidden lives, under assumed names, while their sons and daughters were left to live in constant fear and suffering, without any closure or resolution.

With the help of one of Jessica's aunts, John Walsh began a thorough investigation, determined to bring this fugitive pedophile and his wife to justice. Between 1990 and 1992, *America's Most Wanted* aired three programs about the case. The first two broadcasts yielded no solid leads, but minutes after the third show aired, a woman from California called in and gave the operator a crucial tip: the couple they were looking for had left her house a few hours ago. The woman had cleaned her house and the man did odd jobs and had fixed her car. The caller told the operator that the couple lived on a boat. She gave the operator directions to where the boat was docked. An FBI agent was dispatched, and Jessica's grandparents were promptly arrested, extradited to Massachusetts, and sentenced.

John Walsh was outraged and disgusted by this case—so outraged and so disgusted that he ultimately included Jessica's grandparents among "America's Worst Criminals" in his book on true crime, *No Mercy*. In his book, Walsh reported that Jessica's grandfather "was charged with nine counts of incest and rape of a child . . . and given a sentence of thirty-six to fifty-four years in prison. He will be eligible for parole in the year 2016, when he is eighty-five years old— although with his list of crimes it's unlikely that he'll get out even then, if he lives that long." Jessica's grandmother "was charged with three counts of failure to provide care and protection. . . . She got two years."

The sentencing was a formal resolution, but the residual trauma lingered and affected family members in different ways. For some family members, there was ambivalence and guilt over the fate of Jessica's grandmother, a masochistic, brainwashed woman who had herself been viciously abused by her husband all through their marriage. Others felt little if any mercy for her and blamed her for allowing her own children to be abused for so many years. After Jessica's grandmother had served her two years and was released from prison, she moved to a town close to the prison where her husband was incarcerated. When John Walsh followed up on the case, he discovered a bizarre twist: Jessica's grandmother visited her husband in prison nearly every day and remained "totally devoted" to him.

Not long after Jessica's grandparents were apprehended, one of her aunts drank herself into a stupor and wandered deep into the woods on a bitterly cold night. Her body was found the next day in a creek. She had frozen to death. Some labeled the death an accident. Others suspected that, like the death of Jessica's uncle several years before (he had gotten on his motorcycle with no shoes or helmet on and had zoomed ahead at full speed straight into a Mack truck), the death of Jessica's aunt might very well have been a suicide.

Jessica was disturbed by the untimely deaths of these relatives. She felt shocked, uncomfortable, dirty, and ashamed of the crimes her grandparents had perpetrated. Yet she never discussed these feelings with anyone.

"This was supposed to be a family secret," Jessica murmured. "My dad really doesn't like to talk about it, because it hurts him inside. He just doesn't want to think about it. I never really wanted to know about it. I've never straight-out asked him, 'Why did Grandpa do that?' It scared me. I didn't want to know."

As Jessica was growing up, she felt tremendous pressure to right the wrongs of the past. She wanted to replace sadness with happiness and was desperate to please her father, her mother, and her stepfather. Eager to make her parents proud, she painstakingly cultivated and maintained her reputation as a model child. Yet just beneath the surface, Jessica hid her own mountain of secrets. In retrospect, her stepfather said, "Jessica was too perfect." He shook his head. "Way too perfect."

When her mother and stepfather were away, Jessica's house became known as the place to party. Jessica quickly got caught up in a fast crowd. Unbeknownst to her parents, she lost her virginity at age fourteen. By tenth grade, she had been in and out of four sexual relationships, driven not by love but by her craving for attention and validation.

Jessica found that she was attracted only to black men. Her friends didn't bother setting her up with white guys, because they knew she probably wouldn't be interested. Halfway through her junior year, a friend introduced Jessica to Dwayne, a high school dropout who wasn't part of their usual crowd. At nineteen, Dwayne was three years older and slicker and more street-smart than the guys Jessica had dated. He was known to be a drug dealer. Jessica didn't let that faze her. Tired of what she perceived to be her bland, monotonous daily routine, Jessica welcomed Dwayne's aura of danger, adventure, and transgression.

"When I met Dwayne," Jessica recalled, "I thought that he was gorgeous. I looked at him like 'Oh my God, he is *fine!*' Me and Dwayne started sleeping together after a couple of weeks. It felt like we'd known each other forever. . . . I think I got pregnant the first time we had sex."

The night that ended with Jessica's getting pregnant began with a group of teenagers driving around in search of a good time. Jessica and Dwayne were part of the group, along with another young couple. Shortly after midnight the teenagers headed out of town to pick up some liquor because the stores in Pittsfield shut down early on weekends. After driving around aimlessly for several hours and getting trashed, the teenagers somehow found their way back to Pittsfield at about five in the morning.

Jessica had made plans to sleep over at her friend's house, so no one was waiting up for her at home. She was buzzed, groggy, and completely exhausted. More than anything, she wanted to curl up on a comfortable bed, lay her head down on a soft pillow, and drift off into a deep, deep sleep. However, because she didn't have her own transportation, Jessica was at the mercy of her friends, who weren't ready to call it a night.

The teenagers decided to hang out at the home of one of Dwayne's friends. Upon entering, Jessica's friend rapidly vanished behind closed doors to make out with her date. Jessica found herself alone in a room with Dwayne. He kissed her, and one thing led to another. Jessica made it clear that she didn't want to have sex. She said no several times but eventually surrendered, too tired to fight about it. The moment she caved in, a thought flashed across her mind, *I might as well just get it over with.*

Jessica didn't want to deal with Dwayne being angry with her. She placed conflict avoidance at a premium. At that particular moment, she wasn't confident that she had the physical and mental strength to assert her will. Getting out of this bad situation seemed difficult, complicated, and messy. Surrendering to Dwayne's desire seemed much easier. In her previous sexual encounters, the boys Jessica had been with had used condoms. Dwayne didn't offer to use any protection. Not wanting to make a big deal out of it, Jessica went ahead and had unprotected sex, ignoring the risk of sexually transmitted diseases and never for a moment dreaming that she would be unlucky enough to get pregnant the very first time she had sex with a new partner.

In the weeks following her sexual encounter with Dwayne, Jessica remained convinced of her good luck, her immunity to risk, and her own invincibility. When she missed her period, she quickly repressed her worry that she might be pregnant. Three more months went by and despite missing a second, third, and fourth period, Jessica went on with her life as if everything were completely normal.

Jessica's father suspected something was very wrong when one afternoon, after a routine visit, his daughter asked him to drop her off at a friend's place instead of at her mother's house. Robert followed Jessica's directions and they ended up at a decrepit apartment complex. Rap music was blasting. Drug dealers were lounging around. Robert flat-out refused to stop the car. Enraged, he screeched out of the parking lot. A huge fight between father and daughter ensued. Robert told Jessica that she was crazy if she thought he would ever let her off at a place like that. Jessica insisted that her "friends" lived there and that it was perfectly safe. Later that night Robert got a call from Doris, who suggested that he had overreacted and had upset Jessica. Robert reminded Doris how much he cared about their daughter and said that he wasn't sure if he had been overprotective or if there was indeed serious cause to worry. Doris insisted that their daughter was doing just fine.

In hindsight, Jessica's stepfather offered the following explanation for his wife's failure to see the warning signs that suggested something was terribly wrong.

"I think Doris had got that ostrich thing going on," said Bill. "You know, stick your head in the sand and if you don't know it's happening, then basically it's not happening—until it comes up and slaps you dead in the kisser!"

For six months, despite seeing Jessica nearly every day, not a single member of the family suspected that she might be pregnant. Robert worried that Jessica might be at risk for teen pregnancy but didn't think it had already happened. Bill and Doris were preoccupied with problems in their marriage. Adding to the stress in their home, their younger daughter, Catherine, had been acting out, stealing and failing tests at school. She was the one they were anxious about, not Jessica. As time passed, Jessica became more and more stressed-out about hiding her pregnancy. Her family's living quarters were cramped, and privacy was virtually nonexistent. She was terrified of being discovered.

Seeking refuge in secrecy and denial, Jessica hid under baggy sweatshirts, ashamed of her condition and fearful of disappointing her family. She longed to rewind her life back to the day before she got pregnant and fantasized that somehow by ignoring the pregnancy, she could magically turn back time and reverse the consequences of unsafe sex with Dwayne. Resisting the impulse to confide in a relative, teacher, doctor, nurse, or friend, Jessica clung to her unrealistic wish for her stomach to shrink so that her old jeans would zip right up without a hassle. But as the months passed, her pregnancy didn't disappear. All that disappeared were her choices.

Jessica's silence was a time bomb. By not speaking up for so long, she deprived herself of medical care, psychological support, and advice that could have benefited her during the first two trimesters. She also missed the opportunity to seriously consider and discuss one major alternative: a safe, early abortion.

When Jessica was six months pregnant, she broke down and wrote a note to her mother. As word spread quickly through Pittsfield that Doris and Bill's "Little Princess" was pregnant, Jessica was barraged with an unpleasant assortment of facts about Dwayne that she had previously been unaware of. Jessica realized that although it had felt to her as though she and Dwayne had "known each other forever," they had dated for only just over a month. In fact, she knew astonishingly little about the father of her baby.

People in the community came forward and told Jessica that hers would not be Dwayne's first child. Jessica was shocked to discover that he had already fathered three children with two other young mothers. Dwayne was arrested and jailed for assault and battery of one of his other girlfriends and was behind bars, far from the delivery room, on the day Jessica gave birth to their son, whom she named Ezakeil.

Inside the stark, white hospital room, as Jessica stared at Ezakeil's brown face, black hair, and dark, shining eyes, she felt the weight of Dwayne's absence bearing down on her. Disappointed by his irresponsible behavior, no one in her family had ever even met Dwayne. At the mention of Dwayne's name, Bill would clench his fist, tensing up his whole body, as his face reddened with anger.

"If I were to meet the father of Jessica's baby, I don't think I'd say a whole lot," he fumed. "He's older and he's got three other kids with as many girls. . . . I don't think there'd be anything for me to talk about! I think I'd just go straight to physical. That's why it's best that I haven't met him, because assault is a terrible thing, and I'm already on probation for drunk driving!"

Single motherhood at such a young age destroyed Jessica's autonomy. Suddenly she couldn't even consider going away to college, because she needed her family around her to help care for the baby. The little money she made had to go toward supporting the baby, and in order to remain eligible for welfare while she was still a minor, she was required to remain in a supervised setting with a parent or responsible adult—for the near future, that meant living with Doris and Bill.

"Since I was fourteen, I've always been working," Jessica said matter-of-factly. "I've always wanted to make my own money. I don't like taking money from other people, like my mom, or anything, 'cause then I gotta pay her back. Might as well make my own money. Then I don't got to pay anyone back."

More than anything, what Jessica wanted out of a job was a sense of personal fulfillment and the knowledge that her work made a difference. The money was important, but a sense of satisfaction and being able to take pride in her work was more important—and much, much harder to find. Her work history was long, varied, and littered with a string of disappointments.

"My first job was at McFarlane Office Products," Jessica explained. "It was a desk job, boring, didn't like it. Moved to Burger King. I got sick of that and went to Rave, the clothing store. I didn't get along with my boss, so I moved on to Pretzel Time. It was just a quick little job in the wintertime just to make some extra money. Then I went to Bonanza. I had to wear a stupid outfit and a stupid hat and I looked corny. I got out of there smelling like meat and potatoes. So then I got a job at Edgecombe Nursing Home. I love the elderly, they're wonderful, and Alzheimer patients, I mean, you can just sit there and listen to all their stories because they'll come up with anything."

During the first year of her son's life, Jessica felt inadequate because the money she was making working at the nursing home after school and on weekends wasn't enough to provide her son with all the things she wanted him to have. She devised a plan with a friend who worked behind the counter at a store in the mall. This girl agreed to let Jessica through the checkout line without ringing her up on the register. As Jessica tried to leave the store with a bagful of merchandise she hadn't paid for, a security guard grabbed her. Within minutes the police were on the scene and she was arrested for shoplifting.

"I had stolen this really nice baby mobile, some baby clothes, a child's car seat, a baby monitor . . . just stupid stuff," said Jessica, shaking her head in disbelief over her own impulsive actions. "The police slapped handcuffs on me. I had to go to jail and get fingerprinted. The police took my picture. It wasn't a pleasant experience. What I did was so stupid and immature. I shouldn't have done it. I had money in my pocket, and my son was only a couple of weeks old."

Jessica's father contacted a friend of the family who was a lawyer, and he succeeded in getting Jessica out of the mess with a clear criminal record and a serious warning. Frightened by what had happened, Jessica realized that as a single mother, she could not flirt with danger or take any unnecessary risks. She suddenly understood that she had to be extraordinarily responsible in every area of her life because if anything happened to her—be it illness or injury or trouble with the law—there was no father to step in and take care of her son. Jessica accepted that with Dwayne still in jail, all the pressure of raising their son and supporting him fell squarely on her shoulders. As Jessica's parents drove her away from the police station, she resolved that rather than crack under the weight of such enormous responsibility, she would become strong enough to deal with it.

Despite Dwayne's absence and his failure to pay any child support, Jessica continued to make efforts to get him involved in her son's life. She took Ezakeil to visit his father in jail, hoping that Dwayne would bond with the infant. When Ezakeil was six months old, Dwayne got out of jail.

"He didn't call or show up to see how his son was doing," Jessica reported.

Anguished and reeling from Dwayne's neglect, Jessica temporarily cut off all contact with him. A few months later she heard from friends that he was back in jail. For several months Jessica decided not to take Ezakeil during visiting hours. That was her way of punishing Dwayne for being a bad father.

"I have no contact with my son's father," she explained. "I prefer it this way because I don't want him floating in and out of my son's life, messing his head up."

At the Teen Parent Program, Jessica was able to work through some of her disappointment with her son's father when she attended the writing workshops conducted by Carol Gilligan and Normi Noel. Considering that teen mothers such as Jessica stored up massive reservoirs of pent-up stress and rage with few available constructive outlets, Carol and Normi made every effort to create a safe haven that could contain and support the release of these ragged emotions so that rather than being turned inward in a silent, self-destructive way, these feelings could be discussed.

Carol and Normi discussed Charity Royall, the teenage character in Edith Wharton's novel *Summer*, who is constantly in conflict over how to express her seething rage. When Charity, knowing she is pregnant, sees her friend Ally mending an extravagant lace blouse for Annabel Balch, the rich socialite who is her rival for her lover's affections, she explodes, rips the garment out of her friend's hands, and tears it to shreds: "She had never known how to adapt herself; she could only break, tear and destroy. The scene with Ally left her stricken with shame at her own childish savagery. . . . But when she turned the incident over in her puzzled mind, she could not imagine what a civilized person would have done in her place."

When Carol asked the teen mothers in the workshop to write two letters to the fathers of their babies—one conventional, safe letter that they would be willing to send, and the other one that they would hide in the back of their minds, unwritten and unsent because it contained seeds of rebellion—Jessica seized the moment, put her thoughts down on paper, and read the letter she would not send out loud to a rapt audience:

> *Dwayne, I hate you! You are the most horrible man I have ever met. I never wanted to have sex with you in the first place! When I look at you, you make me sick. I don't understand how you can take care of your other three children but pay no mind to mine. I would really like to punch you in the head. Maybe that would knock some sense into you. When we first met, you were so kind. But you changed so quickly. Why couldn't you have stayed the same? Maybe we could have raised our son together—if you weren't such an asshole!*

The act of writing the letter entailed confronting the origins of the strong feelings of sadness and rage that had driven away words in the first place. Rather than splitting off into denial and justification for being treated badly, the girls were encouraged to venture into territory they felt was dangerous and provocative. They were encouraged to have higher expectations of themselves and to take more control over their relationships with the men in their lives.

Jessica's line "I never wanted to have sex with you in the first place" was one of several comments she made that implied the first time she and Dwayne had intercourse, resulting in her pregnancy, was not totally voluntary. Jessica made it clear that she did not view the experience with Dwayne as rape: she saw it as her own failure to enforce what she wanted, and felt that her ambivalent silence and passive submission had constituted consent. She therefore took full responsibility for her involvement in the encounter and for the fact that she had been drinking that night; nevertheless, she wished in hindsight that she had handled the situation differently.

Though Jessica had regrets about the night her son was conceived, she had no regrets about keeping her baby. "I could never give my baby up for adoption," she said tenderly. "Every day I would wonder where he was, how he looked, what he was doing. . . . I love my son to death. He is my love."

Preoccupied with Ezakeil, work, and studying for final exams, Jessica steered clear of dating and sex, consoling herself with the thought that "dating isn't worth it 'cause men are nothing but trouble."

Her attitude changed when tickets went on sale for the senior prom. Jessica longed to go. She went to the Berkshire Mall and tried on elegant floor-length strapless dresses and glamorous high-heeled shoes. She experimented with different makeup and hairstyles, and imagined herself walking down the red carpet on the big night. Jessica had saved up enough money to buy the gown of her dreams and two tickets to the prom, but there was one big problem: she didn't have a date. After much deliberation, she finally mustered up the courage to ask friends to help her find someone to escort her. They found a guy who said he was up for it. Jessica was ecstatic. Her fantasy had morphed into reality—or so she thought.

"The prom in Pittsfield is supposed to be a fun thing, but it wasn't fun for me," said Jessica. "I found a guy to go with but he backed out, so I didn't get to go. He told me the day before that he wasn't going, so I didn't have any time to find someone else to go with. I had a brand-new dress that was altered to fit me, and nowhere to go in it."

Jessica shook her head in despair as her memories transported her back to the disappointing night.

"I stood outside and watched people going into the prom, what fun! But I didn't get to go in 'cause I didn't have anyone to go with. I sat home with my son and did nothing. All because of that freakin' idiot."

For weeks Jessica's brand-new ethereal peach ball gown hung forlorn on a wire hanger, covered in plastic, gathering dust. It had been painstakingly altered to fit every curve of her slender body, so she could not return it to the store. Jessica was sure she would never have another opportunity to wear such a fancy, exquisite dress. She saw herself as a Cinderella-like character: the prom had been her ball, the one magic occasion in her otherwise uneventful life. When family and friends tried to console her with the idea that surely she would have other special events in the future, Jessica shook her head mournfully.

"Where am I gonna go?" she asked, her humor barely masking the despondency beneath it. "If only I hadn't had the dress altered," she bemoaned. "Then at least I could have returned it and gotten my money back."

Jessica's stepfather wore a pained expression on his face as he witnessed Jessica's crushing disappointment and deflated spirits. He blamed her pregnancy for causing her to become isolated from what he referred to as "the mainstream." He felt that her social life had suffered immensely on account of having a baby and that while the Teen Parent Program had its benefits, being surrounded by teen mothers day after day hadn't exactly increased her chances of meeting a cool, nice guy who might be reliable and fun to date. Bill drew attention to the fact that in the two years since Jessica had gotten pregnant, she hadn't been asked out on any dates. Not a single one.

As Bill talked about time lost, a very subdued Jessica listened. Her characteristic sharp wit, warm laughter, vibrant energy, and boundless enthusiasm had deserted her. Unafraid to speak the truth, Bill had hit on two of Jessica's vulnerable points. Beneath her cheerful optimism and tenacious resilience lay her gnawing worry that she was missing out on the joys of being a young, attractive, sexy single woman. She worried that lots of guys would never want to seriously date, let alone marry, a teenager who already had another guy's baby. Jessica took a deep breath and gathered her strength to respond to Bill's comments about her lack of a social life.

"It's true, but so what! Men are nothing but trouble. Maybe someday I'll find one who will change my mind, but for now I'm too busy goin' to school, goin' to work, and being a mom. I don't have time for anything else."

While raising Ezakeil was hard work, the baby was Jessica's main source of joy. Days went by when she felt unappreciated by her employers, exasperated by her family, frustrated by school, and trapped in Pittsfield, but her son never failed to surprise her with unexpected demonstrations of love, affection, and appreciation.

"My favorite moments are when Ez gives me big hugs out of the blue. When I'm lucky, he'll come up to me and squeeze me tight and give me a big kiss. I love that."

A few weeks after the prom, Jessica graduated from Taconic High School with honors. Ezakeil sat in the bleachers of the gymnasium with his grandparents, watching the ceremony with a huge smile on his face. He loved the way his mommy looked in her bright yellow cap and gown, holding a red rose. Out of the blue, he gave her a big hug.

Jessica's father was immensely proud of his daughter. He constantly reminded her how crucial it was for her to continue her education and develop a trade. His dream was for her to become a nurse. Jessica adopted her father's goals and enrolled in the nursing program at Berkshire Community College, a ten-minute drive from the house where she still lived with her son, Bill, Doris, and Catherine. Initially, Jessica was worried about how she would pay for a college education, but the issue was resolved with the assistance of her welfare worker and the financial-aid advisor at the college.

"College was offered to me for free. For having a kid, I get a grant each semester for two thousand dollars and that's plenty for what I need. I don't use the whole two thousand. I usually get a thousand back, so it's like they're paying me to go to school.

"When I meet with my welfare worker, I always ask what programs are available—if you don't ask, no one's gonna tell you. An organization called Berkshire Works pays for my books, and they pay for my uniforms for nursing. They're going to pay for my testing when I get my RN licensing. Every time I call them I say, 'Thank you so much.' Day care is offered to me for free through an organization called Resources for Child Care. They offer my son good meals, every day. It seems like everywhere you turn, people are willing to help you. That's one of the reasons why I'm still in Pittsfield."

Despite having these services at her fingertips, Jessica had her hands full keeping up with college and her part-time job at the nursing home. However, all these challenges paled compared with the challenge of learning how to adapt and evolve as a single mother in order to keep up with the different phases of her child's development, each with its own demands, challenges, and pitfalls.

"Ezakeil is now eighteen months old and he's a very active eighteen-month-old. I'm glad I'm young," said Jessica, "or I wouldn't be able to keep up with him! I never get a full night's sleep! Never! Ezakeil goes to bed at eight-thirty and wakes up once or twice in the middle of the night. He usually cries and wants to sleep in my bed. I get up and get him something to drink. Sometimes I have to change his diaper. For a while he was having night terrors. He would scream and cry, and if you touched him, he would just get worse. It was like he was in the middle of a nightmare and he looked awake, but he was really asleep. He just had no idea what was going on. There was nothing I could do to make him feel better. All I could do was make sure he didn't fall out of his bed or hurt himself somehow. Every day I get so tired. People told me that Ezakeil waking up at all hours of the night would end when he turned one, but it hasn't ended. He still does it. Every single night."

Because of the lack of space in her parents' house, Jessica and her son had to sleep under the eaves of the roof in a windowless corridor that connected Bill and Doris's room to Catherine's. Whenever the baby cried, it was hard, if not impossible, for anyone in the house to sleep.

Catherine complained, "Ez doesn't sleep through the night because you baby him too much!" Stung by her sister's criticism, Jessica's eyes narrowed defensively.

She fired back, "You try having a baby, Catherine. It's not as easy as people think!"

Jessica persevered through her first two years at Berkshire Community College, where she pursued a degree in nursing while continuing to work part-time with the elderly at a local nursing home for an hourly wage of $7.25.

"Welfare gives me five hundred dollars a month," Jessica explained. "I work one day a week because I go to school full-time, so I can't work any other days. So welfare takes that thirty-four dollars I get from working those hours and subtracts it from the five hundred dollars, and then I'll get the remainder. If I work a couple of extra hours they'll take those extra hours out of the five hundred, so no matter what, I'm only getting five hundred dollars a month. And five hundred dollars is nothing . . . you can't live on five hundred dollars a month. I mean, I obviously live on five hundred dollars a month, but you can't get things that you want. You have to pay your bills and just get regular household stuff like dish detergent and clothes, if you need clothes. My rent is a hundred and forty-three dollars. My cable is usually like forty dollars. My phone bill is usually like eighty or ninety. My electric bill is like fifty-four dollars. My car insurance is sixty dollars. There's other stuff, and it all adds up to a lot; and by the end of the month, I'm broke. I don't have any more money to save.

"I hate being on welfare," said Jessica, "but I have to, there's no way around it. I can't work full-time and go to school—it's impossible. If I could, I would; I don't want to be on welfare. I'm trying to do what I have to do to get off of it. I don't want to be stuck in the system, but thank God for the system.

"Welfare does help me. It really does. I don't know what I'd do . . . I mean, 'cause Dwayne was in jail . . . I never could've . . . I mean, I'm only . . . I'm young. I can't get a full-time job with college and a two-year-old. So welfare was the only thing I could do. I'm so thankful for it, for real, I really am. I don't know what I'd do without it—I mean, of course I know what I'm gonna do without it in the future. That's why I'm going to college. So I don't have to be on welfare. So I can have a good life and make my own money.

"Once I get my registered nursing license, I'll probably work in a hospital for a while, in the ER or pediatrics. I have to get my bachelor's after I get my RN, and then I'll work in delivery. My income is going to increase a lot once I get my registered nursing license. By the time I get up there, it'll probably be like twenty-four dollars an hour."

During Jessica's first two years at Berkshire Community College, her home life became more difficult. Her stepfather's drinking got out of hand, and the cops had to be called to break up a violent fight he had with her mother. Doris began to spend more and more time skydiving by herself at a new drop zone. One afternoon Bill followed Doris to a trailer park and spied on her. He caught her having an affair with one of her fellow sky divers.

"I was a basket case," recalled Bill. "I went between suicidal and homicidal. . . . You know, back and forth, back and forth, back and forth. Kill myself, kill her, kill myself, kill her, ah, fuck it—I'll kill her, then I'll kill myself!"

In the wake of this event, Doris shocked her daughters by announcing that she was moving out. Enough was enough. A teen mother and the veteran of two marriages, Doris longed for time to herself. She was sick of being tied down, and tired of all her responsibilities. Most of all, she was fed up with Bill's drinking.

"There were good times and bad times," said Doris, her voice tinged with sadness. "It was like a cycle with Bill. He would go months and months and months and not drink, and it would be good. When he got sent away the first time, after he got out, he went for two years without drinking, and that time was great. But then it started again. It was 'Oh . . . I'll just have one.' That lasted for a little while and then it was 'Oh, I'll just have two,' and of course he started again.

"I tried not to let the kids see it, but I think the mood that it put me in affected them more than him actually drinking himself.

"When he would drink, he would do it late at night when the kids were sleeping. He wouldn't come home. I wouldn't know where he was. He'd be spending a ton of money, so I was on edge all the time and I didn't have the patience I should have had with the kids because I was upset with Bill."

As her marriage collapsed, Doris reflected on the consequences of becoming a teen mother before having the chance to define herself independently as an adult.

"I felt that I was always Bill's wife or the girls' mother, it was never just me. When I started skydiving—that's part of what broke

Bill and I up. I mean, there was definitely troubles before that . . . lots of troubles . . . but skydiving made me more independent, and he didn't like that. He used to say, 'It always used to be "Bill and Doris," and now it's not anymore.' I couldn't make him understand that it wasn't that I didn't need him or that I didn't want him . . . I just realized that I could do stuff for myself."

Doris told Jessica, Catherine, and Bill that she had signed a lease on an apartment a few blocks away. She made it clear that she expected the girls to remain at the house, living with Bill. She pulled out a stack of boxes and started packing up her belongings.

The day before Doris was scheduled to move in to her new apartment, Bill went to a drop zone in New York, got hammered with his friends, and then tried to drive home. He drove about fifty yards from the bar before being busted by the cops for DUI. The cops discovered that Bill had been arrested on similar charges before and that his license had been taken away. At the time this incident occurred, Bill was on probation and was explicitly forbidden from getting behind the wheel. By driving without a license and being outside the state of Massachusetts, Bill was violating his probation—and on top of that, he was driving while intoxicated. In the courtroom, the judge was not sympathetic when Bill tried to explain that his car had swerved because he bent down to pick up a CD case that had fallen on the floor. The gavel came down hard. Bill was sentenced to six months in jail.

"Actually, going to jail was probably the best thing that happened to me because it gave me time to sit back, it definitely took me out of the loop. I had no dealings with Doris and her boyfriend. I just got totally out of it," Bill said, winding his fingers together and bending them backward until his knuckles cracked.

In spite of Bill's unexpected incarceration, Doris felt compelled to move in to her new apartment. Never mind that it meant leaving her two teenage daughters to their own devices. After all, she had signed the lease and put down the deposit. Claiming her independence had been a big step for Doris, and she wasn't going to be diverted by what she considered to be Bill's childish antics. Seated on a sofa in her own apartment, Doris talked about how much her life had changed since leaving Bill.

"When you're young and you have kids, you're tied down, that's it," she explained. "You have no life until they're grown. Now I can enjoy the freedom that I have. I can come and go as I please."

Bill's incarceration, compounded by Doris's abandonment, left Jessica, at nineteen, completely in charge of Ezakeil, who was just a toddler, and Catherine, who was sixteen. In addition, she had to shoulder the added burden of handling all the household affairs. Bill's aging mother still lived in the front apartment and checked up on the girls from time to time, and Doris, living nearby, had them over for dinner a few nights a week and poked her head in regularly to make sure everyone had enough to eat and that the house wasn't falling to pieces. Her affair with her fellow sky diver was going well, and to the girls, she seemed happier and more relaxed than she'd ever been.

In contrast, Jessica was extremely stressed-out. Pounds began dropping off her. Exhausted, pale, and emaciated, she attributed her significant weight loss to the fact that she was anxious all the time and, as a result, was suffering from terrible stomach cramps. She described a typical day, which began with her waking up at four in the morning to the sound of Ezakeil crying because he was hungry, and then consisted of her running from day care to college classes to a welfare meeting to the grocery store and then back to day care before going home to clean the house and pay a stack of bills. The pressure of her everyday life was killing her appetite.

Jessica had never imagined that she would get stuck managing a household while being a surrogate parent for her sixteen-year-old sister and dealing with what she referred to as her son's "terrible twos," on top of attending Berkshire Community College as a full-time student. As if that weren't already a heavy enough load, Jessica was also working part-time as an activities assistant at a nursing home, supervising games, arts and crafts, and other projects for Alzheimer's patients.

"Living with Catherine and Ezakeil without my parents is totally different than what I thought it would be," said Jessica. "I thought it would be easier and that I wouldn't have to worry about my mom saying stuff like 'Don't you think you should give Ezakeil a bath now?' I just thought that I'd be able to do what I want to do, but it is so not fun. I feel like a thirty-year-old woman. It's hard. And my sister, she doesn't have a job or anything, and her friends come over and I buy the groceries and I come home and everything is gone."

Jessica applied for subsidized housing, eager to be on her own with Ezakeil. She was put at the end of a long waiting list. She had no idea when there would be an opening. She waited and waited. In the dead of winter, the heating suddenly stopped working. Jessica couldn't afford to buy a new heating system, so she, Ezakeil, and Catherine moved in with Doris. Jessica slept on the couch until finally she received a letter in the mail saying there was an apartment available for her at the Wilson projects, near the center of Pittsfield. She was given a duplex, and for the first time, she had privacy and a space she and Ezakeil could call their own.

Jessica got very worried about Ezakeil when she observed that he couldn't play with other kids for long periods of time because he was allergic to dust and had trouble breathing. After a few minutes of play, his eyes became itchy and watery. He tired easily and often had to sit down in the grass and catch his breath. One day Jessica took him to a store and after a few minutes of excited exploration, he started coughing, choking, and vomiting. Similar episodes kept oc-

curring, and when Jessica took Ezakeil to the doctor, he was diagnosed with severe asthma. Jessica was given prescriptions for Claritin and Singulair as well as a nebulizer, a device that uses pressurized air to turn liquid medication into a fine mist for inhalation. Ezakeil relied on his nebulizer two or three times a day.

Jessica had her hands full balancing work, school, and taking care of her son. She became friendly with Dwayne's mother and sister, who often stayed in her apartment, sometimes for days at a time. They looked after Ezakeil when Jessica had to go out. Robert helped her as often as he could. Some days Ezakeil went to day care, other days he went to his grandfather's art studio. Robert taught the little boy how to paint and draw. He was amazed by the toddler's intelligence, curiosity, and wide-eyed innocence. Grandfather and grandson developed a close attachment. The adoration was mutual. As soon as he could talk, Ezakeil called his grandfather "Pa."

"Ez and my dad are best friends," said Jessica. "My dad taught him how to ride a bike and taught him how to swim. They go hiking in the woods. My dad means the world to me and to Ezakeil. The world."

Jessica was extremely grateful for her father's help and involvement; her main regret was the continued absence of her son's biological father.

"Dwayne's been in jail mostly all Ezakeil's life. I was pregnant, he was in jail; I had the baby, he was in jail. Now he's back in jail. But Ezakeil knows his father. We visit him in jail, so he knows him from going to see him there, and Ezakeil has seen him for a few months in between. Like on Halloween, we went trick-or-treating together."

When Dwayne got out of jail, he approached Jessica about re-kindling their relationship. Jessica wavered, tempted to get back to-gether with him. After several failed attempts to woo Jessica back sexually, Dwayne abruptly curtailed his visits to Ezakeil. Despite the temptation and her desire for Ezakeil to have a father in his life, Jessica resisted.

"After Dwayne got out of jail the last time, he got back with his baby's mother, the one who has his other son. They got in a fight and he hit her and now he's back in jail for a year and a half because he can't keep his hands off his girlfriends. He just can't stay out of jail. I don't know why he keeps hitting people."

At the Pittsfield police station, a computer search of the names of the fathers of the six teen mothers' babies revealed more than sixty police reports. The policeman who conducted the search ex-plained that certain basic reports were available to any American citizen under the Freedom of Information Act, provided that the names of victims and witnesses are blacked out. Many of these reports documented arrests for assault and battery, restraining orders, and larceny charges, in addition to describing altercations or incidents involving harassment.

Jessica knew that Dwayne had a violent streak but was shocked when she was presented with copies of page after page of police reports that featured the name of her son's father. There had been many more arrests than even she had suspected. The majority of them were for assault and battery of other women—particularly the mothers of his other children.

Previously, Jessica had disassociated herself from what she knew about Dwayne's violence. She preferred not to know about it and was eager to minimize its implications. Because of the brevity of their relationship and Dwayne's having been behind bars for most of the time they had known each other, Jessica had thankfully never been a target of his assaults.

"I've never been hit by any of my boyfriends, even though they've hit their other girlfriends. I would never stand for a man hitting me," Jessica insisted. "I would do everything in my power, if a man hit me, to hit him back. I just wouldn't be with them. But it doesn't matter if you're in jail or not. I mean, a man can be a lawyer and beat the crap out of you. Or a man can be in for attempted murder and not beat the crap out of you."

Jessica couldn't pretend that the stack of police records sitting in front of her didn't exist. No longer able to deny the reality of the violent nature of the man whom she was dealing with, Jessica acknowledged how painful and difficult it was going to be to explain to Ezakeil why his father kept going to jail.

"Ez just loves his dad. I know he loves his dad. Every day he says, 'Daddy,' every day he wants to know where his father is. It's just really hard not knowing what to say. I mean, what am I supposed to say to a two-year-old? And when he gets older, what am I supposed to say? 'Your dad's working,' or 'Your dad doesn't care about you, Ez, and he doesn't want anything to do with you'? I can't imagine how Ezakeil's gonna grow up not having a father figure. A child needs a father."

Jessica was also upset that Dwayne never contributed a dime of child support. As he kept screwing up every chance to make a difference in Ezakeil's life, her disappointment slowly fermented into rage.

"He didn't even give me . . ." Jessica's voice broke. She slowed down and gathered her thoughts. "I asked Dwayne for ten dollars for Ezakeil's birthday cake. His birthday cake cost twenty dollars, I asked him for ten. He wouldn't even give me ten dollars and he didn't even call on Ezakeil's birthday. He's not gonna live that down. I am through with him. Ezakeil is better off. It's hard to say that, though, because he needs his father. But not like he is now. I'm through with people that go to jail. I mean, I'm not really through with people that go to jail, I'm just through with having to go and visit, and having to bring my son there. I just don't like going."

Sensing that the past was colliding with the present, she paused for a moment, overwhelmed with emotion.

"I remember ever since I was, like, seven years old, visiting a family member in jail. And now, it's still the same thing. Everyone that I love just keeps going to jail, everyone that I care about. I'm just tired of it. It's really depressing. Here one minute and gone the next for a long time. I just . . . It's just too much for me. I don't like seeing people I love locked up. Just the thought of people being in there . . . You just wish they didn't do what they did. But, I mean, if they're gonna go do that, then they have to suffer the consequences. Sometimes I don't really mind bringing Ezakeil to jail. It's the real world."

Jessica rationalized that because so many of her friends and family had been in and out of jail, it couldn't be possible that everyone who was incarcerated was a bad influence or in fact dangerous. She often sympathized with the inmate's side of the story, regardless of whether it was the truth or lies. As a result, her judgment suffered and she often underestimated the negative influence of the people she continued to surround herself with.

Rather than meeting new friends at college or at one of the hospitals or nursing homes where she worked, Jessica remained loyal to her old peer group, many of whom went in and out of jail and were involved with drugs. Within this peer group, Jessica had to hide her intelligence. Her kindness and generosity were taken advantage of. Jessica admitted that she was "too nice" but continued to associate with friends who had less going for them than she did.

Jessica felt ambivalent about her pursuit of a higher education and her aspirations for a steady job and a better life—as if somehow her choice to chase these dreams meant that she was indirectly criticizing and rejecting the circle of friends she had grown up with. She didn't want to feel that she was "better" than they were. Jessica wanted to fit in and feel accepted, terrified that outside this small circle she might not have a place in the world. At times she realized that her allegiance to this old peer group might be holding her back from reaching her full potential, but she found it difficult to break away.

Jessica was apprehensive about entering new social circles. She worried that guys she met in the college environment would be critical of her being a single mother with a son of mixed race. Sadly, her experience proved that her fears were well founded.

"The men in college—I'm just not attracted to them. I have not met . . . oh my God . . . yes I did—I met this guy named Eric. Oh my God, he's so sexy. He is the finest man in the entire world. He's white and he is so fly. He wanted me to go out to dinner with him. One time he asked me to just go sit out and watch the stars and just relax and talk. I said, "I can't. . . . My son is here.' And he said, 'Your son?' That screwed everything up."

A friend invited Jessica on a road trip, telling her that she and her boyfriend were going to visit his brother, Wes, who was incarcerated at Bridgewater Prison. Jessica snapped her son into his car seat, and they went along for what turned out to be the first of many visits.

"Jess let it slip one day that she was going to Bridgewater," recalled Doris. "I said, 'What are you going there for?' She said, 'To see Wes.' I said, 'Jess, why are you bringing Ez there?' She said, 'Oh, well, Wes is there, he's all by himself. We're friends, we're just gonna go and visit him.' I wasn't thrilled with her going that far and taking Ez there," said Doris, shaking her head. "It's a good two hours at least."

"I met Wes a long time ago," explained Jessica. "He was friends with my son's father and my best friend's boyfriend. So I just knew him from around town. I knew him from seeing him from when I was even younger, like sixteen and seventeen. He used to call me Blue Eyes. I'd be walking down the street and he'd be, like, 'Hey, Blue Eyes!' I never knew who he was, so I'd just keep walking.

"Nothing really serious happened then because I wasn't really interested in him, but when he went to jail, we started corresponding through letters. Finally we just decided to form a relationship. We committed ourselves to each other, and everything just evolved from there."

For reasons Jessica didn't understand, she equated sexual attraction with violence and repeatedly found herself drawn to men with criminal records.

"Wes was convicted of rape," said Jessica, "but he says he didn't do it. In jail they have this rape class you can take if you're convicted of that sort of crime, and he won't take it.

"Wes said he would die for me. I mean, that's probably what every man says and I just . . . I don't know . . . I like how he talks. I like how he acts. I just . . . He just attracted me. I thought it was kinda crazy.

"My friends were like 'That man has got six to nine years left in jail. You're gonna wait for him? You've never been with him before! You never had a relationship with him before! You don't even know what it's like to live with the man!'

"I said, 'I know . . . but I love him. . . .' It'll work out. We're meant for each other."

Jessica visited Wes regularly, taking three-year-old Ezakeil with her.

"When you go to visit—every jail is different," Jessica explained, "but at the prison Wes is in right now, you have to wait in this long line to give your paperwork to the people. You have to give your license and your birth certificate to prove who you are. Then you go into another room, where the lockers are, and you put all your valuables in the lockers. Then you wait until they call who you're going to see and you stand up and they search you. They feel your body to see if you have anything on you, and they ask you to stick out your tongue, take off your shoes, take off your belt, unroll your pants, and undo your hair—you can't have anything in your hair and you can't wear any jewelry. You go through a metal detector. You have to get buzzed into the visiting area through two doors, and once you get into the room you have to give your paperwork to the officers—there's like six of them bad boys!

"The chairs are lined up facing toward you, so you pick a chair and you wait another fifteen minutes and then your visitor comes out. You can stand up and hug and kiss at first, for the initial greeting, then when you sit down you have to sit knee to knee. There's a lot of people visiting and there's like six or seven guards and they just go up and down the rows and make sure you're knee to knee. You can't lean over. That's against the rules. If you do it twice, they'll terminate your visit. That's pretty much how the visit is, and it can last three or four hours.

"When Ezakeil visits Wes, he says, 'We're going to the big one?' He's used to seeing his dad in the little one. At Wes's prison, they have a playroom. Ezakeil and the other kids have a designated person in there that watches them. The guards search the kids. They have them stand with their hands wide open. They go around them with the handheld metal detector. If the kids have their cuffs rolled up, they'll undo the cuffs. Sometimes they'll check the babies' diapers. So they do pretty much the same search on the little kids as they do for us."

Because of the distance and her busy schedule, Jessica didn't visit Wes more than once a month. However, the two maintained a constant correspondence via letters and phone calls. Jessica regarded Wes as her boyfriend, and for more than a year she didn't date anyone else, convinced they would end up living together as soon as he got out.

"I love him to death," Jessica said, lost in reverie. "He calls me his queen and he's my king."

Wes told Jessica he would give her a little girl as soon as he got out of jail. The obvious irony, as Jessica's friends were quick to point out, was that iron bars protected her from actually having anything even remotely resembling a real relationship. The distance allowed Jessica to inhabit a safe, idealized fantasy world, where violent, dangerous predators were magically transformed into gentle, charming, valiant kings. Carrying on this rigidly regulated relationship with Wes under the watchful eye of prison guards who monitored their every move gave Jessica an illusion of power and control over the romance and allowed her to hold on to the hope that love could heal the legacy of violence that, in her mind, was inextricably connected to sex—it allowed her to be in a romantic relationship that had firm boundaries and could not, by its very nature, involve a sexual component.

The fairy tale that Jessica had concocted didn't last. Wes became verbally abusive and started arguments with Jessica during visits and phone calls. Determined to exert power and control, Wes told Jessica that he didn't want her going out with her friends and that he didn't want her having any friends over to the apartment. He started referring to himself as her "husband" and kept asking her to marry him in jail.

Jessica managed to keep the relationship a secret from her dad until one evening Robert recognized the sketches she had posted on the walls of her apartment—they were prison drawings. Jessica told him that her friend, Wes, had paid other guys in prison to draw these pictures for her. Robert shivered, eerily reminded of the drawings of

Care Bears he used to lovingly make for his daughter when he was in jail. Jessica had saved all of Wes's letters and had propped up her favorites on the television stand. When his daughter wasn't looking, Robert stuffed some of the letters underneath his shirt and smuggled them home. A few days later he managed to steal a few more letters. By the time Jessica caught him red-handed, he had managed to skim through most of the correspondence and was in a deep panic.

The sinister letters Wes wrote to Jessica were full of romance, promises, sweet talk, manipulation, and commands. Within months, Wes had convinced Jessica to assume power of attorney for him and to open a joint bank account in both their names. Even from the confines of his cell, he managed to control Jessica, telling her what errands to run for him, what letters to type on his behalf, and whom to see. Jessica did whatever he told her to do, including filing his medical and legal records in her apartment.

Robert asked Jessica if she was naive enough to think that she was the only girl Wes was brainwashing and manipulating. Jessica refused to accept this interpretation of her relationship with Wes and continued her regular visits and phone calls. Deeply alarmed and worried, Robert begged Jessica to cut all ties to Wes, for the sake of her son. For months his pleas fell upon deaf ears.

The situation exploded when Wes wrote to Robert—a letter that opened with insults and ended threateningly with Wes demanding Jessica's hand in marriage.

"Over my dead body," Robert told his daughter.

Doris sat down with Jessica and told her in no uncertain terms that she wanted her to break up with Wes immediately. Then she dared ask her daughter a pressing question that had been on her mind for years.

"What do you have against white guys?" she inquired.

"I've just never dated a white guy before," said Jessica. "I'm not objecting to them. I mean, if I find the right white man, so be it, but I'm more attracted to black men. God knows why, but I just am attracted to the bad ones that are in jail, who don't know how to work. It is so weird, but I always do it. I like rough guys. I don't know why."

Robert became more and more hysterical about Jessica's relationship with Wes. He interrogated Jessica and expressed his disapproval, certain that her relationship with Wes would lead to disaster. Robert knew his daughter was an adult, and although he feared losing her by interfering in her personal life, he could not remain on the sidelines and watch his precious daughter being subjected to a life full of pain, trauma, and abuse—a life he was all too familiar with.

"My dad said that if I kept having a relationship with Wes, I was gonna be pregnant and barefoot as soon as he got out of prison. He said that I'd be poor forever and that I'd have eight kids and that Wes would beat me. And he said that I'd never have Christmas because Wes believes in the Muslim faith."

Robert and Jessica had screaming matches that often pushed their relationship to its breaking point before ending in tears and reconciliation. Finally, Jessica began to see that beneath her father's rage was deep, genuine love and concern for her and Ezakeil. Robert's emotional demonstration of his love and his assertion of paternal protective instincts gave Jessica the strength and conviction to end her relationship with Wes. Jessica's phone rang for weeks as Wes repeatedly called her collect from jail, eager to win her back. Jessica refused to accept his calls and stopped responding to his letters.

"The last letter I got was an angry letter," she reported. "Wes is mad at me because I broke up with him. He wrote, 'See you in 2006! I'm gonna cause you even more pain than you caused me.' "

Jessica's mother shook her head when Wes's name came up. She had seen all of Wes's letters posted around Jessica's apartment, and there was no doubt in her mind that he was dangerous. Though she was relieved that the relationship had ended, she still worried about Jessica and was critical of the decisions her daughter had made.

"Jessica's life is very hard because of having Ez," observed Doris, "and, you know, if she hadn't had him, she probably wouldn't even be around here. She was talking about going to college down in Georgia, where her aunt lives. I know Jess doesn't want to stay in this area, so I'm hoping she'll be done with school and have a good job, making good money by the time Wes gets out of prison. I'm really hoping she'll be far away from this area before there's any chance of him getting out."

Doris complained that "Jessica just makes choices that make her life so much harder than it needs to be. I mean, look at her, she's not even twenty-two years old and she's got a kid who's nearly four, and she's working three jobs and trying to get through nursing school. She's got a car that's falling apart around her ears, and that alone is hard enough, and then she keeps letting these men in her life that add even more stress to it."

When Dwayne got out of jail, he began seeing Ezakeil from time to time. Although he and Jessica didn't get back together, Dwayne felt he had a right to enter her apartment whenever he pleased, and Jessica didn't feel it was necessary to get a restraining order.

"I'm his baby's momma," she said in a resigned effort to explain their renewed contact. One day Jessica refused to give Dwayne the keys to her car. He demanded that she drive him to the store.

"Dwayne threw a fit," said Jessica. "He went ballistic with Ezakeil right in front of him. He smashed a glass against the wall and cut himself. He got blood everywhere, blood all over my nice couch and blood all over my nice rug. The glass went everywhere. I'm still finding glass to this day underneath the couch and underneath the cushions. And then Dwayne kicked in my front door. It's still broken. He's just ridiculous. He's got some serious malfunctions."

Soon after that incident, Jessica's father gave Ezakeil a radio as a gift. At nearly four years of age, the little boy was articulate, sensitive, and perceptive. He told his grandfather that he could listen to the radio at the art studio but that he didn't want to take it home. He was terrified that his daddy would come over and break it.

The relationship between Ezakeil and Dwayne continued to be problematic. Jessica had wanted her son to have his father involved in his life, but she began to see that it just wasn't going to work out—she began to accept that Dwayne's presence hurt rather than helped Ezakeil. He routinely taunted the little boy, calling him a punk and a sissy.

"Ez can ride a bike without training wheels," said Jessica. "My dad taught him how. He does wheelies and everything, and he wanted to show his dad. So Dwayne walks outside and looks for two seconds and then walks back in the house. Ezakeil yelled for him to come back, and Dwayne was, like, 'Uh, hold on, Ezakeil, um . . . uh . . . I seen you, man, I seen you.'

"I said, 'Dwayne, you're ridiculous! Ezakeil is proud of himself that he learned to ride a bike. Why can't you be, like, 'Ezakeil, that is so good, I am so proud of you'? That makes a person feel good. . . . I don't think Dwayne ever had that.

"Dwayne just makes me sick about the things he does," Jessica continued. "Like, he cannot get a job. He's got four kids and don't take care of one of them. I never filed for child support myself because I just—I'm too nice. I just didn't, so welfare had to do it. I mean, thank God they did. I mean, how can someone like Dwayne have four children and not even give a damn? I had to change my whole life around for one child, and he hasn't changed anything for four!

"I just can't stand Dwayne. I let him get away with everything, but I've had about enough. I've said it about a thousand times that I've had enough with him, but this time I really and truly have had enough. I will see him in court. If he doesn't get a job, he goes to jail, and if he tries to run away and doesn't check in with his probation officer, they'll issue a warrant and if they find him, they'll arrest him for child support."

Jessica was particularly concerned about getting her son's father to start paying child support because she would soon no longer be eligible for federal assistance under the terms of the 1996 welfare reform bill, which had replaced AFDC with TANF, restricting people to five years maximum on welfare.

"I got on welfare before I got into college," Jessica explained, "and the RN program is a four-year program when you add up all the prerequisites—English, math, science, sociology, psychology—so I'm not gonna make the whole four years on welfare. I had to take some summer months off from welfare so that I could work and then add the welfare time onto my school months. Right now, I'm taking a semester off and working three jobs so that I can save up money so that it will all work out.

"When I'm in school I want to be able to be dedicated to school and to only have to work a couple of days a week. When I go back next semester, my program is going to be very intensive; three days a week you have in-class studying, where they teach you about medications and about everything you need to know about being an RN. The other two days you go into a hospital and you take care of patients for the day and report back to the RN on how the patients are doing. You have to write in a journal and do all kinds of paperwork.

"Right now, I'm a certified nursing assistant and I work at an agency where they tell you what nursing home to go to. When I have elderly clients, I go to their homes and get them ready for the day. I get them in the shower, make breakfast, and clean their houses. I make sure everything is neat and tidy so that they don't trip on anything. I also work at a nursing home as an activities assistant.

"I will finish school. I will become a registered nurse. There's no doubt about that. I will get a car that doesn't need its door held closed with a bungee cord, and I'll have a nice house someday. As for romance—I don't know. I'm gonna try to find a man that will treat me nice and give me something in return for what I give.

"Ezakeil will be starting school in September. When I brought him in, the teachers were just amazed because he is so intelligent. It's amazing. I mean, he's tiny, really small for his age, but I always encourage him to do everything. He gets along with other kids really well. No matter if they're older, younger, girls, boys—he makes friends wherever we go. I really encourage him to do that because you have to be able to socialize with all different people of all different races."

Ezakeil loved listening to music. Rap was his favorite. Jessica was astounded that her four-year-old knew almost every word of most Eminem songs that played on the radio.

One morning while Jessica was driving Ezakeil to school, her cell phone rang. There was bad news. Dwayne had been arrested again in relation to a shooting incident that had occurred the night before. Jessica turned the radio down. Ezakeil turned it back up. Jessica turned it off.

"Daddy's in big trouble," she said. Ez didn't say a word. He just stared out the window at the rows of worn houses. His faith in his father had run out a long time ago. Nothing his mother said surprised him.

A few days later the story of Dwayne's arrest appeared in the local newspaper. Dwayne had gone to a man's house after midnight. The two had gotten into a drug-related argument. Worried about being robbed and fearing for his life, the man had fired shots at Dwayne, apparently in self-defense. With Dwayne momentarily distracted, the man had then fled from his own apartment. He sought refuge at the home of Sheri's mother, Pat, who was known to be heavily involved in the neighborhood drug scene.

Dwayne pursued the man to Pat's house and bashed a hole right through the front door with his head. Pat hid in a closet, terrified. Dwayne pointed a handgun through the hole in the door, but before he could fire, the man inside Pat's apartment fired at him. The stray bullet hit the door. Dwayne ran away but then returned to Pat's house a few hours later, threatening to kill the man if he found him. He was promptly arrested.

The assistant district attorney asked that a high amount of bail be set for Dwayne "because he has a criminal record that includes six convictions for assault and battery, as well as threatening to commit a crime, operating a motor vehicle to endanger, and operating a motor vehicle after his license has been revoked. . . . His New York state record also includes using a different last name."

Dwayne was charged with two counts of armed home invasion, carrying a firearm without a license, and attempting to break and enter in the nighttime with the intent to commit a felony. Bail was set at $100,000. Jessica expected that her son's father would be put away for a long time. Her little boy might be a man by the time his father got out of jail. If the sentence wasn't that long, Jessica had no doubt that the next one would be. Back at the Wilson projects, Jessica watched Ezakeil playing animatedly with his toy cars. She walked over and pulled him toward her in a gentle, firm, protective embrace.

"Wanna go outside?" she asked him. He nodded. Jessica pulled a hat over her son's ears. As the sun lingered overhead, they played together in the last of the dying autumn leaves.

When Jessica's stepfather, Bill, got out of jail, he moved back into the house where he and Doris had raised the girls. The once

noisy rooms were now silent. No arguing voices, no giggling teenagers, no loud rap music, no crying infants. It was just Bill, a beer
in one hand and a cigarette in the other, screening calls to avoid the
creditors who kept harassing him.

"After my mother passes, I'm gonna sell this mausoleum," he said.
"My ass is going to Belize, because I don't know anyone there. . . . No
one knows me. . . . I know there are places to skydive and a warm
ocean and I know I can turn a dollar down there. God knows I'm a
handy kinda guy . . . just gotta get the hell out of here. Pittsfield leaves
nothing to offer, and if the girls were smart, they'd get the hell out of
here, too."

"I am not living in Pittsfield all my life," Jessica vowed. "When
I get my RN, I am not staying here. Ezakeil will not grow up in this

town. There's nothing here. You get stuck. There's nowhere to go. You go to freakin' Berkshire Community College, so what? No, no, no. We're leaving. . . .

"My son—he's gonna be something special. He is something special. He amazes me every day. He's the best thing I could have ever wished for. He is precious."

chapter eight

COMMUNITY

"I wish I could think of you as happier, less lonely. . . . Things are sure to change for you, by and by."

"Things don't change at North Dormer: people just get used to them."

The answer seemed to break up the order of his prearranged consolations, and he sat looking at her uncertainly. Then he said, with his sweet smile: "That's not true of you. It can't be."

The smile was like a knife-thrust through her heart: everything in her began to tremble and break loose. She felt her tears run over, and stood up.

"Well, good-bye," she said.

She was aware of his taking her hand, and of feeling that his touch was lifeless.

—Edith Wharton, Summer

TEEN MOTHERS WERE ON TINA PACKER'S MIND. HER husband, Dennis Krausnik, was adapting Edith Wharton's novel *Summer* for the stage, and during their frequent conversations about the book, Tina found herself marveling at just how contemporary the book's themes remained despite the passage of more than eighty years since its publication back in 1917. Tina knew that minutes from her home in Stockbridge, numerous unwed pregnant teenagers throughout Berkshire County shared the predicament of Wharton's tragic heroine, Charity Royall. She wondered how she could make a difference in their lives.

Sixty and still pulsing with the passion and exuberance of her British youth, Tina was dedicated to her role as artistic director of Shakespeare & Company, the theater group she had cofounded in 1978 with renowned voice teacher Kristin Linklater. Based in Lenox, Massachusetts, Shakespeare & Company was headquartered fifteen minutes from Pittsfield, on the grounds of Edith Wharton's former estate, The Mount. Tina had rescued this beautiful historic property from neglect after happening upon it by chance and discovering that the once-grand mansion had fallen into dilapidated disrepair.

Over the years, as Shakespeare & Company established strong roots in Berkshire County, an outdoor main stage was constructed near the imposing mansion. Every year the company presented two full seasons of plays by a variety of authors, focusing on but not limited to their two natural favorites, Shakespeare and Edith Wharton. Wharton's former stables were converted into theater space, and her parlor became the setting for more intimate productions. Many student performances took place at a lovely Greek theater hidden in a clearing sheltered by the woods bordering the property.

The breadth of Shakespeare & Company's activities quickly expanded far beyond professional performances, into the realm of educational outreach and teacher training. For more than two decades, Tina Packer, Dennis Krausnik, and the company's directors of education, Kevin Coleman and Mary Hartman, have remained steadfast in their devotion to administering the educational outreach program that has brought Shakespeare to more than one hundred public elementary, middle, and high schools.

"Right now we're working in ten high schools, four middle schools, and four elementary schools," said Tina. "We also work in the juvenile justice system, and the kids can choose: they can either do community service if they've done something which is against the law or they can come to us. The children who are in foster care, mostly because their parents are drug addicts and have neglected them or deserted them, come to us and we act out the Shakespeare plays with them using Shakespearean language, but sometimes we actually go to their life stories as well. The themes in Shakespeare often help inspire kids to articulate things that they're thinking and feeling but haven't previously had the words to say."

Teaching the kids to read and act Shakespeare entailed shepherding them through a process of socialization, collaboration, and self-exploration. Researchers from Harvard's Project Zero evaluated the effectiveness of Shakespeare & Company's educational outreach program and gave it rave reviews, concluding that mentors with experience as actors and directors nurtured the imagination, self-awareness, confidence, communication skills, judgment, knowledge base, intellectual curiosity, and emotional growth of the students who participated.

In support of its educational outreach efforts, Shakespeare & Company has been awarded many prestigious grants, including several from the GE Fund totaling more than $600,000. The philanthropic foundation of the General Electric Company "invests in improving educational quality and access, and in strengthening community organizations in GE communities around the world." One of the foundation's programs aims to "double the rate of college attendance in low-income, inner city schools in GE communities." It is precisely this kind of partnership between a mammoth corporation and a dynamic artistic organization that promotes a sense of hope, providing joy, innovation, the satisfaction of accomplishment, and a valuable opportunity for thousands of children, all very much in keeping with the spirit of GE's new slogan, "Imagination at Work."

"When kids are being creative, they're much more capable of dealing with the problems of their life, rather than just receiving the blows of fortune," explained Tina. "They are able to think creatively about how they can change their circumstances, and able to think creatively about how it feels to interact with other people and make a difference. The plays are an art form that spiritually transports the kids to another place and gives them a bigger palette to work with other than just 'I hate school' or 'I hate my family.' Through performing these plays, kids can actually acquire the tools to think in a bigger way about what's going on, and that to me is a godsend, it's a lifeline."

In March 1999 Tina contacted Helen Berube, the director of the Teen Parent Program in Pittsfield, and asked if she would be interested in hosting a Shakespeare & Company residency. Helen responded with hesitation, explaining to Tina that the teen mothers were very secretive and reticent and very stressed-out and overburdened with responsibilities. She wasn't sure that they would be interested in or, for that matter, willing to perform Shakespeare.

Tina suggested a writing workshop that incorporated some theater training as an alternative to the time-intensive process of mounting a full-scale student production. She explained that her theater company was doing a production of Edith Wharton's *Summer,* which dealt with the story of a teenager in Berkshire County who got pregnant, and that the workshops she envisioned would meet one hour a week for a period of six weeks during school hours, using the text of Wharton's novel to inspire writing, reading, and discussion, perhaps culminating in a staged reading. The director agreed to Tina's proposal, and tentative dates for the workshop were set.

Tina then approached her close friend psychologist Carol Gilligan, who lived twenty minutes from Pittsfield, in West Stockbridge. Renowned for her seminal writing about adolescent girls, she was, in Tina's mind, the perfect person to lead the seminars. Over the course of three years, Carol had conducted workshops with girls ages nine through eleven as part of a Harvard research project called Strengthening Healthy Resistance and Courage in Girls. Accompanied by

Normi Noel, a Linklater voice teacher and theater director, and by Annie Rogers, a colleague from Harvard, Carol had worked within the public school system in the Boston metropolitan area. Using voice exercises, writing exercises, and improvisational theater games, they had developed a method of working to empower young girls.

Carol and her colleagues sought to help each girl they worked with to establish a stronger, more active, articulate presence in her own life. The alternative they had observed and were trying to counter was the adolescent girl's retreat into passivity, repression, dissociation, and silence. Their work with the girls in Boston focused on strengthening three different levels of relationships: the girls' relationships to one another, which involved their sharing thoughts and feelings with a group, resulting in the realization that they were rarely isolated or alone when it came to their perceptions and experiences; the girls' relationships to nonjudgmental mentors who acted as guides and facilitators along their paths of self-discovery, without limiting or constraining them to conventionally accepted thoughts, behaviors, or emotions; and finally, the girls' relationships to the community at large, a connection that was established at the end of the workshop, through a publicly staged reading of the girls' own writing.

When Tina asked Carol and Normi if they would adapt their approach to fit the special needs of students at the Teen Parent Program in Pittsfield, they enthusiastically agreed. Their workshops with the teen mothers in Pittsfield were funded in part by a grant to prevent repeat pregnancies, which represent more than 20 percent of teen births. One of the biggest risks for teen pregnancy is a previous pregnancy. Almost one out of every three young women whose first birth occurs before the age of seventeen has a second child within twenty-four months. Thus, the population of teen mothers with one child is a group for whom successful intervention can be key in preventing the compounded economic and social risks that are intensified by having two children at such a young age.

Carol and Normi's objectives included enhancing the teen mothers' access to their own voices and improving their grasp of language as a means of self-expression so that when it came time for them to communicate their needs for respect and protection within a relationship, they would be more likely to have the confidence and conviction to assert themselves, to stand up for what they valued, and to be present in an active, influential way, shaping their destiny instead of just passively letting events unfold.

As soon as Carol and Normi started working with the teen mothers, they realized that many of these girls had been wounded by society's negative reaction to their predicament and deeply affected by the labels and stereotypes that defined them as "bad girls" solely on the basis of their being young, visibly pregnant out of wedlock, and determined to keep their babies. When Carol read parts of Edith Wharton's novel *Summer* aloud, she made a point of stressing that a prominent, prolific American author had written an entire novel about a girl in their situation, demonstrating that empathy and compassion were indeed possible responses.

"Charity Royall wasn't just condemned and humiliated," said Carol. "Wharton described her as a girl with a lot of integrity. My hope was that reading the book would give the girls a sense that language, culture, and art were capable of holding complicated truths, and would help them to understand that not everything needed to be defined in black-and-white terms as either 'good' or 'bad.' "

The workshops also aimed at helping the teen mothers feel more connected to the community by including them in cultural events. In addition to Shakespeare & Company's *Summer,* the Berkshire Opera Company was presenting its own production of Wharton's novel. Affiliated with both organizations, Carol made arrangements to reserve some complimentary tickets for the teen mothers. However, when the staged reading of the teen mothers' writing was scheduled and publicized, some people in the community voiced their opposition to the prospect of this particular group performing.

"Initially," recalled Carol, "when we announced that we were going to involve the girls in the community celebration of Wharton's novel *Summer,* the response of some people was 'You can't do this. The community doesn't want to see these girls.' I remember reading letters that criticized us for giving these girls special attention, and more or less implied that instead of being put onstage as if they were heroes, these teen mothers should be covered with shame and hidden from sight as if they didn't exist.

"If teen mothers get that message from society, their voices recede and they feel that they have nothing to say and that they're not of value," said Carol. "To encourage the voice that in fact would work against teen pregnancy, you have to first start by creating a place or an atmosphere that invites their voices. You have to want to hear what they have to say."

Too young to vote, most teenage girls have no political voice, and when it comes to important debates about the very circumstances that define their lives, to a large extent they remain silent and excluded. Whenever teen parenthood is filtered through the media, so often the national spotlight remains fixed on the moral and theoretical battles waged between liberals and conservatives. Each side comes to the table armed with competing agendas regarding sex education, contraception, abortion, family values, and the relationship between church and state. In contrast, most pregnant and parenting teens remain sequestered on the fringes of society, represented as statistics, deprived of a forum to refute those who stereotype them, positioned helplessly as scapegoats, and powerless to contradict those who have written them off as ignorant, irresponsible youngsters with doomed futures.

"Prior to Carol and Normi's workshops using Edith Wharton's *Summer,* we had never ever done a program specifically for young girls who were in the predicament of teen pregnancy or motherhood," explained Tina Packer, "but I actually think theater is one of the ways out of a predicament like that, because it entails articulating what you think and feel and presenting yourself and being able to say to a large group of people what you think is going on. It strengthens your voice, and the voice is the most important thing. One of the primary functions of theater is to articulate what is not being said within a society. Within a community, if you don't hear what teenagers are saying and if they sense they are not being heard, it's difficult to make progress in getting them out of that cycle."

Reflecting on her work with the teen mothers, Carol said, "That very brief experience in the Berkshires with our very short program suggests that a program that is coherent and focused on voice and relationships, and that uses the arts to give girls a vehicle for discovering what in fact they think and feel, can help girls to be present with one another in an honest way and can help them to see themselves as connected with the world, rather than shunned by the world. I think that integrating those particular concepts into a larger teen pregnancy program would be another step forward for prevention. What I've found in all my work with girls is that they are constantly underestimated."

Six weeks after beginning the writing workshop, Jessica, Liz, Colleen, Sheri, and Amy sat on chairs staggered along the stage of Shakespeare & Company's marvelously austere, naturalistic Greek theater. As the warm June sun danced upon the slim, gnarled branches of the trees, creating soft shadows, each teen mother read her own writing out loud to an attentive audience composed of Shayla and other classmates from the Teen Parent Program, as well as friends, teachers, affiliates of Shakespeare & Company, and a few parents. Carol Gilligan and Normi Noel beamed with pride as each teen mother read her own writing aloud in a clear, confident voice.

"What I've learned from my work with these girls," said Normi, "is that with whomever it is you are mentoring, you better know how to show up yourself, and you better be able to find your own humility in that position because it requires you to have the courage to stand openly with another person and to be in the presence of the currents of truth that they are looking for.

"I once saw a street sign pasted up on a window of an abandoned building," Normi recalled. "It said, 'The greatest teachers of all are ice cubes.' What I interpreted that to mean is that as a teacher, you need to be able to melt in the water, you need to be able to disappear. You're with the kids, and then in the end you need to gracefully let go of that position when you have supplied something for them that other people have done for you, which is simply being there and listening."

————

A week after their staged reading, several of the teen mothers attended Shakespeare & Company's production of *Summer*. As the houselights dimmed and the curtain lifted, they sat back and watched, captivated, as Charity Royall's destiny played itself out right before their eyes. The story was one that by then they knew well:

Charity Royall hates her life, has a tense relationship with her foster father, and dreams of escaping North Dormer. She pins her hopes on a handsome young architect from the city who visits the library where she works to do research on old houses in the area. Before long, Charity and this seductive stranger are romantically entangled. After a few months of reckless passion and exquisite pleasure, Charity discovers that she is pregnant. Before she even has a chance to share this news with her lover, she learns of his grievous betrayal. Too proud, too heartbroken, and too bewildered to confide in anyone, Charity decides to hide her pregnancy while she explores her options. Her own parents are not around to advise her. Her biological father is in jail for murder, and she has long been estranged from her mother, an impoverished alcoholic and former prostitute who lives in a decrepit shantytown on the peak of a foreboding mountain.

Removed from her mother's home at age four, Charity has been raised by her foster father, Mr. Royall. After the premature death of his wife, Royall disgusts Charity with his drunken binges and his inappropriate sexual advances. There is no one Charity trusts, no one she feels she can turn to for guidance. She feels totally alone in the world. Determined to keep her pregnancy a secret, she struggles for months, until the changes in her body begin to make the truth visible. At that point, she is forced to make a difficult decision about her destiny and the future of her unborn child.

When *Summer* was first published, it was viewed as scandalous and incendiary. People were taken aback by Charity's raw eroticism and disgusted by the incestuous undertones of her relationship with her foster father. Readers were stunned that Edith Wharton, a woman so cushioned by wealth all her life, had dared step away from familiar terrain to take a hard, critical, unflinching look at the sharp divisions between social classes, zeroing in on the darkest of subject matter: hopelessness, despair, crime, alcoholism, prostitution, incest, abortion, absent parenting, and premarital sex.

In the novel, Edith Wharton contrasts the beautiful freedom of nature and the transcendence of unbridled passion with the unrelenting constraints of Charity's life in an oppressive, stifling small town, spiraling downward, bereft of hope and opportunity. The profound inequality inherent to American society is personified by Charity and her rival for her lover's affections, the fabulously wealthy, elegant, refined, city-born-and-bred, blond-haired, blue-eyed Annabel Balch.

Incisive and unrelenting, Edith Wharton's social conscience was ahead of its time and remains to this day at the center of her indelible legacy. Perhaps most notable is Wharton's blatant refusal to whitewash her perceptions of what went on "behind the paintless wooden house-fronts of the long village street or in the isolated farm-houses on the neighboring hills."

In her memoir, *A Backward Glance,* Wharton offered the following response to critics of her stark, brutal realism:

> *Summer* . . . was received with indignant denial by many re-
> viewers and readers; not the least vociferous were the New
> Englanders who had for years sought the reflection of local

life in the rose-and-lavender pages of their favourite author-
esses—and had forgotten to look into Hawthorne's.

"Here in Pittsfield, we're heavily involved in dealing with sexual
abuse," said Captain Patrick Barry, speaking from a dimly lit room at
the police station where old records were stored. "One of our day
detectives handles sex crimes and he focuses almost exclusively on
child abuse sex cases. The Department of Social Services reports
information to the district attorney's office and then it comes to us.
We also get some reports directly in cases where a child may disclose
something to the other parent or a friend or relative or a teacher or
a doctor. There are certain mandated reporters. Under the law they
have to report suspected abuse. Priests, by the way, were never mandated but now they will be after that scandal."

In a discussion of the results of the ACE (Adverse Childhood
Experience) study, Dr. Felitti, Dr. Anda, and their colleagues raised
several questions, including the issue of "whether sexual abuse during
childhood is the primary destructive force or simply a dramatic
marker for a severely dysfunctional family." Statistics show that a
significant number of teen mothers such as Liz have painful histories
indelibly marked by sexual trauma. In July 1998 the *Journal of the
American Medical Association* published a review of several of the most
conclusive research studies to date regarding the significant links between sexual abuse and teen pregnancy:

Child and adolescent sexual abuse is a risk factor for teen
pregnancy on two levels. First, sexual abuse is a common

antecedent of adolescent pregnancy, with up to 66% of pregnant teens reporting histories of abuse. Conversely, sexually abused adolescent girls are significantly more likely to have been pregnant than teens without abuse histories. A history of sexual abuse has been linked to high-risk behaviors that may account for increased risk of early unplanned pregnancy, including young age at initiation of sexual intercourse, failure to use contraception, prostitution, engagement in relationships involving physical assault, and abuse of alcohol and other drugs. Moreover, girls with histories of sexual abuse have been found to have a greater desire to conceive and increased concerns about infertility than girls without abuse histories.

At age eight, Liz found a way to tell the story of her molestation to a judge, but how many young girls and teenagers remain silent, repressing, suffering, and disassociating as the abuse goes on, sometimes for years, as it did in the traumatic case of Jessica's grandparents and their children? How many doctors neglect to ask pregnant teenagers if they have ever been sexually abused? Every day in this country, how many sex education classes are taught in which the phrase *sexual abuse* is never even mentioned? Can sex education classes that promote "abstinence only" give teenagers and preteens the knowledge, comfort level, and negotiation skills to defend themselves against molestation, incest, date rape, and sex described as "voluntary but not really wanted"?

For years a cloak of silence, denial, and discomfort has covered sexual abuse in medical and educational settings and within American society at large, preventing the public from clearly seeing key factors that are inextricably entwined with the roots of teen pregnancy. The scandal within the Catholic Church has opened up a dialogue about sexual abuse, but perhaps even more difficult for society to stomach is the thought of sexual abuse occurring with alarming frequency within the four walls of the family home. Without widespread acknowledgment of the prevalence of childhood sexual abuse in all its forms and a strategy to address this particular risk factor, plans for significantly reducing teen pregnancy remain incomplete, like a puzzle missing a crucial, central piece.

After years of experience counseling teen mothers, Joann Oliver accepted the position of clinical coordinator at Berkshire County Kids' Place, a child-advocacy center in Pittsfield that specializes in treating children who have disclosed sexual abuse. Within the comfortable, homelike environment of Kids' Place, young victims of sexual abuse receive services from a multidisciplinary team that includes trained clinicians, police officers and detectives, the district attorney's office, and pediatricians. Kids' Place coordinates and unites these separate organizations so that they can act as a team to represent the best interests of each child.

In her mid-thirties and a mother of two, Joann is passionately committed to counseling and mentoring the children who are referred to her. She estimates that approximately one hundred new sexual-abuse cases are referred for treatment every year. The vast majority of the children and adolescents are residents of Pittsfield.

Although Joann counsels some teenagers and small children, most of her clients are between the ages of eight and eleven. In addition to all the new referrals, there are roughly 175 children in ongoing treatment for traumas such as sexual abuse, physical abuse, and witnessing domestic violence.

"I don't think that once the damage occurs, that's it," said Joann. "I think education is a big part of recovery. I think if the child has a good support system, that's very important. If there's just one person in their life who believes their account of the abuse and takes them seriously, that can be very helpful."

One of the biggest challenges Joann faces in her job is explaining the family dynamics within which sexual abuse occurs. Often these dynamics are either not well known or are misunderstood.

"We're often asked by the police or the D.A.'s office, 'Why didn't this kid tell, if the abuse has been going on for five years?' I have to explain that maybe a young girl didn't disclose because the perpetrator said that her family would fall apart and her mother would kick her out. And, in fact, when she does tell, that's exactly what happens."

Joann is familiar with the varying degrees of household dysfunction and abuse described by Sheri, Nadine, Colleen, Shayla, Jessica, and Liz. In her line of work, she comes across similar stories every day.

"In households where there's sexual abuse and/or domestic violence, there are not good boundaries in place," Joann explained. "There's a lot of sexual innuendo and a lot of situations where boundaries just are not defined. If a young girl is in the bathroom taking a shower and her father or stepfather or brother comes in to go to the bathroom, even if they don't look at her, they are showing no regard for boundaries and no respect for her space.

"Then when these girls grow up and they end up in a relationship where the other person is possessive and likes to know where they're going and what they're doing all the time, they actually see that as loving and caring rather than as controlling. They often think, 'Oh, this person cares so much about me. He doesn't want me to see my friends, he only wants me to be with him.' I don't even think these young women see their bodies as their own. They find love by physical contact and they end up in these relationships where they're not able to say, 'Stop!' or, 'We need to use protection!' "

Over the years, Joann has closely observed and documented the symptoms exhibited by teenagers who have been sexually abused. Suffering immensely, these troubled adolescents often engaged in high-risk, self-destructive behaviors such as self-cutting, drug use, excessive drinking, promiscuity, and running away. As Joann astutely pointed out, these symptoms were identical to the high-risk behaviors that resulted in their getting into situations in which they faced a huge risk of getting pregnant. When Liz ran away at thirteen to escape her abusive, promiscuous mother and the host of boyfriends drifting in and out of the family home, she subsequently sought food and shelter in the apartments of adult men who were able to convince her that they "loved" her.

Joann has seen numerous cases like Nadine's, in which adolescents' accounts of intolerable home situations were contradicted by their parents and simply not believed by the Department of Social Services or the police, resulting in the teenagers being shuttled from one foster home to another in between repetitious stints in their original malignant home environments.

"A lot of the struggles we have with the different professions and agencies we have to work with relate to the problem that sometimes the high-risk self-destructive behaviors ruin the girl's credibility," explained Joann, "so then when she comes forward and says that she has been sexually abused, oftentimes a parent or family member may say, 'Well, she's always running away, or she's always lying to me. Now she's lying about this, too.' It's a double-edged sword because the very symptoms that are due to the sexual abuse often confuse people into thinking that the girl is not credible.

"Most of the time if a child or teen discloses and the mother does not support them or believe them, the chances of them recanting are pretty high," said Joann. "We've had a number of cases with teen girls where they've disclosed and the perpetrator has been the mother's boyfriend or their stepfather. What happens then is that the mother doesn't believe the girl partly because of those acting-out behaviors I spoke about earlier. So she's forced to make a decision to kick the father out or to put the child in foster care. Oftentimes the girl goes to foster care and the mom continues living with the perpetrator. In those situations, those girls are at a much higher risk for teen parenthood."

Compounding the problems that abused girls face in their own homes is a foster care system that is often extremely impersonal. Liz, Sheri, and Nadine reported being extremely unhappy with their foster home placements; yet instead of someone helping them adjust and find their way into a more stable situation, often anonymous workers within the bureaucratic system actualized the girls' fears of upheaval and transience by arbitrarily returning them to their original home environments and then reassigning them to a new foster home when trouble inevitably arose again. None of these girls ever had a sense that one mentor within the system was consistently concerned and looking out for them and making sure to place them in a supportive, nurturing foster home where they might thrive. Where they ended up just seemed to be the luck of the draw, reinforcing their sense that they had no control over their own lives.

Between 1995 and 2000, while Liz estimates that she was in and out of twelve foster homes, the number of children in America's foster care system doubled, from 250,000 to roughly 560,000. In November 2000 *Time* magazine ran a cover story titled "The Crisis of Foster Care." The article addressed several key factors that were responsible for the bureaucratic system's failure to ensure the welfare of the children it was supposed to protect. The list included poor, archaic recordkeeping (hardcover binders as opposed to a centralized national computer database), inadequate monitoring of individual cases (missed visits, bad decisions about placements), and a huge turnover of social workers (close to 70 percent in some states). One lawyer the journalists interviewed remarked dryly, "You can't even run a Burger King with a seventy percent turnover!"

At Kids' Place, Joann Oliver made sure she maintained a consistent, relatively long-term presence in the lives of the children she treated. Girls whom Joann had treated when they were nine were encouraged to stop in to see her as teenagers. She tried to maintain her connections with these kids and made it clear that if at any point in their lives they needed advice, guidance, or services, they could count on her being a phone call away. Joann realized that her steady, predictable presence in their lives was vital, particularly in cases where a girl's disclosure of sexual abuse had severely impaired her relationship with her mother and splintered her family, leaving her with few if any sympathetic, receptive elders to turn to.

"We've had situations where even though the case has gone to court and the stepfather has been found guilty and sentenced to jail for fifteen or twenty years, the mother still will not make reparations with the girl," said Joann. "That kind of mother-daughter relationship is really damaging to the young girl's development. Those teenagers are much more at risk of ending up in really bad relationships and becoming pregnant."

Joann frequently talked to teenage girls who believed that giving their mothers grandchildren might be the first step toward mending their fractured relationships. All too often, this was proven to be true, at least in the short term. Sheri and Liz both reconciled with their mothers temporarily during their pregnancies, and the arrival of Colleen's baby, Jonathan, did indeed bring joy and cohesion to a depressed household.

In addition to treating children who had disclosed sexual abuse, Joann treated boys and girls who had witnessed domestic violence. She found that when very young children witnessed their mothers being battered, it was as detrimental to them psychologically as if they themselves were the victims because at that age, they had not yet separated from their primary caretaker, so watching their mother being abused was just as damaging as it would be if the pain were inflicted directly upon them.

"There's a lot of research that has indicated that boys who have witnessed domestic violence are much more likely to become sexual perpetrators," said Joann. "The element in common seems to be power. When young sexual offenders perpetrate sexually, they feel powerful and don't have that feeling of helplessness that they had when they stood by and witnessed their mothers being battered."

The numerous arrests, prosecutions, and subsequent incarcerations of the fathers of Shayla's, Jessica's, Colleen's, and Nadine's babies on charges of assault and battery reflected the police department's hard-core approach to addressing the problem of domestic and dating violence, particularly in households where young children were living with young mothers. Some of these perpetrators, who had fathered children with one or more teen mothers, had reportedly witnessed their own mothers being battered at some point during their childhood. These were not isolated, unusual cases.

Domestic and dating violence among teenagers is a nightmare that America is slowly waking up to. According to estimates from the U.S. Centers for Disease Control and Prevention, 22 percent of high school students are victims of nonsexual dating violence, with girls slightly more likely to report being victims. Even more teens experience verbal or emotional abuse. A similarly disturbing statistic surfaced in an article published in the July 2001 issue of the *Journal of the American Medical Association* featuring a study led by Jay G. Silverman of Harvard University's School of Public Health. Silverman's research sample was composed of 4,163 students who attended public schools in the state of Massachusetts. More than 70 percent of the girls who participated in the study were white. Participants were asked if they'd ever been shoved, slapped, hit, or forced into any sexual activity, including rape, by a date. They were also asked about recent risky behavior. The results indicated that "one in five high school girls had been physically or sexually abused by a dating partner, significantly increasing their risk of drug abuse, suicide and other harmful behavior. Victimized girls were about eight to nine times more likely to have attempted suicide in the previous year and four to six times more likely to have ever been pregnant."

Colleen's and Nadine's brutal victimization during their pregnancies was sadly and alarmingly a common thread that connected their experience to those of other pregnant teenagers across the country. Violence expert James Makepeace explained that "because teenagers are lacking in the developmental maturity and self-control that ideally should accompany sexual intimacy, there is a greater risk that they will use violence to vent frustration, punish their partner, or in an attempt to terminate an unwanted pregnancy." A survey administered to pregnant adolescents in metropolitan areas yielded the following results: "Of the more than two hundred pregnant teens surveyed, twenty-six percent reported they were in a relationship with a male partner who was physically abusive. Of those females being abused, forty to sixty percent stated that the battering had either begun or escalated since discovery of the pregnancy. Even more alarming was the fact that sixty-five percent of those abused had not talked with anyone about the abuse, and no one had reported the abuse to the law enforcement agencies." The study concluded that "battering during teen pregnancy is potentially a major adolescent health problem, jeopardizing adolescent and infant health. Women abused during pregnancy are at greater risk for medical complications of pregnancy, delivery of low birth-weight babies and homicide."

As director of the Berkshire Violence Prevention Center in Pittsfield, Katrina Mattson-Brown chose to dedicate herself to teaching high school students. Whenever she guest-lectured health classes, her goal was to teach teenagers how to identify the components of abusive relationships, and to then explain why it was essential for them to get out of such situations. Limited by funding constraints, Katrina could spend only two days at each high school. She made the most of what little time she had.

Katrina devoted one day to gender identity. She led discussions that explored how kids felt about the ways in which the media, popular culture, and their own friends and families defined the roles and expectations for male and female behavior. Her perception was that as patterns of abusive relationships observed during childhood repeated themselves from one generation to the next, they were often characterized by heavy gender-stereotyping: women were more likely to assume the passive role of victim, and men were more likely to assume the active role of perpetrator.

Katrina observed that as many teenagers struggled to define themselves and sought status and popularity within their peer groups, they often experimented and role-played, trying on new "adult" identities, often going to extreme caricatures of masculine "macho" and feminine "submissive" behaviors in their efforts to conform to distorted, archaic gender stereotypes. Sometimes adolescents who felt the desperate need to boldly assert their masculinity or femininity resorted to using teen parenthood to bolster their efforts, assuming the generic roles of "mother" and "father" while searching for authority and self-esteem somewhere within the fragile narcissistic gran-diosity they felt when relating to a helpless, dependent child.

However, because developing a mature, integrated identity is by its very nature a long-term process entailing a period of psychological growth that stretches into young adulthood and often beyond, the expectation that teen parenthood could provide a shortcut to self-definition usually turned out to be a fleeting illusion that quickly soured into bitter disappointment. As in the case of C.J. and Shayla, the reality was that more often than not, the strain of teen parent-hood produced feelings of profound inferiority, particularly in the young fathers who found themselves incapable of meeting the needs of their girlfriends and children. Physical aggression was a last resort, a desperate attempt to assert power, enforce control, and prove one's masculinity.

"When we talk to teenagers about the different types of abuse," said Katrina, "one of the things we talk a lot about is sexual assault and rape and another kind of sexual violence—being pressured to have sex. With teen pregnancy, what sometimes happens is that the girls are in an abusive relationship and don't feel powerful enough to say no."

During her presentations Katrina always discussed the controver-sial issue of sex when a female is intoxicated. "We explain to the kids that if a girl is drunk, sex may be considered rape. We tell them that the law is quite clear that if someone is drunk, it's very ques-tionable as to whether or not they are capable of consenting. Most kids are pretty surprised about that. When they leave, they're asked to fill out evaluation forms and there's a section of fill-in-the-blanks. Almost all the boys and girls write: *One thing I didn't know before this course was . . . the law about rape and alcohol and consent.*"

In classrooms all over Berkshire County, Katrina ventured beyond the physical, concrete aspects of violence to address the more complex psychological characteristics of abusive relationships. Wherever she lectured, she brought along a large piece of white fabric on which the forlorn life-size outline of a person was traced. This "person" appeared completely empty and expressionless, devoid of any defining features and characteristics. Katrina hung this dull, lifeless, limp "person" up on the blackboard and wrote five haunting words above its head: "Could This Happen to Me?"

A few boys usually tittered nervously before silence descended upon the class and all eyes gravitated toward the front of the room where the empty "person" hung. When she was confident that she had captured everyone's attention, Katrina proceeded to hand out pads of Post-it notes in a rainbow of colors and asked each teenager to write down words that represented something about themselves and their lives that was very personal, very important, and very precious—something that they would never allow anyone to take away from them.

Pens scribbled and a few minutes later Katrina asked the students to share with the class what they had written. Some teenagers who had answered with the words "my family" explained that their parents and grandparents and siblings provided unconditional love, confidence, and positive reinforcement. Some who had written "being good at soccer" or "basketball" explained that they liked being part of a team and that they liked games and competitions because those events gave them something exciting to work toward and look forward to. Others who had written "doing well in school" said that getting good grades gave them hope and a sense of pride and accomplishment. Others wrote "friends" because they valued the support of their peers.

After listening to all the responses, Katrina asked the students to stick their Post-it notes on the "person," who was suddenly transformed from a blank, depressing canvas into a colorful, vibrant, multilayered figure adorned with all the words that described the things that were most precious and most important to the students. Katrina then began a discussion that centered on how the items the teenagers had written down and posted fed "the person's" self-esteem. Then using an interactive question-and-answer method that involved the kids' ideas and participation, Katrina proceeded to construct a story in which she demonstrated how an abuser could strip these positive attributes away from the "person."

"Your family doesn't like your boyfriend," Katrina said. "They think he treats you badly and they tell you to stop dating him. What do you do?" she asked.

"Keep dating him anyway," agreed a few girls, giggling.

"So the abuser has already created a wedge between you and your family," said Katrina, removing the fluorescent yellow Post-it upon which the words "my family" were written.

"Your boyfriend says that he loves you and that he's jealous of the time you spend with other people. He makes it clear that he wants you to spend all your free time with him and says that if you really loved him, you would. So you want to make him happy . . . What do you have to give up in order to do that?"

The classroom was quiet.

"Well, if you're spending all your free time with your boyfriend, how are you gonna keep up with your other friends? And what about soccer practice?"

Katrina removed the lime green Post-it notes upon which the words "my two best friends" and "soccer" were written. She proceeded with this line of thought until every single Post-it note—fluorescent yellow, lime green, orange, turquoise, and hot pink—had been removed, leaving the "person" blank and colorless.

"So what's left to fuel this 'person's' self-esteem?" Katrina asked before explaining that because "the person" had allowed the abuser to make her give up all the other sources of pride, accomplishment, companionship, and support in her life, she was now dependent on him for all those things, so it became that much harder to leave him, because the connection with her abuser was the only thing sustaining her. Now she would go to great lengths and tolerate more abuse in her repeated attempts to win back the love and approval of the abuser who had suddenly become the most important person in her life. Why? Because she had allowed the abuser to become the sole provider of her self-esteem, validation, and sense of identity, all of which she craved desperately and felt empty without.

"This is what it feels like to be trapped in addictive, abusive relationship," Katrina concluded, pointing to the blank, lifeless outline of a person hanging limply from the blackboard at the front of the classroom.

In another visually captivating classroom demonstration, Katrina drew a giant heart up on the blackboard. She asked the teenagers to identify things they felt were healthy in a relationship and things they felt were unhealthy. As each student named behaviors, situations, and feelings, Katrina wrote their words inside the perimeter of the heart. On the left side of the heart she wrote things that were positive and healthy, and she wrote things that were negative and unhealthy on the right side. She explained that abusive relationships don't always start out with violence, that at first there was usually a honeymoon period in which the couple fell in love and everything went smoothly. Then one day that honeymoon period was shattered by a seemingly spontaneous episode of physical or verbal abuse, followed by more romantic, loving moments. The problem was that over time the abuse often overshadowed the romantic, loving moments, yet the two still coexisted within the relationship, which made it all the more difficult to walk away.

"Most women stay with their abusers because they keep wishing and hoping and believing that things will go back to being great again," said Katrina, "but more often than not, once violence makes itself known, it doesn't just go away even though there are still some good times."

Like Shayla and Colleen, many teenagers tended to think of relationships as either good or bad, and it was hard for them to comprehend how a relationship could be good and bad at the same time. Within their relationships with the fathers of their babies, Colleen and Shayla defensively split off from the negatives, pushing the abuse out of their consciousness and denying its implications while romanticizing and magnifying the small embers of love they stoked as they clung to their increasingly unrealistic hopes that their boyfriends would morph into the idealized men they fantasized about. Both teenagers suffered the consequences of remaining trapped in abusive relationships for too long. Katrina's objective was ideally to intervene in the lives of teenagers such as Shayla and Colleen before they got trapped in abusive relationships that rendered them powerless and at risk for pregnancy.

"Every time I finish a presentation a few kids come up to me," said Katrina. "They usually say something like 'This really hit home' or 'Can I talk to you about my relationship?' In some schools we used to provide office hours. We would be on-site one day a week so that if our presentation triggered something and the kids needed to talk to us privately, they could come see us. We're not able to do that anymore because of funding. We just can't afford to. Our program used to receive state funds from the Department of Education, but then one Friday, last September, when the governor was on her way out, all of a sudden we heard that all our funding had been completely cut. We knew budget cuts were coming, but we mistakenly thought that our program to prevent teen dating violence was safe."

Worse lay ahead for Katrina and other dedicated workers. In January of 2003, Mitt Romney was sworn in as governor of Massachusetts. Facing a $650 million budget gap, he promptly resorted to using emergency budget-balancing powers and announced plans for enormous cuts, including $114 million from local aid, $41 million from education, and $133 million from social and health-care programs. Programs to prevent teen pregnancy suffered.

Statewide, anxious administrators of these and other youth-oriented programs racked their brains for ways to slash costs, determined to keep their doors open so that their young people would not be shortchanged. Months went by, and with America in a recession and billions going toward national defense and the war in Iraq, many wondered how, where, when—and if—their country would be able to find the resources necessary to ensure the welfare of its many children at risk.

Despite falling upon hard times, Katrina refused to sacrifice her idealistic objectives.

"We're committed to continuing our work," she insisted. "We're still going into almost every school in Berkshire County. We always leave the kids making sure they understand how to access services at Kids' Place and at the Elizabeth Freeman Center, which is Pittsfield's shelter for battered women. We give the kids these telephone numbers and we tell them, 'This is where you can call, this is what you can do.' We remind them that the school counselor is there to listen to them and we stress that if kids disclose anything, they will be sure to get access to the right services."

At Pittsfield High School, guidance counselors have caseloads of 250 to 260 students each, and as much as they try to stay involved in the lives of students, the reality is that they are spread too thin. *The Berkshire Eagle* featured an article titled "Mission Impossible?" in which the director of guidance at the high school bemoaned that "counselors spend most of their time on problems like why kids are running away from home or won't do their homework rather then on what colleges they should apply to. 'We are trying to find out why a lot of kids seem to have no connection to what's going on,' she said. 'They are living day-to-day and I am living six months in their future. I can see the consequences of not doing something today and they are struggling with things at home.' "

"Our schools are conscious of the fact that a lot of the things parents and families used to do for children, schools are now expected to do," said Pittsfield's mayor, Sara Hathaway. "Unbelievable demands are being placed on the community and on the school system, and on the after-school programs, too. We have a great Boys and Girls Club, we have Boy Scouts, Girl Scouts, and Cub Scouts. We have team sports and organized sports outside of the schools and leagues. We have all kinds of activities available for young people, and I think that all of the adults that are affiliated with these groups are reaching out constantly. But I think a lot depends on the parents. Did they read to their kids? Did they talk to their kids about drugs? Do they sit down around the table and eat dinner and ask their kid how their day was? What kind of rapport do they have with their children? Where do they take up the responsibility of paying attention to their kids? There's only so much the schools can do."

During the past decade, many factors have contributed to this increasingly relevant and controversial issue of the widening gap between where a parent's responsibility ends and a school's begins. The number of households headed by single women who have children grew nearly five times faster in the 1990s compared with the number of married couples with children. Less than a quarter of American households are made up of married couples living with their children, and more than 40 percent of female-headed families live below the poverty line. Six years after the 1996 national welfare reform law went into effect, it was declared by many to be an unequivocal success, with advocates pointing to data showing that "welfare rolls have plummeted by more than 50% and child poverty is at its lowest point in more than twenty years."

But behind these new and improved statistics were many single mothers such as Liz, Sheri, Amy, and Shayla who worked long hours at grueling, monotonous, low-wage jobs, and Jessica, who went to college and worked part-time. While these young single mothers attended work or school, their small children spent most of their waking hours in day-care centers that varied enormously in terms of quality and reliability of personnel, as was evidenced in Katherine Boo's shocking investigation of Washington, D.C., day-care centers and by Shayla's terrible experience of seeing her son coming home with mysterious bruises, thinking he must have gotten them while playing, and then finding out that the woman who ran his day-care center had overdosed on heroin and died.

It won't be long before Jaiden, Kaliegh, Marcus, Peter, Ezakeil, Caleb, Jonathan, and Leeah and other children like them start turning to their schools in search of the guidance, nurturing, and adult mentorship that was so sparingly rationed to them by their hardworking parents during their early years. The growing void when it comes to the social and emotional nurturing of young children across the country presents an enormous challenge, and many schools have not yet begun to adjust their curriculums because they lack either the inclination or the resources, or both. Nobel laureate economist James Heckman believes that earlier intervention costs less and is more effective and that as children become teenagers and teenagers become

adults, the cost of intervention goes up as the rate of intervention success goes down. Thus, says Heckman, "It pays to invest in the young."

Heckman questions the prevalent tendency among American educators to overemphasize cognitive skills as measured by academic achievement or IQ tests while virtually ignoring "the critical importance of social skills, self-discipline and a variety of non-cognitive skills that are known to determine success in life." He believes that "one can make a bigger difference and have more of an impact with children during the early years because the social skills they learn in the very early years set a pattern for acquiring life skills later."

Some of the very same issues of emotional maturity, social skills, and life skills are at the core of President George W. Bush's Marriage-Incentive Program. Eager to increase success rates of marriages and to restore the shattered institution of America's nuclear family so that

more children can grow up in loving two-parent homes, the current administration has allocated funding for marital counseling, mentoring, and educational programs that aim to help married couples stay together. Following the logic of James Heckman, wouldn't some of this money be better spent nurturing the emotional, social, and life skills of the very young?

Across the country, a handful of bold educators familiar with Howard Gardner's theory of multiple intelligences and Daniel Goleman's theory of emotional intelligence have pioneered innovative new programs that place a premium on what James Heckman calls "noncognitive skills." Within galvanized curriculums, these educators are actively addressing the enormous importance of their students' emotional competence, motivation, and stress management. They are prioritizing the development of the ability to relate to others effectively and with empathy, and they are recognizing the need for activities that serve as rites of passage for adolescents as they approach the transition to adulthood. Rather than lamenting or evading their students' growing need for guidance and mentorship in all areas of their lives, these educators are confronting it and attempting to offer leadership and counsel.

One of the most impressive curriculums created to address the social, emotional, and spiritual needs of adolescents is the Council Program, founded in 1980 by Jack Zimmerman, educator, therapist, and president of the Ojai Foundation.

"Inspired by the Native American tradition of council, the program is based on the belief that respectful listening and speaking from the heart are central to creating a sense of community," explained Zimmerman. "These concepts are represented by the form of the circle, within which close, sustained, open interaction between elders and the younger generation is possible."

After its initiation at a small experimental school in the early 1980s, the Council Program was incorporated into the curriculum at the Crossroads School in Santa Monica, California. At this private school, the course was nicknamed "Mysteries" because in each group the teachers asked the teenagers to share their deepest questions, thoughts, fears, and feelings. Every year, the course retains a degree of flexibility and can be broadened and enhanced to address the issues that are of greatest concern to the students in any given group. One of the reasons adolescents love "Mysteries" so much is because they actively collaborate with their teachers to help create the curriculum, thus playing a central role in determining, shaping, and influencing what they learn.

Back in 1982, Jack Zimmerman and his colleague, Ruthann Saphier, wrote in their mission statement:

> We have discovered that our young people have unspeakable fears about the future and that they yearn for a sense of *meaning* or *purpose*, which they don't know how to find.

These young people long to connect to something larger than themselves. They long to find their place in creating and participating in a new, more hopeful paradigm. We must dare to create in our schools a place to begin to meet those needs. "Mysteries" arose from and thrives from a bold re-envisioning of the meaning of education, health, and citizenship for the twenty-first century. . . . "Mysteries" aims to help teenagers from all walks of life come to terms with matters such as the erosion of family and community, a changing economy, the changes in the American workplace, a mass media wildly at odds with traditional values, the destruction of our biosphere, the untenable balance of resources in our country and our world, and the threat of more immediate destruction still posed by nuclear weapons.

In the more than twenty years that have elapsed since this mission statement was first written, American society has endured many destabilizing shifts: an increase in single-mother families; constantly evolving definitions of gender roles; the pressing moral and ethical questions posed by corporate corruption; the pollution of the natural environment; the widening income gap; the recession; the stressful, heightened presence of chemical and biological warfare; terrorism's encroachment on daily life; and the threat of weapons of mass destruction. All have intensified the sense of anxiety, alienation, emptiness, and confusion about the future that so many teenagers experience, making the Council Program and its "Mysteries" curriculum more compelling, relevant, and vital than ever before.

At the Crossroads School, the Council Program is integrated into life-skills seminars administered by the Human Development Department. These seminars convene for roughly ninety minutes once a week, during which time the comprehensive "Mysteries" curriculum sets out to reduce stress and self-destructive behaviors among adolescents in grades six through twelve by "building identity definition and self-esteem; setting goals and strengthening the will; creating and instituting rites of passage, both on the school premises and on multiday retreats that bring the kids closer to nature; developing communication and decision-making skills, as well as nonviolent exploration and resolution of conflicts; nurturing imagination, intuition, and a mind-body connection; offering preventive health education about sexuality, drugs, and gender identity; fostering access to feelings of playfulness and joy; celebrating human diversity; discussing the importance of self and group validation; encouraging divergent thinking; exploring group problem solving; discussing the meanings of friendship and intimacy; teaching personal and social responsibility; and enhancing spiritual education that stems from developing a sense of meaning and purpose through storytelling about one's own life in a way that evokes a sense of personal myth."

The program at the Crossroads School culminates in a five-day rite-of-passage ceremony for seniors. This retreat takes place on the grounds of the Ojai Foundation. From start to finish, the program provides a form and context within which each teenager can engage in a process of self-definition that occurs internally and through the experience of being witnessed by others.

The curriculum and teaching methods Zimmerman and Saphier pioneered have since been expanded and refined by several innovative and dedicated educators, including Maureen Murdock, Rachael Kessler, and Peggy O'Brien. Kessler has written extensively about her work in the area of social and emotional learning in a book titled *The Soul of Education: Helping Students Find Connection, Compassion, and Character at School.* Following the years she spent as chair of the Department of Human Development at the Crossroads School, Kessler became director of the Institute for Social and Emotional Learning. She provides workshops for educators all over the country and consults with schools that want to develop curricula like the Council Program. Kessler emphasizes the importance of "Passages," which she defines as the series of transitions that characterize the adolescent's journey into adulthood.

"What distinguishes the 'Mysteries' and 'Passages' curriculum from many of the other programs in social and emotional learning," writes Kessler, "is that it also recognizes spiritual development in the adolescent and provides an opportunity for students to explore meaning and purpose in life, to experience stillness, silence, and solitude, to express their yearning for transcendence, joy, and creativity, and to experience a deep connection to themselves, others, and the wholeness of life. Thus 'health education' is returned to the original meaning of health, 'to make whole.' Health from this perspective is defined as the integration of mind, body, community, spirit, and heart."

The Palms Middle School is one of several public schools in the Los Angeles Unified School District that have adopted the Council Program. Jack Zimmerman estimates that the cost of delivering the program to the twelve hundred Palms sixth and eighth graders is about $125 per student per year and can run up to $250 per student for some programs depending on their size and scope. Not a huge price to pay for enhancing the development of the next generation, who will inherit the responsibility of nurturing and sustaining a very diverse, very complex America.

"We just got a grant from the Annenberg Foundation," Zimmerman reported jubilantly. "It's to help the Palms Middle School become an Institute for Council Training so that more teachers can come and learn how to replicate the Council Program in their schools."

Like the Council Program, the Children's Aid Society-Carrera Program, created by Dr. Michael Carrera, takes a comprehensive, long-term approach to youth development. Unlike the Council Program, which has been integrated directly into the school curriculum at private and public schools, the Carrera Program meets after school at different sites in indigent neighborhoods across the country and is geared toward adolescents who are at high risk for teen pregnancy and parenthood. The program's curriculum aims to fill the frequently unsupervised hours between late afternoon, when school ends, and evening, when parents get off from work, provided that they only have one job and work the day shift. The curriculum is designed to work with eleven- to twelve-year-olds who meet five or six days a week, twelve months a year, for five to seven years, until they graduate from high school.

An intensive evaluation of the Carrera Program conducted by Douglas Kirby for the National Campaign to Prevent Teen Pregnancy "demonstrated that, amongst girls, it significantly delayed the onset of sex, increased the use of condoms and other effective methods of contraception, and reduced pregnancy and birth rates." Supported over the years by the Robin Hood Foundation, the Bernice and Milton Stern Foundation, and the Charles Stewart Mott Foundation, the

Carrera Program costs $4,000 per child per year and encompasses "family life and sex education, individual academic assessment, tutoring, help with homework, preparation for standardized exams, and assistance with college entrance. It provides opportunities for self-expression through the arts and participation in sports activities. It makes available comprehensive health care, including mental health and reproductive health services and contraception. In addition, it offers work-related activities, including a job club, stipends, individual bank accounts, employment, and career awareness."

When it comes to sex education, the current administration has been strident about allocating federal support to "abstinence only" programs. The success of the Carrera Program shifts the spotlight away from the government and illuminates the vital, pivotal philanthropic role that can be played by private, family, and corporate foundations that take the initiative and follow their own independent agendas. According to the Charles Stewart Mott Foundation newsletter: "The Carrera program, which currently serves more than 2,000 adolescents annually, is considerably less expensive than the public cost of teenage pregnancies, estimated by the National Campaign to Prevent Teen Pregnancy at more than $7 billion each year for health care and financial assistance to teen mothers and their children."

A five-year replication project costing about $10 million is currently under way to bring the Carrera Program into even more communities. Five regional training centers have been established across the United States, and each will manage seven Carrera-based teen pregnancy prevention programs.

No plans or funding are yet in place to open a Carrera-based program in Pittsfield. In 2001 the city faced a budget deficit of $8–

$10 million. A state oversight board was closely monitoring its finances. In city council meetings that addressed how to reduce Pittsfield's expenditures, several people suggested turning off the streetlights.

Mayor Sara Hathaway was elected in 2002. She faces many obstacles in her quest to help Pittsfield and its citizens into a phase of recovery, renewal, and self-definition, yet like the creators of the Council Program and the Carrera Program, she embodies a spirit of courage, optimism, idealism, and innovation. A native of Michigan, Sara Hathaway upset Pittsfield's entrenched old boys' network when she defeated nine male opponents to win the election. To many citizens of Pittsfield, the swearing-in of this bright, focused, strong, compassionate, energetic woman in her late thirties symbolized their ability to initiate change in their community through participation in the democratic process.

With a degree in urban planning and previous experience as senior planner of the Berkshire Regional Planning Commission and as State Senator Andrea Nuciforo's chief of staff and district director, Mayor Hathaway brought expertise to the table. She formulated a detailed plan to revitalize Pittsfield's downtown using funds from a settlement with GE and has expressed her dedication to improving educational opportunities and vocational training. She dreams of starting a performing arts magnet school in Pittsfield that would draw on the region's wealth of talent and train a new generation of actors, musicians, filmmakers, composers, dancers, theater directors, and production designers.

Mayor Hathaway remains committed to ensuring that all citizens of Pittsfield have direct access to her and are allowed to have their say when it comes to determining how their city should be run. In her inauguration speech she vowed, "While I am your mayor, no one person, no one business, no one group, no single elected official, no single special interest, will decide how we will do things in this city." Right after being elected, true to her word, Mayor Hathaway began hosting coffee hours at locations across the city, including the library and the local bagel shop. These events were open to the public, and the mayor made sure that people knew she was approachable, eager to hear their thoughts and opinions, and very open about sharing her own.

During her first year in office, Mayor Hathaway made a special visit to the Teen Parent Program. "I sat in the chair at the front of the room, and each one of the teen mothers talked a bit about their lives. They all said that they were tired. Whether they were pregnant or they had already given birth—they were very tired. I asked them about the things they had to give up. One of the girls had been a great basketball player and she couldn't do it anymore. I asked them what their boyfriends were like—that was a sore subject. None of them were happy with the men who had participated in the situation. I tried to draw them out a little bit about what their hopes were for the future. It was clear that these lives were being drastically affected by pregnancy and parenthood. On the other hand, one of the girls said, 'I'm getting the best education I've ever gotten out of being in this program because it's individually geared to the level I'm at, and that's what I needed. I wish I could have had tutoring before I was pregnant.' There were some strange ironies that my visit to the Teen

Parent Program raised, like how sad it is that we had to wait until this child was in crisis before this level of individual attention was made available to her."

"I think Mayor Hathaway's burden is to translate her good intentions into a large, community-organizing process," observed local documentary filmmaker Mickey Friedman. "Many, many people are exceedingly cynical that anything can be done in Pittsfield. You've got to convince them that there's a reason for them to get involved. The older people are tired and worn down, and the younger people don't have an awful lot of hope."

Captain Barry sat at his desk at the Pittsfield police station, surrounded by photographs of his ancestors. "I like helping people," he said. "I enjoy making a difference in their lives. I always wanted to do this. It's in my blood. My dad wanted to be a police officer, but at the time they had a height requirement and he was a quarter inch too short. My grandfather was a vice squad detective during Prohibition and his father, Daniel Barry, was a detective here in the 1800s. Now it's my job to serve and protect, and I take it very seriously. I want Pittsfield to be a good, safe community for the people that live here."

Years ago when Captain Barry was in the Air Force and the Air National Guard, he had the chance to travel extensively. Occasionally he found himself wondering what it would be like to live somewhere else, somewhere far away from Pittsfield. But every time he contemplated moving, he ended up appreciating where he was.

"Recently," he said, "I took a train to Albuquerque to see a friend of mine who was in the Air Force, and the most beautiful scenery I saw was in South County on my way out of Pittsfield. I realized that Berkshire County is a beautiful place to live and that although I like the warmer climate as I get older, I still like it here. I like going out with my dogs, Snoopy and Snoopy Two. Those beagles are my best buddies. I got Snoopy when I got out of the Police Academy. She'll be fourteen in March. I picked up Snoopy Two when I was in charge of the city dog pound a couple of years ago. I felt sorry for him because he had been living there for about four months and because he was such a menace to society, nobody wanted him. So I took him."

Captain Barry paused and looked out the window. The sky was gray. Snowflakes were falling. "I like it here in Pittsfield, and I want to stay here," he murmured. "There are beautiful mountain views and I like the four seasons. We have a lovely autumn and I like that. . . . This is the path I chose, so I'll be here for the long haul."

Although Carol Gilligan commuted to New York City several days a week to teach and traveled all over the world for conferences, home was Berkshire County. "The community is going to live with the consequences of what happens here," she said, "and in spite of all efforts to prevent it, some girls do get pregnant and it seems very shortsighted to pull resources away from these girls or to condemn them. The fact about these girls is that they have become pregnant and they have given birth to babies and they are still very young, so you have their lives and you also have the lives of their children, so it's a very good place to put community resources to try to prevent this cycle from going on into the next generation.

"When you look at a teen mother like Jessica—she made some good decisions, like going back to school, and she made some bad decisions—but all people make good decisions and bad decisions," said Carol. "The problem with these girls is that there is no safety net. The absence of resources really needs to be addressed. I remember being shocked that they were going to school and taking care of their babies and working and earning so little money and staying up all night with their babies, ratcheting up the stress level to the point where the consequences would be borne by them and by their children. If you don't put resources behind this—it's like not having prenatal care—then you have trouble."

———————

Back in her apartment on April Lane, Sheri stood in her kitchen, heating up some macaroni and cheese for Leeah's dinner. She set the steaming bowl down in front of her daughter and sat beside her while she ate.

"When I was pregnant," said Sheri, "lots of people told me, 'You're gonna be a teen mom—your life is over.' Whoever says that to teen mothers is lying. My life is just beginning."

NOTE ON METHOD

It was Carol Gilligan who first invited me to come to Pittsfield to videotape the workshops she taught with Normi Noel at the Teen Parent Program and offered to allocate some grant money she had received toward this purpose. Our relationship dated back to the Boston Festival of Women's Cinema, where in 1998 she had moderated a discussion following a screening of a documentary film I had produced and directed, *Inside Out: Portraits of Children*. That particular screening happened to be a benefit for the Guidance Center, a multicultural nonprofit organization in Cambridge that addresses the needs of economically and socially challenged families. Their mission is "to provide innovative prevention, intervention, and educational programs that empower families to confront challenge and crisis proactively."

Carol was deeply moved by my film about the imaginary worlds of children. She encouraged me to consider making a documentary film about teen motherhood. A year later, I joined her in Pittsfield to explore this possibility.

During the first workshop session I attended, Carol showed the teen mothers a section of my previous film, which was narrated exclusively by its subjects, children between the ages of five and twelve. After the screening, I asked the teen mothers how they would feel about being in a documentary and explained what this endeavor would entail. First and foremost, they had to want to be seen and heard. They had to believe that what they had to say was valuable and important. They had to have the courage to place their thoughts, feelings, emotions, and intimate family histories and relationships under a microscope in front of a judgmental public. They had to be strong enough to confront their own vulnerability and live with it. Each girl had to be driven by the desire to shatter what up until now had been her own private silence.

A few members of the group were interested and felt strong enough to attempt it. Those who were game tested the waters and allowed me to interview them. Those who felt comfortable being videotaped identified themselves as being interested in participating as subjects. Aware of the level of intimacy, involvement, scrutiny, and commitment that the project required, they agreed to let me into their world.

Recognizing that their lives were incredibly stressful and busy, I made myself available to meet with them completely on their terms, at home, at work, at school, and at social gatherings. We caught up with one another during their fifteen-minute lunch breaks, between classes, late at night after their kids were fast asleep, early on bitterly cold days when their early-morning shifts were slow, in between customers at the drive-through if the manager happened to be on break, and on weekends, if and when they were lucky enough to have half a Saturday or Sunday off from work.

Occasionally the teenagers would lose track of time and forget to call to cancel scheduled meetings when excursions to the lake or the mall lasted longer than expected or when they were overwhelmed with errands or doctor's appointments or when they had to work late unexpectedly or if transportation got tricky. In those instances when they were late or didn't show up at all, I would wait in my car, often for hours, parked on street corners or in the parking lots of housing projects, staring out my window, watching children playing, mail being retrieved from mailboxes, snowflakes falling, leaves burning, raindrops splattering on the windshield, and people coming and going.

Ultimately, this patience and unwavering dedication constituted the foundation upon which our relationships were built. As the teen mothers witnessed my respect for them, and my commitment, I was rewarded with their trust and raw honesty.

Not too far removed from the ups and downs of my own adolescence, I empathized with their fluctuating moods and their many conflicting obligations. I was sensitive to the crushingly high levels of stress that saturated their daily lives. We shared good days, bad days, and many ordinary days. I witnessed private and public moments. As they introduced me to the fathers of their babies and to their parents, slowly I began to get a sense of their romantic relationships, their friends, and their family histories. What initially had been

a blank canvas began to take on color, shape, and dimension as I learned more and more about the different layers of their lives.

The short documentary we made during the first few months we worked together was screened at venues ranging from the Museum of Tolerance in Los Angeles to Harvard's Graduate School of Education in Cambridge, HBO's Frame by Frame Film Festival in New York City, and the health class at Reid Middle School in Pittsfield. The film was distinguished as one of the outstanding short documentaries of 1999 by the Academy of Motion Picture Arts and Sciences and was screened in its annual documentary series at UCLA.

This documentary covered the teenagers' lives through their last months of high school. After the documentary film was completed, the teen parents and I agreed to continue videotaping interviews with the objective of creating a book. Over the course of four years I continued to interview them and their families while simultaneously operating a handheld Sony VX-1000 mini-DV camera, relying on natural light and trying to be as unobtrusive as possible. I also continued to photograph and videotape them as they went through their days, visiting them at home, at work, at their parents' homes, and, in the case of Jessica, at Berkshire Community College.

I attended children's birthday parties, the senior prom, graduation, family barbecues, and other special events. We spent a substantial amount of time hanging out, driving around, and talking when the camera wasn't running. In addition to all the videotaped material, some interviews were audiotaped, conducted over the telephone or in person. All the interviews were transcribed and edited, with an emphasis on maintaining the integrity of each voice while trying to extract the most clear, vivid story from hours of material.

I began this project without any agenda other than curiosity about the lives of teen mothers, which at the outset, I knew very little about. All my subsequent research was motivated and spurred on by the content of the oral histories I collected. The interviews with the teenagers and their families left me with many questions. As a voracious reader, I began my search for answers in books and gradually expanded the scope of my interviews to include people like Captain Patrick Barry, Mayor Sara Hathaway, Nicole, Katrina, Joann, Mary, Jack Zimmerman, and Dr. Vincent J. Felitti.

The one book that inspired me most and galvanized me every day was

NOTE ON METHOD

Dorothy's Allison's stark, incisive, courageous, gripping memoir, *Two or Three Things I Know for Sure*:

> Behind the story I tell is the one I don't. Behind the story you hear is the one I wish I could make you hear. Behind my carefully buttoned collar is my nakedness, the struggle to find clean clothes, food, meaning and money. Behind sex is rage, behind anger is love, behind this moment is silence, years of silence.

> *Two or three things I know for sure, and one is that I would rather go naked than wear the clothes the world has made for me.*

NOTES

Many excellent works influenced this book and are referenced in the notes below. Among them, Kristin Luker's *Dubious Conceptions: The Politics of Teenage Pregnancy* provided me with an essential conceptual framework for understanding the complex construct of teen parenthood. Positioned somewhere between the liberal and conservative perspectives, Luker views teenagers as capable of making their own decisions but emphasizes that often these decisions are strongly influenced by environmental factors. For facts about the General Electric Company's history in Pittsfield, I am indebted to Thomas F. O'Boyle's book, *At Any Cost: Jack Welch, General Electric, and the Pursuit of Profit*, and to two professors of anthropology, each of whom wrote incredibly detailed books set entirely in Pittsfield: June C. Nash, author of *From Tank Town to High Tech: The Clash of Community and Industrial Cycles*, and Max H. Kirsch, author of *In the Wake of the Giant: Multinational Restructuring and Uneven Development in a New England Community*. I am also indebted to Mickey Friedman, who spent ten years making the documentary *Good Things to Life: GE, PCBs and Our Town*, and to *The Berkshire Eagle*, for their outstanding coverage of local events. I have identified direct quotations from printed sources. Other quotations are from personal interviews conducted between 1999 and 2003.

Chapter 1: Pittsfield

3   Catherine—not her real name.

7   The Alan Guttmacher Institute regularly publishes outstanding reports on teen pregnancy and parenthood. For detailed information about the history of adolescent health services under the umbrella of what is now the

Department of Health and Human Services (DHHS) and for details about the legislation enacted to support institutions like the Teen Parent Program in Pittsfield, refer to the Guttmacher Report on Public Policy 3, no. 3 (June 2000).

8   While the number of national teen pregnancies, abortions, and births began to decrease about 1991 and have continued to decline every year since, in certain economically depressed communities, such as Pittsfield, teen birthrates have remained persistently high and are not showing as much improvement when it comes to prevention.

In his report *Emerging Answers: New Research Findings on Programs to Reduce Teen Pregnancy,* Douglas Kirby writes:

> Teen birth rates are now at their lowest recorded level ever. But even with recent declines the United States still has the highest teen pregnancy and birth rates among comparable industrialized nations. More than four in ten teen girls still get pregnant once before the age of 20 which translates into nearly 900,000 teen pregnancies a year. In addition, between 2000–2010 the population of teen girls aged 15–19 is expected to increase by nearly 10%—which means that even declining rates may not necessarily mean fewer numbers of teen pregnancies and births (pp. 1–4).

This report can be viewed on the National Campaign to Prevent Teen Pregnancy website, www.teenpregnancy.org.

8   *Adolescent Births: A Statistical Profile,* Massachusetts, 2000. Massachusetts Department of Public Health: Bureau of Family and Community, Office of Statistics and Evaluation; Bureau of Health Statistics, Research and Evaluation. Refer to Table 24, "Trends in Birth Rates Among Women Ages 15–19 for Selected Communities, Ranked by Teen Birth Rate, Massachusetts: 2000." See also 1995, Table 24, "Births by Mother's Age and Race/Hispanic Ethnicity for Selected Communities, Massachusetts: 1995." Both tables are available at www.state.ma.us/dph.

8   Including Nadine, five out of the seven teen mothers in this book are white; one is black; and the other is half white, half Hispanic. Often when the American public and media discuss teen motherhood, they tend to associate it with the African American and Hispanic populations, feeding stereotypes connecting poverty and social adversity to minorities while turning a blind eye to the fact that while the teen parenthood rates are indeed significantly higher within these populations—more than twice as high as that of white teenagers (a fact that merits major attention, resources, and targeted intervention), in sheer numbers, white births account for the largest proportion of teen births. In other words, most American teen mothers are indigent and white.

    In *Dubious Conceptions,* Kristin Luker addresses this issue:

> Although African Americans do account for a disproportionate share of births to teenagers and unmarried women, unmarried African American teenage mothers are not, statistically speaking, typical unwed teenage mothers. . . . In 1992, for example, about 60% of all babies born to unmarried teenage mothers were born to whites. Some commentators, among them, Charles Murray, say that the rising birthrates among white unmarried teenagers presage the growth of a white underclass, which will take its place alongside historically disadvantaged African Americans. In essence, Murray argues that as racial differences become less important in the life of the country, Americans will separate into two nations—no longer black and white, but married and affluent on the one hand, and unmarried and poor on the other (p. 7).

    Bell Hooks raises the issue of the racial stereotyping of poverty, welfare, and teen parenthood in her startling chapter "White Poverty: The Politics of Invisibility" in *Where We Stand: Class Matters:*

> Today most people who comment on class acknowledge that poverty is seen as having a black face, but they rarely point to the fact that this representation has been created and sustained by mass media. Concurrently, reports using statis-

tics that show a huge percentage of black folks in the ranks of the poor compared to a small percentage of whites make it seem that blacks are the majority group in the ranks of the poor. Rarely do these reports emphasize that these percentages are based on population size. The reality they mask is that blacks are a small percentage of the population. While black folks disproportionate to our numbers are among the poor, the vast majority of the poor continue to be white. The hidden face of poverty in the United States is the untold stories of millions of poor white people (p. 117).

Similarly, the stories of white teen mothers more often than not remain obscured from the public eye, leaving millions of young mothers silenced, disenfranchised, isolated, and unrecognized—apart from their inclusion in mass, depersonalized national and state statistics.

8   Census 2000, Redistricting Data (Public Law 94-171) Summary File. Geographic Area: Pittsfield city, Massachusetts, available at http://factfinder.census.gov.

9   June C. Nash, *From Tank Town to High Tech,* pp. 29–92. Traces industrial evolution of Pittsfield throughout nineteenth and twentieth centuries.

10   Ibid., p. 27. For details about GE's defense contracts.

10   Ibid. During the postwar period three-fifths of Pittsfield's workforce was employed by GE. See pages 100–104 for a discussion of Pittsfield's economic vulnerability and dependency on GE.

10   Thomas F. O'Boyle, *At Any Cost: Jack Welch, General Electric, and the Pursuit of Profit,* pp. 48, 57–66. For an account of Welch's arrival and seventeen years spent in Pittsfield, see Chapter 2, "Passing the Baton."

10   Nash, p. 104. "Eight of eleven city council members worked for GE."

11   Max Kirsch, *In the Wake of the Giant.* For an analysis of the structure of Pittsfield's economic dependency, see page 4. See also pages 59–60:

"When the umbrella of the corporation started to break down during the 1970s, Pittsfield became analogous to a small colonial state that had just been granted independence: it had no mechanisms in place to deal with its new status."

11   Nash, pp. 232–33. Nash describes GE's "shift in production from blue-collar assembly work to steel collar robots," and discusses GE's entry into and prioritization of high-tech and financial operations.

11   Janet Lowe, *Welch: An American Icon*, pp. 240–41.

12   Nash, p. 5. In 1986 GE announced the closing of its Power Transformer Division, "downsizing" its electrical machinery plant in Pittsfield.

12   Lowe, pp. 88–89. "The Companies General Electric Dumped: No More Weapons of War." In 1993 GE sold its aerospace division to Martin Marietta for $4 billion in cash and preferred stock. In 1995 Martin Marietta merged with Lockheed Corporation to become Lockheed Martin.

12   Nash, pp. 9, 235. GE Plastics Worldwide Headquarters housed the corporation's Advanced Plastics Technology Center "in a new facility that employs around 700 people, for the most part highly skilled and educated engineers, designers and managers, and despite high sales in the first few years of its development, it is not expected to increase employment by more than 30%, since there will be no production work on the site. . . . Production might be done in one of the dozen plastics injection and mold businesses that have grown in the city."

12   Pittsfield Economic Revitalization Corporation, *An Economic Base Study of Pittsfield and Berkshire County* (Pittsfield, Mass., 1988).

14   R. Calahan and S. Watson, *A Strategy for Economic Development in Berkshire County*. See also Max Kirsch's discussion of this report in his chapter "Development Strategies," pp. 54–55.

14   Educational attainment: Pittsfield city, Massachusetts Data Set: Census 2000 Summary File 3 (SF 3)—Sample Data DP-2. Profile of Selected Social Characteristics: 2000, available at http://factfinder.census.gov.

14   In *At Any Cost*, Thomas F. O'Boyle chronicles other casualties that were once "pillars of the GE Empire." His list includes "Schenectady, which has twenty-two thousand fewer GE jobs than it did in 1978; Erie, Pennsylvania, six thousand fewer; Lynn, Massachusetts, seven thousand fewer; Fort Wayne, Indiana, four thousand fewer; Louisville, Kentucky, thirteen thousand fewer; Evandale, Ohio, twelve thousand fewer. . . . All these communities have the same worn, dazed look that puts one in the mind of a losing prizefighter about to answer the bell for the fifteenth round."

What happened in Pittsfield is, according to O'Boyle, "a story that's repeated a thousand times in cities across the once vibrant industrial heartland, repeated with such frequency that America has become inured to it, much like stepping over a drunk in the street" (p. 32).

Max Kirsch's *In the Wake of the Giant* cites other corporations that through downsizing have dramatically transformed industrial communities: the Sunbeam Corporation in Biddeford, Maine, and the Thunderbird plant in Lorain, Ohio, and Youngstown, Ohio, formerly a thriving auto-producing community, are situations he uses as comparisons to the situation in Pittsfield with GE (pp. 111–12).

15   O'Boyle's chapter "Great River of the Mountains" contains a detailed discussion of the history of synthetic chemicals, the mixing of PCBs to create Pyranol, and the use of this fluid in three plants, two on the Hudson River and one in Pittsfield, and describes the increased incidence of cancer and premature mortality in workers who worked in Building 12 at the Pittsfield Plant (pp. 183–209).

15   I interviewed Mickey Friedman, the producer, director, and editor of a ninety-minute documentary film titled *Good Things to Life: GE, PCBs and Our Town*. Mickey spent ten years interviewing GE workers and following the progression of the toxic-waste disaster in Pittsfield. His documentary is ex-

tremely thorough and includes interviews, footage of the land testing and former dump sites, footage of the river being dredged, scenes of meetings and negotiations between GE and the EPA and the people of Pittsfield, as well as presentation, analysis, and discussion of many documents—including articles from *The Wall Street Journal* and *The Boston Globe,* results of the EPA's studies regarding levels of PCBs in Pittsfield, and a few pieces of GE's internal correspondence throughout the twentieth century on the subject of PCBs. In addition, Mickey was a co-founder of the environmental activist group Housatonic River Initiative. To view further information related to PCBs in Pittsfield and the efforts of this group to hold GE accountable for the contamination, go to www.housatonic-river.com.

To order a copy of the video, contact Mickey Friedman at Mfried@ bcn.net.

17 In late 1997, *Inside Edition,* television's longest-running nationally syndicated newsmagazine show, aired an investigative report questioning whether GE had for years, knowingly and deliberately, covered up the fact that it was dumping dangerous PCBs in Pittsfield. This episode aired on CBS and was titled "Living with Danger." It was produced by Scott Rappoport and James Bogdanoff. For information on how to purchase this video, visit www.insideedition.com.

18 David Stout, "G.E. Agrees to Clean Part of Tainted River in Massachusetts," *The New York Times,* Sept. 25, 1998; Scott Allen and Peter Howe, "GE Accepts $150M Plan to Clean Pittsfield Sites," *The Boston Globe,* Sept. 25, 1998; "Pittsfield Officials, GE Tout Cleanup Plan Seen as a Key to Revitalizing City," *The Boston Globe,* Oct. 15, 1998; Associated Press, "GE to Pay $150 Million to $200 Million to Clean Up New England River," *The Washington Post,* Sept. 25, 1998; Jack Dew, "GE Challenges Cleanup Cost Complaint Targets New Method of Accounting," *The Berkshire Eagle,* Feb. 5, 2002.

19 This EPA report on PCB-related health hazards in Pittsfield was dated June 4, 1998, and appears in Friedman's documentary.

19   Alan Guttmacher Institute, "Occidental Report—Teenagers' Pregnancy, Intentions and Decisions, 1999."

20   The issue of the environment and peer pressure is key when it comes to at-risk girls such as Shayla who get pregnant on purpose. There are many who believe that taking an at-risk child out of one environment and putting her in a different school could help reduce the risk of her becoming a teen parent.

In *Dubious Conceptions,* Kristin Luker writes: "A young black or white woman who is poor, having trouble academically, and becoming convinced that she is unlikely to get ahead is better off—whatever her individual risk factors—if she is in a good suburban school where a majority of her peers view pregnancy as an obstacle to achievement" (p. 116).

Reading the above passage, I am reminded of Francie, the ebullient thirteen-year-old who is the central character in Betty Smith's classic, *A Tree Grows in Brooklyn*, later turned into a terrific movie directed by Elia Kazan (1945). Like the small tree near her tenement, Francie seeks out the light as she struggles against poverty and a life overshadowed by her father's alcoholism and her parents' strained relationship. One day while walking outside the periphery of her destitute neighborhood, Francie wanders into a wealthier area and sees a beautiful school. She longs to go there instead of to the grim one she attends. Her father comes up with a scheme. They take down a random address of a house in the wealthy neighborhood near the school, and her father writes a letter requesting a transfer, claiming that he's moved there. The request is granted, and Francie's life changes.

The No Child Left Behind Bill offers parents the option of transferring their children out of failing schools. In addition, through their foundations, philanthropists such as Theodore J. Forstmann, John T. Walton, and Bill and Melinda Gates have allocated substantial grants to help parents in need with tuition so that they can transfer kids into private elementary schools (in the case of the Children's Scholarship Fund) and to support parents in sending their kids to smaller, alternative schools (in the case of the Gates Foundation).

For more information, see www.scholarshipfund.org and www.gatesfoundation.org.

21   Jim Bouton, *Foul Ball: My Life and Hard Times Trying to Save an Old Ballpark.* A former major-league pitcher for the New York Yankees recounts "the battle waged in Pittsfield over whether to build a new stadium to replace 83-year-old Wahconah Park, a contentious struggle that pitted the wishes of the people against those of the local power elite."

In light of the budget deficit Pittsfield faced in 2001 (which was in the realm of $8–10 million), residents voted by a narrow margin not to establish a new $18.5 million stadium to lure a new minor-league baseball team.

21   See website for the Colonial Theatre, www.colonialtheater.org.

23   In addition to interviewing Captain Barry at the police headquarters, I referred to a document he provided me, a research report he had commissioned internally on the subject of the history of the drug trade in Pittsfield.

25   Tony Dobrowolski, "Heroin Rears Its Ugly Head in Pittsfield," *The Berkshire Eagle,* Nov. 10, 2002.

25   Ibid. See also D. R. Bahlman, "City Ordinance Aims to Leash Vicious Dogs," *The Berkshire Eagle,* Oct. 14, 2002, and "Vicious Dog Rule Endorsed," *The Berkshire Eagle,* Oct. 24, 2002.

36   Rebecca Maynard, ed., *Kids Having Kids: Economic Costs and Social Consequences of Teen Pregnancy.*

> Early childbearing and youth crimes are linked. . . . If young teens delayed their first childbirth until ages 20 or 21, their child's risk of incarceration would fall by an estimated 12% and the correction costs incurred by more than $900 million. . . . The age of the mother has less of an effect on delinquency than other differences in the circum-

stances facing the children of young teen versus non-teen mothers (pp. 16, 252).

See also Jeffrey Grogger, "Incarceration-Related Costs of Early Childbearing," in ibid.

Children of young teen mothers are almost three times as likely to be behind bars at some point in their adolescence or early 20's in comparison to the children of mothers who delayed childbearing.

36 According to statistics compiled by Adolescent Pregnancy Prevention, Inc. (APPI), a nonprofit service agency in Fort Worth, Texas, children born to teen mothers are:

More likely to be low-birth weight and have developmental problems

More likely to be victims of abuse

More likely to repeat a grade

Males are more likely to be incarcerated, and females are more likely to become teen parents themselves.

The APPI website, www.appifw.org, lists a compilation of data from a variety of sources, including the Alan Guttmacher Institute; National Center for Health Statistics; Texas Department of Health; National Campaign to Prevent Teen Pregnancy; Annie E. Casey Foundation, 2000 Kids Count Report; Youth Risk Behavior Survey, 1995; Centers for Disease Control; Time/CNN poll, 1999; Kaiser Family Foundation; Sexuality Education and Information Council of the United States; Advocates for Youth; *Pediatrics*, Feb. 2001; *Men's Health,* June 2001; APPI independent surveys.

38 James Gilligan, *Violence: Reflections on a National Epidemic.* An eloquent explanation of the theory that violence often arises out of a deep desire to correct/counter a perceived injustice.

38 For demographics of Pittsfield by race, see U.S. Census 2000 at www.census.gov.

40   Martin Kasindorf and Haya El Nasser, "Impact of Census' Race Data Debated: Some Say It Will Divide Country; Others Say Unite," *USA Today,* March 13, 2001.

> By 2050, 21% of Americans will be claiming mixed ancestry, according to projections in 1999 by demographers Jeffrey Passel of the Urban Institute and Barry Edmonston of Portland State University in Oregon. . . . More and more of us will look like singer Mariah Carey, who has a half-Venezuelan, half African-American father and an Irish mother. Or like golfer Tiger Woods, who describes himself as "Cablinasian," an amalgam of Caucasian, black, American Indian—from his father, Earl Woods—and Asian from his mother, Kultida Woods, a Thai, partly of Chinese origin.

Michael Lind of the New America Foundation, based in Washington, D.C., is one of several scholars who believe that "with race due to fade as a basis of social distinctions and government policies, new lines may be based on socioeconomic class, geography, education or other factors."

41   Paul Krugman, "For Richer: How the Permissive Capitalism of the Boom Destroyed American Equality," *The New York Times Magazine,* Oct. 20, 2002, compares the wide income gap that defines contemporary American society and draws a parallel with the era of the Great Depression.

See also Edward N. Wolff, *Top Heavy: The Increasing Inequality of Wealth in America and What Can Be Done About It.*

41   Marc L. Miringoff, *The Social Health of the Nation: How America Is Really Doing,* p. 104.

In a comparative study of teen parenthood rates (1991–95) in six industrialized countries conducted by the Alan Guttmacher Institute, the U.S. ranked highest with a teen parenthood rate of 9 percent, Great Britain second with 6 percent, then France with 2 percent, and Germany, Poland, and Japan with 1 percent.

41   Kristen Luker, *Dubious Conceptions,* pp. 107-108.

For detailed statistics on what percentage of teen mothers come from low-income or poor families, see the Alan Guttmacher Institute's *Teen Pregnancy and Welfare Reform Debate* and *The Politics of Blame: Family Planning, Abortion, and the Poor.*

> Poor and low-income teenagers, whose prospects for a good education, a decent job and marriage are dim or nonexistent, often have little incentive to delay childbearing. As a result of differences in pregnancy and abortion rates, *poor and low-income teenagers account for 83% of adolescents who have a baby and become a parent and 85% of those who become an unwed parent.* By contrast, higher income teenagers who make up 62% of all women aged 15–19 represent only 17% of those who give birth. . . . Many teenagers who become mothers would have been poor later in life even if they had not had a baby.
>
> Almost three-quarters (70%) of higher income teenagers who become pregnant have abortions; they choose to postpone childbearing so they can complete their education, get a good job, establish their financial independence and get married before they can start a family.

41   Kristin Luker, "Dubious Conceptions: The Controversy Over Teen Pregnancy," in Andrew Cherlin's *Public and Private Families.*

41   Luker, *Dubious Conceptions,* p. 182. She sees teen parenthood as a symptom of "the toll that a bifurcating economy is taking on Americans" and asserts that young, poor women have babies in a search for meaning and purpose, desperately seeking the right to make some kind of claim on society that is achieved in small but meaningful ways when they have babies.

42   Ibid., p. 154. Luker discusses the various factors that influence whether a teenage girl has an abortion. In addition to class, race, and socioeconomic status, she comments on the roles of significant others in the girl's

life. She then goes into a detailed analysis of the legislation and policy surrounding teenage abortions in various states, and she addresses the issues of access, funding, and parental consent.

43   Vincent J. Felitti, Robert F. Anda, Dale Nordenberg, and David F. Williamson, "Relationship of Childhood Abuse and Household Dysfunction to Many of the Leading Causes of Death in Adults," The Adverse Childhood Experiences (ACE) Study, *American Journal of Preventive Medicine* 14, no. 4 (May 1998), pp. 245–58. See also Vincent J. Felitti, "Adverse Childhood Experiences and Adult Health: Turning Lead into Gold," *Permanente Journal* 6, no. 1 (Winter 2002), available at www.drfelitti.com.

When I met with Dr. Felitti in San Diego, where he heads the Department of Preventive Medicine at Kaiser Permanente, we discussed his work with patients who have experienced childhood sexual abuse, which is one of the areas the ACE Study has pinpointed as a category of risk. Felitti's view is that although it is uncomfortable for physicians to integrate questions regarding sexual abuse into their routine evaluations of patients, it is necessary for them to be trained to overcome this reluctance. He feels strongly that a direct, open, clinical approach is essential when it comes to patients who present the psychosomatic symptoms often seen in people with histories of childhood sexual abuse, symptoms that include but are not limited to chronic depression, obesity, gastrointestinal distress, chronic headaches, and chronic sleep disturbance.

Dr. Felitti has found that a significant number of patients who come to him with these complaints have kept memories of childhood sexual abuse secret for decades and that often once they disclose them and discuss them and deal with the trauma, some of their symptoms begin to disappear. This was most visually apparent in his work with obese female patients, many of whom lost weight rapidly after disclosing memories of child abuse and discussing them in the open, supportive environment of the clinical setting.

43   Vincent J. Felitti, Susan D. Hillis, Robert F. Anda, and Polly A. Marchbanks, "Adverse Childhood Experiences and Sexual Risk Behaviors in

Women: A Retrospective Cohort Study," *Family Planning Perspectives* 33, no. 5 (Sept.–Oct. 2001).

45   Robert Coles, *The Youngest Parents,* pp. 6–7.

45   Shayla's comment regarding her fantasy that having a baby would "change things" made me think of a metaphor used by Kristin Luker in *Dubious Conceptions*. She compares a disadvantaged teenager's fantasy of having a baby to a lottery ticket: "It brings with it at least the dream of something better, and if the dream fails, not much is lost" (p. 182).

46   David Simon and Edward Burns, *The Corner: A Year in the Life of an Inner-City Neighborhood*, p. 235.

46   Coles, *The Youngest Parents*, pp. 78–79.

47   Tony Dobrowolski, "Pittsfield Lays Off 96 Teachers," *The Berkshire Eagle*, May 2, 2002.

49   No Child Left Behind website at www.nclb.gov.

50   Katherine Boo, "Welfare Reform Series" from *The Washington Post,* Dec. 15, 1996–Dec. 21, 1997. Portraits of individuals and institutions engaged in the daily struggle of coping with various aspects of welfare reform.

50   Martha Matthews, "Teens and TANF: Welfare Reform Could Have Major Impact on Youth," *Youth Law News* 14, no. 5 (1998). This article provides a thorough review of the impact of welfare reform on pregnant and parenting teens. Although parents under eighteen are only a small percentage of all welfare recipients, teen mothers tend to be blamed for numerous social problems. These youths are specifically targeted by a number of recent changes in federal and state welfare laws— particularly the requirement that to receive federally funded TANF ben-

efits, teen parents must live in adult-supervised settings and attend school or work. The article discusses the need for safe and stable living environments, meeting adolescent educational needs, and advocacy efforts.

Chapter 2: Amy & Bernard

63 Trevor—not his real name.

82 Edith Wharton, *Summer,* pp. 156–57.

102 Bridget—not her real name.

Chapter 3: Liz & Peter

108 Paula—not her real name.

111 Ted—not his real name.

111 Vivian—not her real name.

118 For a discussion of the role of predatory adult men in teenage childbearing, refer to: Joycelyn Elders and Alexa E. Albert, "Adolescent Pregnancy and Sexual Abuse," *Journal of American Medical Association* 280, no. 7 (Aug. 19, 1998):

> Gov. Pete Wilson's Statutory Rape Vertical Prosecution Program and the Teenage Pregnancy Prevention Act of 1995 are two pieces of legislation enacted in California to more aggressively prosecute adult men sexually involved with adolescent girls. Several other states, including Delaware, Georgia, Florida, Pennsylvania, and Texas, have taken steps to punish these "male predators."

125 Ricardo—not his real name.

130 Irene—not her real name.

131 Eric Schlosser, *Fast Food Nation*. In his investigative report on America's fast-food industry, Schlosser highlights the way in which teenagers such as Liz are integral to the operation of places like McDonald's and KFC. He noted that because these teenagers are for the most part unskilled, part-time, willing to accept low pay, and unlikely to start or join a union, they are perfect fodder for these routine assembly-line-style jobs with unorthodox hours. Teenagers such as Liz, Amy, Shayla, Jessica, and Colleen (all of whom have worked at fast-food restaurants) accepted these less-than-ideal circumstances at various points in their lives when they were absolutely desperate to work because they needed the money to support their babies.

Schlosser offers the following critique of what he asserts is the fast-food industry's meticulous plan to exploit adolescent workers in subtle, seemingly benign ways:

> No other industry in the United States has a workforce so dominated by adolescents. About two thirds of the nation's fast food workers are under twenty. Roughly 90% of the nation's fast food workers are paid an hourly wage, provided no benefits, and scheduled to work only as needed. Crew Members are employed "at will" and managers try to make sure that each worker is employed less than forty hours a week, thereby avoiding overtime payments (p. 68).

Chapter 4: Colleen

140 Ryan—not his real name.

144 *Physicians Assistant's Guide to Health Promotion and Disease Prevention*, Emory Medical School, 1996.

149 Mary Pipher, *Reviving Ophelia*. She discusses the case of a teenager named Rita whose upbringing with an alcoholic father conditioned her to be drawn into chaotic relationships with unpredictable men, a pattern that may be observed between Colleen and Ryan. "The familiar was comfortable" (p. 192).

163 Valerie Sinason, *Mental Handicap and the Human Condition*. When I did my M.Sc. at the Anna Freud Centre/University College London, I had the pleasure of meeting and working with Valerie Sinason, who was based a block away at the Tavistock Clinic. Her book permanently altered and enhanced my understanding of primary and secondary handicap and helped me understand how organic disability can often appear much more serious and acute when compounded by emotional disability. A crucial, compassionate book for all parents of mentally and physically handicapped children.

See also Valerie Sinason, *Understanding Your Handicapped Child*.

Chapter 5: Shayla & C.J.

171 Alan—not his real name.

179 For more on how a father's abandonment of his daughter can have lasting effects, including the precipitation of teen pregnancy, see Jonetta Rose Barras, *Whatever Happened to Daddy's Little Girl?: The Impact of Fatherlessness on Black Women*. Barras writes that teen girls who grow up without their fathers tend to have sex earlier than girls who grow up with their fathers; a fifteen-year-old with just a mom is three times more likely to lose her virginity before her sixteenth birthday than one living with both her parents. Based on her personal experience, Barras offers the following explanation for why the idea of getting pregnant is often so alluring to this potentially more vulnerable segment of the female population:

> In our fantasies we try to believe that the man we have chosen to love will not leave—as our fathers did. But we half expect him to; we program ourselves for his inevitable departure. The baby is a feature of that programming. At least when he leaves we will have someone—we won't be alone. In fact we'll still have him, because we have his baby. It's ludicrous, but nevertheless, we cling to this reasoning; it is our life-preserver (p. 70).

188 In roughly 92 percent of all domestic-violence incidents, men commit the crimes against women, and according to a study conducted by the

U.S. Department of Justice, women are five to eight times more likely than men to be victimized by an intimate partner. Because of these statistics, police are much more likely to arrest the male than the female, even if both parties have suffered injuries.

For the National Domestic Violence Fact Sheet and Statistics re: Incidence of Partner Abuse, go to the website www.ndvh.org.

200   Ian—not his real name.

211   Danah Zohar and Ian Marshall, *SQ: Connecting with Your Spiritual Intelligence.*

Chapter 6: Sheri

219   Greg—not his real name.

220   Nadine—not her real name.

220   Steve—not his real name.

224   Steven Greenhouse, "Problems Seen for Teenagers Who Hold Jobs," *The New York Times,* Jan. 29, 2001.

The issues Greenhouse raises brought to mind images of Sheri working from 3 to 9 P.M. as a housekeeper every day after school at age sixteen, and Colleen working long hours after school at Burger King. The article refers to a study conducted by two arms of the National Academy of Sciences—the National Research Council and the Institute of Medicine. This study found that when teenagers work more than twenty hours a week, the work often leads to lower grades, higher alcohol use, and too little time with their parents and families. The article discusses efforts in Massachusetts to enact legislation limiting the maximum hours teenagers are allowed to work:

> In Massachusetts, several lawmakers are seeking to limit the maximum amount of time 16-year-olds and 17-year-olds can work during school weeks to 30 hours, down from the cur-

rent maximum of 48 hours. "We have 16- and 17-year-olds working 40 hours a week on top of 30 hours in the classroom," said Peter J. Larkin, the Massachusetts state representative sponsoring the bill to reduce the number of hours teenagers can work. "Something has to give, and academics seems to be taking a back seat. Sure there is pressure against the bill from employers who need teenage workers to help in a full-employment economy, but many other employers are complaining that the graduates of our high schools are not up to par."

For the complete article, go to the *New York Times* archives at www.nytimes.com.

231   In her book *Of Woman Born,* Adrienne Rich has a wonderful passage that gave me insight into the immense impact of the mother-daughter relationship, specifically when it comes to teen motherhood and relationships like the one between Pat and Sheri and now between Sheri and her daughter, Leeah. In the passage below, Rich takes on the idea of the baby as a wish—and makes the point that in addition to investing their own hopes and dreams in children, mothers need to serve as examples of individuals who are in some way chasing their own dreams, who have not given up on their own lives, and who have not sacrificed their own identities completely and become entirely consumed in their roles as mothers at the expense of their own freedom:

> Only when we can wish imaginatively and courageously for ourselves can we wish unfetteredly for our daughters. But finally, a child is not a wish, nor a product of wishing. Women's lives—in all levels of society—have been lived too long in both depression and fantasy, while our active energies have been trained and absorbed into caring for others. It is essential now, to begin breaking that cycle. . . . As daughters we need mothers who want their own freedom and ours. We need not be the vessels of another woman's self-denial and frustration.

The quality of the mother's life is her primary bequest to her daughter, because a woman who can believe in herself, who is a fighter and who continues to struggle to create livable space around her, is demonstrating to her daughter that these possibilities exist. Because the conditions of life for so many poor women demand a fighting spirit for sheer physical survival, such mothers have sometimes been able to give their daughters something to be valued far more highly than full-time mothering (pp. 246–47).

252 Brad—not his real name.

256 Dylan—not his real name.

265 At various times, the teen mothers in this book were incapacitated by depression. In *The Noonday Demon: An Atlas of Depression,* Andrew Solomon writes: "Depression cuts across class boundaries, but depression treatments do not. This means that most people who are poor and depressed stay poor and depressed; in fact, the longer they stay poor and depressed, the more poor and depressed they become. Poverty is depressing and depression is impoverishing, leading as it does to dysfunction and isolation" (p. 335).

Chapter 7: Jessica

271 John Walsh, *No Mercy: The Host of* America's Most Wanted *Hunts the Worst Criminals of Our Time,* pp. 154–216. Although I incorporated some of Jessica's recollections about her grandparents as well as the recollections from one of her aunts whom I met, I relied on John Walsh's book for the details about her grandparents' trial, the years they spent as fugitives, and the story of how they were ultimately apprehended and sentenced to prison.

275 Dwayne—not his real name.

282 Edith Wharton, *Summer,* p. 157.

283   Jessica's remark "I never wanted to have sex with you in the first place" points to another problem area: the difficulty of a teenage girl asserting to a man that she isn't ready for sex, doesn't want it, and will not do it. This is a serious problem because its roots lie not in the sexual situation but at the heart of the relationship. Has the teenager chosen to date a guy whose behavior in other areas demonstrates that he cares about her, values her feelings, and will respect her wishes? If not, she is already in trouble and at risk by the time she enters a sexual situation. In one large survey, 31 percent of teen girls ages fifteen to nineteen said their first sexual experience was either nonvoluntary or voluntary but not really wanted. See www.appifw.org/statistics.html.

      Joycelyn Elders and Alexa E. Albert refer to the same issue in their *JAMA* article, "Adolescent Pregnancy and Sexual Abuse." They report that:

> [T]he incidence of non-voluntary sexual experiences that occur in adolescence, and thus, could lead to teen pregnancy, appears greater than previously assumed: One study of a mixed-ethnic sample of almost 2,000 middle and high school students in Los Angeles, Calif., found that 20% had unwanted sexual experiences, with 51% of adolescent girls having their first coercive sexual act between the ages of 13 and 16 years.

284   Some teenagers share Jessica's misconception that all adoptions are closed and require complete separation and anonymity between birth mother and child. These teenagers are not informed about the option of an open, private adoption. Justifiably, they fear surrendering their children to what they believe to be the utter unknown and are unwilling to agree to terms that they expect will require complete confidentiality and a severance of all ties with their babies.

      The battle between secrecy and disclosure of adoption records is still being waged in state legislatures and on the federal level, but significant progress has been made. Laws have been rewritten and revised, broadening the spectrum of parents who are eligible to adopt and making it easier for children to find permanent homes. The tide has shifted dramatically over the past twenty years, and the majority of infant adoptions that occur in America are private and open to varying degrees. The Internet has played a huge role in the move toward open adoptions, and all a teenager has to do is log on to websites such as www.birthmother.com or www.adoption.com to get complete information about attorneys and agencies in various states.

Attorneys representing clients who are desperate to adopt will pay to fly a teenager in Jessica's situation all the way across the country, if necessary, to hold interviews in the hopes of arriving at an agreement. In an open, private adoption, a birth mother is often allowed to maintain a relationship with the adoptive parents, who agree to pay for all her medical costs during the pregnancy. The birth mother is free to say yes or no to the prospective adoptive parents after meeting them and getting information about their lives, families, and financial profiles. Similarly, the adoptive parents can interview the birth mother to ascertain that they feel comfortable with the idea of adopting her baby. Although it varies, depending on the specific contracts, often letters, phone calls, and photographs can be exchanged so that a teenager such as Jessica wouldn't have to live a life full of unanswered questions about her son. She'd be able to maintain some level of connection to the child she relinquished. She would be able to know "where he was, how he looked, what he was doing."

For more on how adoption laws are being revised and the expanding role of the Internet, see Adam Pertman, *Adoption Nation: How the Adoption Revolution Is Transforming America*, pp. 1–26, 103–28.

Another issue that cannot be ignored is that most adoptive parents are white and are looking to adopt white children, which could potentially make it more challenging for a baby of mixed race, like Jessica's son, to find a home. In his book *Interracial Intimacies,* Randall Kennedy writes:

> In the 1980s a federal government investigation found that a healthy black infant waited about four times as long for placement as a healthy white infant. By the 1990s the dis-

parity had remained the same or widened. . . . Racial pref-
erence for white children remains a decisive and pervasive
influence within the adoption system (pp. 448–49).

Racial issues aside, it cannot be denied that giving up one's child is a
gut-wrenching process, no matter how great the adoptive parents are.
Making that particular decision requires an unmarried teen mother to
place a higher value on money, security, marriage, a stable two-parent
home, and other environmental comforts she might not be able to provide, as opposed to maternal love, which is one of the few priceless
resources she is capable of offering a child.

In the cases of teen mothers like Liz, who themselves spent time in
foster care, there is the fear that if they put their child up for adoption,
the child could end up unwanted by adoptive parents and be forced to
spend his or her childhood moving from one foster home to another.
That is not a risk many teen mothers are willing to take.

For more on why so few teen mothers choose to put their children
up for adoption, see Kristin Luker, *Dubious Conceptions,* pp. 161–64.

302 Wes—not his real name

Chapter 8: Community

317 Edith Wharton, *Summer,* p. 84.

321 Steve Seidel, "*Stand and Unfold Yourself: A Monograph of the Shakespeare &
Company Research Study.*"

321 For more information about the GE Fund, visit www.ge.com/commu-
nity/fund.

323 Kristin Linklater, *Freeing the Natural Voice.* Kristin Linklater's theories and
approach to the human voice are central to the work of Tina Packer,
Carol Gilligan, and Normi Noel. Linklater explains:
The basic assumption of the work is that everyone possesses

a voice capable of expressing through a two-to-four-octave natural pitch range whatever gamut of emotion, complexity of mood, and subtlety of thought he or she experiences. The second assumption is that the tensions acquired through living in this world, as well as defenses, inhibitions, and negative reactions to environmental influences, often diminish the efficiency of the natural voice to the point of distorted communication. Hence, the emphasis is on the removal of the blocks that inhibit the human instrument as distinct from the development of a skilled musical instrument. The object is a voice in direct contact with emotional impulse, shaped by intellect, not inhibited by it.

323   For more on the work of Carol Gilligan and her colleagues, see Carol Gilligan, *In a Different Voice: Psychological Theory and Women's Development,* and "Joining the Resistance: Psychology, Politics, Girls and Women," *Michigan Quarterly Review* 24 no. 4, pp. 501–36 (presented as the Tanner Lecture on Human Values, University of Michigan, March 16, 1990); C. Gilligan, J. V. Ward, and J. M. Taylor, eds., *Mapping the Moral Domain;* C. Gilligan, T. J. Hanmer, and N. P. Lyons, eds., *Making Connections: The Relational Worlds of Adolescent Girls at Emma Willard School;* and C. Gilligan, A. Rogers, and D. Tolman, eds., *Women and Therapy* (special issue on adolescence), also published as *Women, Girls, and Psychotherapy: Reframing Resistance.*

323   The Alan Guttmacher Institute published statistics on the risk of repeat teen pregnancies in the Guttmacher Report on Public Policy 3, no. 3 (June 2000). This report also addresses the increased number of teenagers who are switching from birth control pills to the contraceptive implant Norplant and, to an even greater extent, the three-month injectible, Depo-Provera. Several of the teen mothers in this book tried "the Shot" as a form of birth control after having their first child. Shayla reported uncomfortable side effects, including chronic migrane headaches, that discouraged her from continuing with this mode of birth control.

324   When I interviewed Carol Gilligan, she mentioned several classics in
      addition to *Summer* that she thought could be used effectively by mentors
      working to strengthen the voices and psychological awareness of adolescent
      girls. All of the books she mentioned have one thing in common: each fea-
      tures an intense, complicated, highly perceptive girl or young woman as
      narrator and/or central figure, and addresses trauma and painful emotions
      in an honest way: *To Kill a Mockingbird* by Harper Lee, *The Bluest Eye* and
      Sula by Toni Morrison, *Jane Eyre* by Charlotte Brontë, *Annie John* and *Lucy*
      by Jamaica Kincaid, and *Harriet the Spy* by Louise Fitzhugh.

329   Regarding the critical reception of Edith Wharton's *Summer* in 1917: in
      her introduction to the Scribner paperback edition, Marilyn French
      writes:

> *Summer*'s excellence was recognized at the time it was pub-
> lished by readers like Joseph Conrad, Howard Sturgis, and
> Percy Lubbock, the latter two of whom compared it not
> unfavorably to *Madame Bovary*. But most Americans were
> scandalized by the book's subject matter, and Wharton was
> reproached for it (p. 41).

In her introduction to the Bantam paperback, Susan Minot wrote the
following about the critical reception of *Summer* in 1917:

> The chapter about a drunken funeral on the Mountain was
> according to Wharton, "received with indignant denial by
> many reviewers and readers," and while she was not re-
> quired to defend her fictional choices, she did reveal that
> the scene was taken directly from an account given to her
> by the rector of the church in Lenox (p. xiii).

329   Edith Wharton, *A Backward Glance,* p. 294:

> In those days the snow-bound villages of Western Massa-
> chusetts were still grim places, morally and physically: in-
> sanity, incest and slow mental starvation were hidden away
> behind the paintless wooden house-fronts of the long village
> street, or in the isolated farm-houses on the neighbouring

hills; and Emily Bronte would have found as savage tragedies
in our remoter valleys as on her Yorkshire Moors.

330 Joycelyn Elders and Alexa E. Albert, "Adolescent Pregnancy and Sexual
Abuse," *Journal of the American Medical Association* 280 (Aug. 19, 1998),
pp. 648–49. This article discusses teen pregnancy as an all-too-common
scenario for 800,000 U.S. adolescent girls each year and examines the
prevalence of sexual abuse among this population, citing data from numerous studies: A 1992 Washington State study of 535 teen mothers revealed
that the first pregnancies of 62 percent of the participants were preceded
by experiences of molestation, rape, or attempted rape. The mean age of
their offenders was 27.4 years (D. Boyer and D. Fine, "Sexual Abuse as a
Factor in Adolescent Pregnancy and Child Maltreatment," *Family Planning
Perspectives* 4, 24, no. 1 [Jan./Feb. 1992], pp. 9–11, 19). A 1986 study of
445 teen mothers in Chicago reported that 60 percent claimed they had
been forced to have an unwanted sexual experience, with a mean age for
the first incidence of abuse being eleven. (H. P. Gershenson et al., "The
Prevalence of Coercive Sexual Experiences Among Teenage Mothers,"
Journal of Interpersonal Violence 4 [1989], pp. 204–9).

Jacqualine Stock et al., "Adolescent Pregnancy and Sexual Risk-Taking
Among Sexually Abused Girls," *Family Planning Perspectives* 29, no. 4
(1997). Data on 3,128 girls in grades eight, ten, and twelve who participated in the 1992 Washington State Survey of Adolescent Health Behaviors were used to analyze the association of a self-reported history of
sexual abuse with teenage pregnancy and with sexual behavior that in-
creases the risk of teen pregnancy. An association between sexual abuse
and teenage pregnancy appears to be the result of high-risk behavior
exhibited by adolescent girls who have been abused.

332 Valerie Sinason, ed., *Memory in Dispute*. Composed of articles by British psy-
choanalysts and psychotherapists, this book explores the many levels of
complexity involved in acknowledgment of child abuse and its consequences, and addresses the clinical challenges these issues present. Chapter
2, "Children Are Liars, Aren't They? An Exploration of Denial Processes in

Child Abuse," by Arnon Bentovim, looks at issues such as children's statements, psychological denial, social denial, denial and the court system, and trauma-organized systems as an exploratory model for denial processes.

332 Judith Herman, M.D., is clinical professor of psychiatry at Harvard Medical School and director of training at the Victims of Violence Program at Cambridge Hospital in Cambridge, Massachusetts. She first published *Father-Daughter Incest* in 1981. When it was reprinted in 2000, she included a new afterword in which she discussed the findings of Andrea J. Sedlak and Dianne D. Broadhurst, who wrote the *Executive Summary of the Third National Incidence Study of Child Abuse and Neglect* (Washington, D.C.: United States Department of Health and Human Services, 1996):

> The most recent survey, conducted in 1996, arrived at a conservative estimate that 217,000 children were sexually abused in that year. Roughly half of these children were abused by their fathers, stepfathers, or other father figures. . . . Unfortunately, the capacity of state authorities to intervene on behalf of abused children has not kept pace with the professional capacity to identify children at risk. As reporting has soared, the number of case investigations has remained static, resulting in a declining percentage of investigated cases. By 1996, only 28 percent of the cases identified by sentinels were officially investigated, even when the children had serious physical injuries. . . . Back in 1990, the National Advisory Board on Child Abuse and Neglect was describing the situation in child protection as a "national emergency." Since then, matters appear to have gotten worse. . . . This crisis in child protective services is but one example of a larger conflict between public concern about the welfare of children and reluctance to intervene or to commit resources on a scale that might realistically be necessary to provide all children with adequate care and protection (pp. 222–23).

333   For more on the complexity of sexual abuse and disclosure, see Herman, *Father-Daughter Incest,* pp. 129ff.

336   Timothy Roche, "The Crisis of Foster Care," *Time,* Nov. 13, 2000.

338   J. G. Silverman and Anita Raj, "Dating Violence and Sexual Risk Behavior Among a Representative Sample of High School Females," *Harvard Children's Initiative,* Harvard University, in *Journal of the American Medical Association* 286 (Dec. 12, 2001), p. 2813.

339   Barrie Levy, ed., *Dating Violence: Young Women in Danger.* The chapter by Judith McFarlane, "Violence During Teen Pregnancy: Health Consequences for Mother and Child," relates directly to Colleen's and Nadine's stories.

339   James M. Makepeace, "Courtship Violence as Process: A Developmental Theory" in Albert Cardarelli, ed., *Violence Between Intimate Partners: Patterns, Causes, and Effects,* p. 33. In this chapter, Makepeace discusses how a high school dating culture that revolves around cars, sex, and alcohol contributes to "terrible and epidemic consequences." For more on interpersonal violence and adolescent pregnancy, go to www.noappp.org.

339   L. Bullock and McFarlane conducted a 1988 survey of pregnant teens in several large metropolitan areas. Of the more than two hundred pregnant teens surveyed, 26 percent reported physical abuse, 40–60 percent stated that the battering had either begun or escalated since the discovery of the pregnancy, and 65 percent of those abused had not talked to anyone about the abuse.

340   For more on extreme stereotyped gender roles and their relation to dating violence within the adolescent population, see Levy, ed., *Dating Violence* pp. 4–5. This book also includes an outstanding, very detailed section on education and prevention projects (pp. 223–78).

346   Rick Klein, "Romney Team Spreads Its Cuts," *The Boston Globe,* Jan. 31, 2003.

346   Erik Arvidson, "Romney Aide: Budget Cuts Spare 'Muscle and Bone'"
       The Berkshire Eagle, Jan. 31. 2003.

347   Pat Nichols, "Mission Impossible?" *Berkshire Eagle,* Oct. 27, 2002.

348   For more on absent parenting and the aloneness of many of today's
       teenagers, see Patricia Hersch, *A Tribe Apart: A Journey into the Heart of
       American Adolescence.* Hersch spent several years documenting the lives of
       teenagers in Reston, Virginia.

348   Eric Schmidt, "For the First Time, Nuclear Families Drop Below 25% of
       Households," *The New York Times,* May 15, 2001:
       > For the first time, less than a quarter of the households in
       > the United States are made up of married couples with their
       > children, new census data show. That results from a number
       > of factors, like many men and women delaying both mar-
       > riage and having children, more couples living longer after
       > their adult children leave home and the number of single-
       > parent families growing much faster than the number of
       > married couples. *Indeed, the number of families headed by women
       > who have children, which are typically poorer than two-parent
       > families, grew nearly five times faster in the 1990's than the number
       > of married couples with children* (italics mine).

348   Marc L. Miringoff, *The Social Health of the Nation:*
       > In 1996, female single-parent households had a median in-
       > come of $16,389 per year, compared to $51,768 for married
       > couples with children. More than 40% of all female-headed
       > families had incomes below the poverty line (p. 128).

349   William J. Bennett and Jack Kemp, "Keep Reforming Welfare," *The Wall
       Street Journal,* Aug. 1, 2002. Bennett, a former secretary of education,
       and Kemp, a former secretary of housing and urban development, cite
       the 1996 welfare reform bill as "one of the most significant and successful

pieces of social policy enacted in the last half century. Welfare rolls have plummeted by 50%, child poverty is at its lowest point in 20 years, poverty levels of black children are at their lowest recorded level ever."

349   Katherine Boo, "Welfare Reform Series," *The Washington Post*, Dec. 15, 1996–Dec. 21, 1997. See Part 4, "Day Care Centers in Trouble."

350   James J. Heckman, *Invest in the Very Young*, published by the Ounce of Prevention Fund, available at www.ounceofprevention.org.

351   See Howard Gardner, *Intelligence Reframed: Multiple Intelligences for the 21st Century* and *The Unschooled Mind: How Children Think and How Schools Should Teach*.

351   Daniel Goleman, *Emotional Intelligence: Why It Can Matter More than IQ*. Goleman makes the case for emotional intelligence being the strongest indicator of human success.

352   Jack Zimmerman and Virginia Coyle, in *The Way of Council*, describe the roots of the Council Program and its application to family life and adult groups, including business organizations, as well as to teenagers in a school setting. Influences discussed include Native American traditions, Quaker Meetings, extended family gatherings, and many contemporary techniques of group dynamics.

352   Jack Zimmerman and Ruthann Sapphier, *The Mysteries Sourcebook and Lesson Plan*. This program was developed with the support of the Ojai Foundation and initiated in 1983 at the Crossroads School in Santa Monica, California, and was expanded to a variety of schools, including the Palms Middle School in the Los Angeles Unified School District. All descriptions of the course were taken from this highly detailed booklet, which contains the course program broken down on a week-by-week basis and lists discussion topics, educational philosophy, assignments, and teaching methodologies.

For information about teacher training and to order this outstanding course book complete with lesson plans, visit the resources section of the website www.counciltraining.org.

355   Rachael Kessler, *The Soul of Education: Helping Students Find Connection, Compassion, and Character at School* and "Passages: Fostering Community, Heart, and Spirit in Adolescent Education." This article is available at www.newhorizons.org.

For information on Kessler's workshops, consultation, and materials, go to www.mediatorsfoundation.org or contact:

> The Passageways Institute for Social and Emotional Learning
> 3822 North 57th Street
> Boulder, CO 80301

More thoughts regarding the importance of rites of passage:

In her book *Promiscuities* Naomi Wolf devotes a section to this topic:

> Anthropologists who look at adolescent rites of passage agree that their importance cannot be overstated, not only for the sake of the developing adolescent, but for the sake of the coherence of a society.

Wolf goes on to argue that in the absence of other rites of passage that are present in other cultures, the transition from girlhood to womanhood has for many American adolescents become defined by sexual availability, and often young girls misinterpret teen pregnancy and motherhood as a confirmation of adulthood in the absence of other indicators (pp. 143–46).

While doing research for this book, I made several visits to Raw Arts Works (RAW), a nonprofit art-therapy organization in the depressed city of Lynn, Massachusetts. This outstanding program offers adolescents two groups that are dedicated to rites of passage, Men 2 Be and Women 2 Be. Through field trips, overnight camping trips, and artistic group projects, this nonprofit organization takes kids at risk who live in nearby public housing projects through steps toward maturation that involve co-operation, exploration of identity, reliability, persistence, and courage. They have seen hardly any teen pregnancies among kids who have participated in their program.

Of particular interest is their exceptional work with middle-school and high-school boys in the Men 2 Be group, led by gifted art therapist Jason Cruz. Below is an example of one of Jason's assignments for the boys:

> *Breaking Broken Records:* Write down on the record the places where you feel stuck, where the "needle keeps skipping," and then smash the record. Take the pieces and create a sculpture that describes changes you want to make in your life. Define how you will change the "Broken Record."

For more on RAW programs, see their website, www.rawarts.org.

355 Jack Zimmerman is currently editing and co-writing a new book with educators who have implemented the Council Program in several schools in different parts of the country. This book will include information about how to implement the Council Program at public and private schools and will be available in 2004.

For updates about Zimmerman's forthcoming book and for information about teacher training, go to www.counciltraining.org.

356 Douglas Kirby, *Emerging Answers: New Research Findings on Programs to Reduce Teen Pregnancy,* the National Campaign to Prevent Teen Pregnancy, May 2001. For a summary of his study of programs with both sexuality and youth-development components and his specific comments on the success of the Children's Aid Society-Carrera Program, see pages 15–17. Kirby's study is available at www.teenpregnancy.org.

357 Tamar Lewin, "Program Finds Success in Reducing Teenage Pregnancy," *The New York Times,* May 20, 2001.

357 "The Carrera Model: A Success in Pregnancy Prevention" was published in the newsletter of the Charles Stewart Mott Foundation, April 2, 2002.

358 I met Mayor Hathaway for the first time at one of the coffee hours she held at the Berkshire Athenaeum in Pittsfield. True to her campaign

promises, in person she was warm, accessible and receptive. She granted me an interview the following day.

362 Alexander Stille, "Grounded by an Income Gap," *The New York Times,* Dec. 15, 2001. Economist James Heckman is quoted in this article expressing a view similar to that of psychologist Carol Gilligan:

> Never has the accident of birth mattered more," he asserts. "If I am born to educated, supportive parents, my chances of doing well are totally different than if I were born to a single parent or abusive parents. I am a University of Chicago libertarian, but this is a case of market failure: Children don't get to 'buy' their parents and so there has to be some kind of intervention to make up for these environmental differences."

BIBLIOGRAPHY

Adolescent Pregnancy Prevention, Inc. *Facts About Teen Pregnancy*. April 1999, from www.appifw.org.

Alan Guttmacher Institute. The Guttmacher Report on Public Policy. *Teenagers' Pregnancy, Intentions and Decisions*. 1999.
————. *Teen Pregnancy and the Welfare Reform Debate*. 1998.
————. *The Politics of Blame: Family Planning, Abortion, and the Poor*. 1995.
————. *Public Policy* 3, no. 3 (June 2000).
————. *Teen Sex and Pregnancy*. September 1999.
————. *U.S. Teenage Pregnancy Statistics*. March 2001.
These reports are all available at www.guttmacher.org.

Allison, Dorothy. *Bastard Out of Carolina*. New York: Plume, 1993.

————. *Trash*. New York: Plume, 2002.

————. *Two or Three Things I Know for Sure*. New York: Plume, 1996.

Alonso-Zaldivar, Ricardo, and Robin Fields. "Latino, Asian Populations Rise Sharply in Census: New Multiracial Figures Find a Substantial Growth of Immigrants in Nontraditional Regions." *The New York Times*, July 31, 2001.

Anda, R. F., and D. P. Chapman, V. J. Felitti, V. E. Edward, D. F. Williamson, J. P. Croft, and W. H. Giles. "Adverse Childhood Experiences and Risk of Paternity in Teen Pregnancy." *Obstetrics and Gynecology* 100, no. 1 (2002), pp. 37–45.

Anda, R. F., and V. J. Felitti, D. P. Chapman, J. B. Croft et al. "Abused Boys, Battered Mothers, and Male Involvement in Teen Pregnancy: New Insights for Pediatricians." *Pediatrics* 107, no. 2 (2001), p. e19.

Anderson, Sherwood. *Winesburg, Ohio.* New York: Bantam Classic, 1995.

Barras, Jonetta Rose. *Whatever Happened to Daddy's Little Girl? The Impact of Fatherlessness on Black Women.* New York: Ballantine, 2000.

Bentovim, Arnon. "Children Are Liars Aren't They?—An Exploration of Denial Processes in Child Abuse," in Valerie Sinason, ed. *Memory in Dispute.* London: Karnac Books, 1998.

The Berkshire Eagle.
    Arvidson, Erik. "Romney Aide: Budget Cuts Spare 'Muscle and Bone.'" January 31, 2003.
    Bahlman, D. R. "City Ordinance Aims to Leash Vicious Dogs." October 14, 2002.
    ———. "Vicious Dog Rule Endorsed." October 24, 2002.
    Carey, Bill. "Crane Wins $336M Currency Paper Contract." October 16, 2002
    Dew, Jack. "Pittsfield, N.A., See Big Drops in Census." October 24, 2000.
    Dew, Jack. "GE Challenges Cleanup Cost, Complaint Targets New Method of Accounting." February 5, 2002.
    ———. "PCB Contamination Experts to Meet for Panel Discussion." February 9, 2002.
    ———. "Coffee Talks Cover the Same Ground; Hathaway Touts Solutions to Pittsfield's Many Woes." October 8, 2002.
    Gosselin, Lisa. "1 Man Nabbed, 1 Man Sought in City Shooting." November 13, 2002.
    ———. "Shooting Incident Suspect Ordered Held on High Bail." November 14, 2002.
    Mehegan, Julie. "Heroin Abuse in Mass. Called an Epidemic." December 18, 2002.

Nichols, Pat. "Mission Impossible?" October 27, 2002.
The above articles are all available at www.berkshireeagle.com.

Bernstein, Nina. "Side Effect of Welfare Law: The No-Parent Family." *The New York Times,* July 2, 2002.

Boo, Katherine. "Welfare Reform Series" from *The Washington Post,* December 15, 1996–December 21, 1997.

Bouton, Jim. *Foul Ball: My Life and Hard Times Trying to Save an Old Ballpark.* North Egremont, Mass.: Bulldog Publishing, 2003.

Bragg, Rick. *All Over But The Shoutin'.* New York: Vintage, 1998.

Brown, L., and C. Gilligan. "Meeting at the Crossroads: Women's Psychology and Girls' Development." *Feminism and Psychology* 3, no. 1, pp. 11–35.

Calahan, R., and S. Watson. *A Strategy for Economic Development in Berkshire County.* Cambridge, Mass.: John F. Kennedy School of Government, Harvard University, 1984.

Cherlin, Andrew J. *Public and Private Families: A Reader.* 2d ed. Boston: McGraw-Hill, 2000.

Coles, Robert. *The Youngest Parents.* New York: Center for Documentary Studies in association with W. W. Norton, 1997.

Dash, Leon. *When Children Want Children: An Inside Look at the Crisis of Teenage Parenthood.* New York: Penguin, 1996.

Dietz, P. M., and A. M. Spitz, R. F. Anda, D. F. Williamson, P. M. McMahon, J. S. Santelli, D. F. Nordenberg, V. J. Felitti, and J. S. Kendrick. "Unintended Pregnancy Among Adult Women Exposed to Abuse or Household Dysfunction During Their Childhood." *Journal of the American Medical Association* 282 (1999), pp. 1359–64.

Ehrenreich, Barbara. *Nickel and Dimed: On (Not) Getting By in America*. New York: Metropolitan Books, 2001.

Elders, Joycelyn, and Alexa E. Albert. "Adolescent Pregnancy and Sexual Abuse." *Journal of the American Medical Association* 280, no. 7 (Aug. 19, 1998), pp. 648–49.

Erikson, Erik H. *Identity: Youth and Crisis*. New York: W. W. Norton, 1968.

Felitti, V. J. "The Relationship Between Adverse Childhood Experiences and Adult Health: Turning Gold into Lead." *The Permanente Journal* 6 (2002), pp. 44–47. Available at www.drfelitti.com.

Felitti, V. J., R. F. Anda, D. Nordenberg, D. F. Williamson, A. M. Spitz, V. Edwards, M. P. Koss, et al. "The Relationship of Adult Health Status to Childhood Abuse and Household Dysfunction." *American Journal of Preventive Medicine* 14 (1998), pp. 245–58.

Friedman, Mickey. *Good Things to Life: GE, PCBs and Our Town*. A feature-length digital video documentary about General Electric and its use and misuse of the toxic chemicals, PCBs. Blue Hill Films, 32 Rosseter Street, Great Barrington, MA 01230. Mfried@bcn.net.

Froomkin, Dan. "Welfare's Changing Face." *The Washington Post,* July 23, 1998.

Gardner, Howard. *Intelligence Reframed: Multiple Intelligences for the 21st Century*. New York: Basic Books, 2000.

———. *The Unschooled Mind: How Children Think and How Schools Should Teach*. New York: Basic Books, 1993.

Gilligan, Carol. *In a Different Voice: Psychological Theory and Women's Development*. Cambridge, Mass.: Harvard University Press, 1982.

————. "Joining the Resistance: Psychology, Politics, Girls and Women." *Michigan Quarterly Review* 24, no. 4, pp. 501–36. Presented as the Tanner Lecture on Human Values, University of Michigan, March 16, 1990.

Gilligan, C., J. V. Ward, and J. M. Taylor, eds. *Mapping the Moral Domain.* Cambridge, Mass.: Harvard University Press, 1988.

Gilligan, C., T. J. Hanmer, and N. P. Lyons, eds. *Making Connections: The Relational Worlds of Adolescent Girls at Emma Willard School.* Cambridge, Mass.: Harvard University Press, 1989.

Gilligan, C., A. Rogers, and D. Tolman, eds. *Women and Therapy.* Special issue on adolescence (1991). Published also as *Women, Girls, and Psychotherapy: Reframing Resistance.* New York: Hayworth Press, 1991.

Gilligan, James. *Violence: Reflections on a National Epidemic.* New York: Vintage Books, 1997.

Goleman, Daniel. *Emotional Intelligence: Why It Can Matter More than IQ.* New York: Bantam Books, 1997.

Goodnough, Abby. "Policy Eases the Way Out of Bad Schools." *The New York Times,* December 9, 2002.

Greenhouse, Steven. "Problems Seen for Teenagers Who Hold Jobs." *The New York Times,* January 29, 2001.

Hathaway, Sara. Mayoral Inaugural Address, Pittsfield, Mass. January 7, 2002.

Heckman, James J. *Invest in the Very Young.* The Ounce of Prevention Fund, from www.ounceofprevention.org/publications/pubindex.html.

Herman, Judith Lewis. *Father-Daughter Incest.* Cambridge, Mass.: Harvard University Press, 1981.

Hersch, Patricia. *A Tribe Apart: A Journey into the Heart of American Adolescence.* New York: Ballantine, 1998.

Hillis, S. D., R. F. Anda, V. J. Felitti, and P. A. Marchbanks. "Adverse Childhood Experiences and Sexual Risk Behaviors in Women: A Retrospective Cohort Study." *Family Planning Perspectives* 33 (2001), pp. 206–11.

Hooks, Bell. *Where We Stand: Class Matters.* New York: Routledge, 2000.

Hymowitz, Kay S. *Ready or Not: Why Treating Children as Small Adults Endangers Their Future—and Ours.* New York: Free Press, 1999.

Jencks, Christopher. *Rethinking Social Policy: Race, Poverty, and the Underclass.* Cambridge, Mass.: Harvard University Press, 1992.

Kagan, Jerome, and Robert Coles, eds. *Twelve to Sixteen: Early Adolescence.* New York: W. W. Norton, 1972.

Kasindorf, Martin, and Haya El Nasser. "Impact of Census' Race Data Debated: Some Say It Will Divide Country; Others Say Unite." *USA Today,* March 13, 2001.

Kennedy, Randall. *Interracial Intimacies: Sex, Marriage, Identity, and Adoption.* New York: Pantheon, 2003.

Kessler, Rachael. *The Soul of Education: Helping Students Find Connection, Compassion, and Character at School.* Alexandria, Va.: Association for Supervision and Curriculum Development, 2003.

———. "Passages: Fostering Community, Heart, and Spirit in Adolescent Education," from www.newhorizons.org.

Kirsch, Max H. *In the Wake of the Giant: Multinational Restructuring and Uneven Development in a New England Community.* Albany: SUNY Press, 1998.

Klein, Rick. "Romney Team Spreads Its Cuts." *The Boston Globe*, January 31, 2003.

Kotlowitz, Alex. *There Are No Children Here: The Story of Two Boys Growing Up in the Other America*. New York: Doubleday, 1991.

Krugman, Paul. "For Richer: How the Permissive Capitalism of the Boom Destroyed American Equality." *The New York Times Magazine,* October 20, 2002.

Levy, Barrie. "Abusive Teen Dating Relationships: An Emerging Issue for the '90s." *Response to the Victimization of Women and Children* 13 (1990).

Levy, Barrie, ed. *Dating Violence: Young Women in Danger*. Seattle: Seal Press, 1991.

Lewin, Tamar. "Program Finds Success in Reducing Teenage Pregnancy." *The New York Times,* May 20, 2001.

———. "Zero-Tolerance Policy Is Challenged." *The New York Times,* July 11, 2001.

Linklater, Kristin. *Freeing the Natural Voice*. New York: Drama Book Specialists, 1976.

Lipper, Joanna. *Inside Out: Portraits of Children*. New York: Ruby Slipper Productions, 1996. www.rubyslipper.net.

———. *Growing Up Fast* (the documentary). New York: Ruby Slipper Productions, 1999. www.rubyslipper.net.

Lowe, Janet. *Welch: An American Icon*. New York: John Wiley & Sons, 2001.

Lukas, Anthony J. *Common Ground. A Turbulent Decade in the Lives of Three American Families*. New York: Vintage Books, 1986.

Luker, Kristin. *Dubious Conceptions: The Politics of Teenage Pregnancy*. Cambridge, Mass.: Harvard University Press, 1996.

———. "Dubious Conceptions: The Controversy Over Teen Pregnancy" in Andrew Cherlin, ed., *Public and Private Families*. New York: McGraw-Hill, 1996.

Makepeace, James M. "Courtship Violence as Process: A Developmental Theory" in Albert Cardarelli, ed., *Violence Between Intimate Partners: Patterns, Causes, and Effects*. Boston: Allyn & Bacon, 1997.

Maynard, Rebecca A., ed. *Kids Having Kids: Economic Costs and Social Consequences of Teen Pregnancy*. Washington, D.C.: Urban Institute Press, 1997.

Miringoff, Marc L. *The Social Health of the Nation: How America Is Really Doing*. New York: Oxford University Press, 1999.

Morrison, Toni. *The Bluest Eye*. New York: Penguin, 2000.

———. *Sula*. New York: Knopf, 2002.

Musick, J. S. *Young, Poor, and Pregnant: The Psychology of Teenage Motherhood*. New Haven: Yale University Press, 1993.

Nash, June C. *From Tank Town to High Tech: The Clash of Community and Industrial Cycles*. Albany: SUNY Press, 1989.

National Campaign to Prevent Teen Pregnancy. *"Just the Facts"*: *Data on Teen Pregnancy, Childbearing, Sexual Activity and Contraceptive Use*. 2000.

O'Boyle, Thomas F. *At Any Cost: Jack Welch, General Electric, and the Pursuit of Profit*. New York: Vintage, 1998.

Ounce of Prevention Publications. *Heart to Heart: An Innovative Approach to Preventing Childhood Sexual Abuse*, from www.ounceofprevention.org/publications /pubindex.html.

Pertman, Adam. *Adoption Nation: How the Adoption Revolution Is Transforming America*. New York: Basic Books, 2001.

Pipher, Mary. *Reviving Ophelia*. New York: Ballantine Books, 1995.

Rich, Adrienne. *Of Woman Born: Motherhood as Experience and Institution*. New York: W. W. Norton, 1976.

Roche, Timothy. "The Crisis of Foster Care." *Time*, November 13, 2000.

Sander, Joelle. *Before Their Time: Four Generations of Teenage Mothers*. New York: Harcourt Brace Jovanovich, 1991.

Schlosser, Eric. *Fast Food Nation: The Dark Side of the All-American Meal*. Boston: Houghton Mifflin, 2001.

Schmidt, Eric. "For the First Time, Nuclear Families Drop Below 25% of Households." *The New York Times,* May 15, 2001.

Seidel, Steve. *Stand and Unfold Yourself: A Monograph on the Shakespeare & Company Research Study*. Project Zero, Harvard Graduate School of Education, 1998.

Silverman, J. G., and Anita Raj. "Dating Violence and Sexual Risk Behavior Among a Representative Sample of High School Females." *Journal of the American Medical Association* 286 (Dec. 12, 2001), p. 2813.

Simon, David, and Edward Burns. *The Corner: A Year in the Life of an Inner-City Neighborhood*. New York: Broadway Books, 1997.

Sinason, Valerie. *Mental Handicap and the Human Condition*. London: Free Association Books, 1992.

————. *Understanding Your Handicapped Child*. Toronto, Ontario: Warwick Publishing, 1997.

Smith, Betty. *A Tree Grows in Brooklyn*. New York: Perennial Books, 1998.

Solomon, Andrew. *The Noonday Demon: An Atlas of Depression*. New York: Scribner, 2001.

Stille, Alexander. "Grounded by an Income Gap." *The New York Times*, December 15, 2001.

Tanner, Lindsey. "Study: Girls Victimized by Dates." Associated Press, July 31, 2001.

Taylor, J., C. Gilligan, and A. Sullivan. *Between Voice and Silence: Women and Girls, Race and Relationships*. Cambridge, Mass.: Harvard University Press, 1995.

Terkel, Studs. *Working*. New York: The New Press, 1974.

U.S. Department of Health and Human Services. *A National Strategy to Prevent Teen Pregnancy*. Annual Report 1999.

U.S. Department of Labor. *About Welfare—Myths, Facts, Challenges and Solutions*. 1998.

Walsh, John. *No Mercy: The Host of* America's Most Wanted *Hunts the Worst Criminals of Our Time*. New York: Pocket Books, 1998.

Wharton, Edith. *Summer*. New York: Bantam, 1993.

————. *A Backward Glance*. New York: Touchstone, 1998.

Wolf, Naomi, *Promiscuities: The Secret Struggle for Womanhood*. New York: Fawcett, 1998.

Wolff, Edward N. *Top Heavy: The Increasing Inequality of Wealth in America and What Can Be Done About It*. New York: New Press, 2002.

Zimmerman, Jack, and Virginia Coyle. *The Way of Council*. Las Vegas: Bramble Books, 1996.

Zimmerman, Jack, and Ruthann Saphier. *The Mysteries Sourcebook and Lesson Plan*, from www.counciltraining.org/resources.html.

Zohar, Danah, and Ian Marshall. *SQ: Connecting with Your Spiritual Intelligence*. New York: Bloomsbury, 2001.

Selected Websites

www.appifw.org—*Adolescent Pregnancy Prevention, Inc.*

www.cdc.gov/nchs—*National Center for Health Statistics of the Centers for Disease Control and Prevention*

www.childstats.gov—*Federal Interagency Forum on Child and Family Statistics*

www.counciltraining.org—*Mysteries Program, council training, and resources*

www.drfelitti.com—*information on the ACE (Adverse Childhood Experience) Study*

www.drugfreeamerica.org—*Partnership for a Drug-Free America*

www.etr.org/recapp/index.htm—*Resource Center for Adolescent Pregnancy Prevention*

BIBLIOGRAPHY

www.growingupfast.com—*book website with photo galleries*

www.guidancecenterinc.org—*Guidance Center Inc.*

www.housatonic-river.com—*Housatonic River Initiative*

www.jama.ama-assn.org—Journal of the American Medical Association

www.mediatorsfoundation.org—*Passageways Institute Connection, Compassion and Character in Learning the Soul of Education*

www.molt.org—*The Charles Stewart Molt Foundation*

www.ndvh.org—*National Domestic Violence Hotline*

www.noappp.org—*National Organization on Adolescent Pregnancy, Parenting and Prevention*

www.nochildleftbehind.gov—*U.S. Department of Education*

www.ounceofprevention.org—*Ounce of Prevention Fund, James Heckman*

www.plannedparenthood.org—*Planned Parenthood Federation of America*

www.pzweb.harvard.edu—*Project Zero, Harvard Graduate School of Education*

www.rawart.org—*Raw Arts, art therapy for youth at risk*

www.rubyslipper.net—*Ruby Slipper Productions*

www.safehorizon.org—*Domestic and dating violence prevention*

www.scholarshipfund.org—*Children's Scholarship Fund*

BIBLIOGRAPHY

www.shakespeare.org—*Shakespeare & Company, Lenox, Mass.*

www.state.ma.us/dhcd/—*Massachusetts Department of Housing and Community Development*

www.state.ma.us/dph/—*Massachusetts Department of Public Health*

www.stopteenpregnancy.com—*Carrera Program*

www.teenpregnancy.org—*National Campaign to Prevent Teen Pregnancy*

www.teenweb.org—*Berkshire Coalition to Prevent Teen Pregnancy*

www.wroc.org—*Welfare Rights Organizing Coalition*

ACKNOWLEDGMENTS

I would like to extend my deepest gratitude to all the people who spoke from their hearts and shared their stories for this book. Thanks to Amy, Bernard, James, Donna, Colleen, Maureen, Shayla, Kelly, Ashley, C.J., Sheri, Jon, Pat, Nadine, Liz, Peter, Jessica, Doris, Bill, Robert, Mary Ann, Captain Patrick Barry, Mary, Nicole, Mayor Sara Hathaway, Jack Zimmerman, Marjorie Cohan, Mickey Friedman, Joann Oliver, Katrina Mattson-Brown, Dr. Scherling, and Dr. Vincent J. Felitti. Thanks also to the late Helen Berube, the former director of the Teen Parent Program, and to B. J. Mancari, who was the social worker in residence the year the documentary film was made. My gratitude also extends to the children I had the privilege of observing from infancy on: Ezakeil, Ka-liegh, Marcus, Leeah, Jonathan, Jaiden, Caleb, and Peter.

Without the participation of these young parents and the adults in Pittsfield who shared their unique perspectives, this book would never have come into existence. I would like to thank them for everything they have taught me, and for giving me a collection of special moments and poignant memories that I will always treasure. Being a vessel for their words and a mirror for their emotions was an enormous honor and an immense responsibility. I can only hope that I have risen to the occasion and done an adequate job of reflecting the character, strength, eloquence, humor, insight, and courage of these young parents, their families, and the people in their community.

I never dreamt that I would be so fortunate as to have an editor like Frances Coady enter my life. Her energy, brilliance, and dedication to this book have been nothing short of phenomenal. With her imagination, empathy, boundless energy, and vivid social conscience, she helped extract, structure, and shape the panorama that became this book—regarding every aspect of the process, from the photography to the videotaped interviews to the writing, with equal respect and meticulous attention, offering strong input while also giving me the freedom to explore and determine my ultimate destination. I thank Frances and all her colleagues at Picador—including Josh Kendall, Christine Preston, Tanya Barone, and Leia Vandersnick—for making the process of writing my first book such an intense, challenging, joyful experience.

Thanks to my agent, Jennifer Rudolph Walsh at William Morris, to Xanthe Tabor, also at William Morris, and to my lawyer, Michael Schenkman, at Bloom, Hergott. Their counsel and expertise have been invaluable.

I would like to thank Carol Gilligan for believing in my work, for inviting me to Pittsfield, for making it possible for me to start this project, and for encouraging me and inspiring me along the way. Similarly, I would like to thank Tina Packer, Jane Fonda, Normi Noel, Kirsty Gunn, and Margaret Mahoney. With their sheer strength, intellect, power, insight, and sensitivity, these trailblazers continue to give me much to aspire to.

While an undergraduate at Harvard, I took courses taught by professors who profoundly influenced my thinking and encouraged me to approach subjects from a rigorous, passionate, interdisciplinary perspective. I extend my gratitude to Elaine Scarry, Philip Fisher, Stanley Cavell, Sacvan Bercovitch, Susan Suleiman, Jerome Kagan, Svetlana Boym, and Patrice Higonnet. Thanks also to Jill McCorkle and Melanie Thernstrom in the creative writing department.

While a graduate student at the Anna Freud Centre and University College London, I attended insightful seminars led by the late Joseph Sandler, Anne-Marie Sandler, Peter Fonagy, and Pauline Cohen. Their emphasis on child development from infancy through adolescence, their focus on observation, and their exploration of the evolution of psychoanalysis from the time of its inception through the present provided me with a rigorous conceptual and historical framework. This background, along with the monumental work of Erik Erikson, helped shape my many questions about an individual's relationship to family and society at various phases of the life cycle.

I would like to thank the Woodhull Institute for Women and Ethical Leadership and three of its board members, Dr. Robin Stern, Erica Jong, and Naomi Wolf, for their support and friendship throughout the writing process, and for hosting the teen mothers at a screening of our documentary followed by an inspiring discussion at Makor. Thanks to Dejan Georgevich and to Raj Guru at Manhattan Color Lab. Gratitude also to Garth Thomas and Barrington Pheloung for their support, friendship, and invaluable contributions to both my documentaries.

Thanks and much love to my family and friends for their love, support, humor, and encouragement. Special thanks to Jim, for being a critical and supportive eye at the very early stages, and to Frederick, Laura, Clara, Catherine, Ezra, Anne, Jenny Lyn, David B., Jeffrianne, Chris, Robert, Nelson, Noga, Peter, Katie, and Zooey.

Walter Ramin took time to assist me at every step of this project, painstakingly transcribing every single interview I conducted, accompanying me on many trips to Pittsfield, and wearing many hats, including that of production coordinator and sound recordist. His efforts were vital in helping bring this endeavor to fruition. For his wonderful friendship and for the warmth and kindness he displayed toward all the subjects in this book and their children, I am extremely grateful. In between trips to Pittsfield and long hours devoted to this project, Walter, a talented musician and the guitarist of the rock band RPC, opened for Ozzy Osbourne and Tool in Prague. I feel so fortunate to have had such a talented, driven, kind, patient, amusing, entertaining comrade on this adventure.

My mother has always been an inspiration to me, both personally and professionally. With love and admiration, I have dedicated this book to her.

J.H.L.
New York City
March 11, 2003